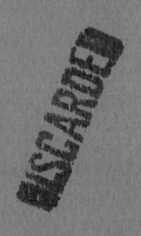

PAPERS ON THE
ARCHAEOLOGY OF

Black Mesa, Arizona

Edited by
GEORGE J. GUMERMAN
and
ROBERT C. EULER

Southern Illinois University Press

Carbondale and Edwardsville

Feffer & Simons, Inc.
London and Amsterdam

Library of Congress Cataloging in Publication Data
Main entry under title:

Papers on the archaeology of Black Mesa, Arizona.

   Bibliography: p.
   Includes index.
   1.   Indians of North America—Arizona—Black Mesa—
Antiquities—Addresses, essays, lectures. 2.   Black
Mesa, Ariz.—Antiquities—Addresses, essays, lectures.
3.   Pueblo Indians—Antiquities—Addresses, essays,
lectures. I. Gumerman, George J. II. Euler, Robert C.
E78.A7P27   979.1′3′00497   75-32340
ISBN 0-8093-0734-0
ISBN 0-8093-0735-9 pbk.

Contents

Part 1   The Archaeology of the Black Mesa Region

Part 2   New Directions in the Archaeology of Black Mesa

List of Illustrations

List of Tables

Foreword

As with most long-term research projects there comes a time when a number of more or less specialized reports are generated. After eight years of survey and excavation on Black Mesa we have elected to publish a number of these in this volume.

The lengthiest of these, and the only descriptive one, is Albert Ward's "Black Mesa to the Colorado River: An Archaeological Traverse." This reports upon survey and excavation accomplished along the route of the coal slurry pipeline that is currently transporting coal from Black Mesa to the Mohave Generating Plant in southern Nevada, a distance of 274 miles. Fifty-eight sites were recorded and six were excavated. Most importantly it presents data on early phases of Kayenta occupation, especially the Dot Klish, along Moenkopi Wash near the western edge of Black Mesa. These data are directly correlatable with our other excavations in the strip mining areas proper.

The other three papers in this volume are more theoretical in nature. Karlstrom, Gumerman, and Euler present what we believe is a dynamic thesis of environmental change that correlates exceptionally well with our independently derived phase sequence. That sequence as tentatively put forth (Gumerman, Westfall, and Weed 1972) was based essentially on ceramic indicators. We have increasingly become aware of the limitations of the more traditional ceramic typology of the Kayenta region, based so intensively on sherd rather than whole vessel analyses. Yet, our belief in the basic and general validity of that traditional system has been bolstered by this cultural-environmental correlation. Parenthetically, it should be noted that these results remain of a tentative nature. The multidisci-plinary paleoenvironmental field research on Black Mesa and its immediate environs is an ongoing project by no means complete.

It is of interest to note that our environmental model, especially as it refers to reasons for population movements in the twelfth century A.D. seems, at first glance, to be at variance with the hypothesis presented for the same movements by Swedlund and Sessions in their "A Developmental Model of Prehistoric Population Growth on Black Mesa." Careful comparison, however, should indicate their supportive nature. The Swedlund and Sessions paper, quite hypothetical in nature, points out types of demographic analyses that may prove fruitful to archaeologists dependent more upon data collected from surface survey than from excavation.

The final paper, "Aspects of Prehistoric Social Organization on Black Mesa" by Robert Clemen, is perhaps the most speculative. It was generated by an earlier paper by David Phillips (1972) that posited a dichotomy of primary and secondary sites during the Toreva phase occupation of Black Mesa, ca. A.D. 1050–1150. Using ceramic design motif data from what in Phillips's opinion was a primary Toreva phase site excavated in 1971, Clemen suggests an occupation by two matrilocal groups that may have developed into a matrilineal clan.

It might be well at this juncture to emphasize that the authors of these theoretical papers, as well as the editors, are well aware of the tentative and, at times, speculative, nature of their remarks. They welcome constructive criticism for this ongoing project. Certainly such exchanges should lead to refinement of our postulates and, in the long run, to a more detailed understanding of the archaeology of Black Mesa and hopefully of anthropology in general.

From the outset of our research, several papers and monographs have been published. None of these carries a particular Black Mesa numerical designation and we have refrained from adding to possible confusion by establishing a special "Contributions to the Archaeology of Black Mesa" numbered series. Therefore, the following complete list of project publications seems advisable.

PUBLISHED CONTRIBUTIONS TO THE ARCHAEOLOGY OF BLACK MESA

Euler, Robert C.
1973a   Attributes of prehistoric Pueblo settlement patterns on Black Mesa, Arizona. *Proceedings of the 40th International Congress of Americanists, Rome, Italy.*

1973b   Exploring the past on Black Mesa. *American West* 10, no. 5, September.

Gumerman, George J.
1970   *Black Mesa: survey and excavation in Northeastern Arizona, 1968.* Prescott, Ariz.: Prescott College Press.

1973   A rural-urban continuum for the prehistoric Pueblo Southwest: Black Mesa and Chaco Canyon. *Proceedings of the 40th International Congress of Americanists, Rome, Italy.*

Gumerman, George J., Deborah Westfall, and Carol S. Weed
1972   *Archaeological investigations on Black Mesa, the 1969–1970 seasons.* Prescott, Ariz.: Prescott College Press.

Karlstrom, Thor N. V., George J. Gumerman, and Robert C. Euler
1974   Paleoenvironmental and cultural changes in the Black Mesa region, northeastern Arizona. In *The geology of northern Arizona with notes on archaeology and paleoclimate,* edited by Thor N. V. Karlstrom. Twenty-seventh Annual Meeting, Rocky Mountain Section, Geological Society of America. Flagstaff.

Olsen, Stanley J.
1972   The small Indian dogs of Black Mesa, Arizona. *Plateau* 45, no. 2 (fall)

One of the difficulties that we have faced recently has involved adequate times for analysis and report writing. We have unavoidably been delayed in publishing some of our descriptive reports, although preliminary statements for each season's work have been submitted to the Smithsonian Institution and the Navajo and Hopi Tribes as called for in our several permits. At this writing, the final reports for the 1971 and 1972 excavations are partially complete; the analysis of the 1973 materials is finished; and, with the 1974 season just completed, those analyses will be started this fall.

G. J. G.
R. C. E.

January 1, 1975

Part 1

**The Archaeology of
the Black Mesa Region**

1

Black Mesa to the Colorado River: An Archaeological Traverse

ALBERT E. WARD

This report and the work which made it possible was sponsored by Black Mesa Pipeline Company and Peabody Coal Company. Our gratitude to these firms and to Gene Richardson and Michael Hunter of the pipeline company is hereby acknowledged. The R. K. Fulton Company also extended many courtesies.

The Navajo and Hopi Tribal Councils granted the necessary permits to excavate. Permits to survey and excavate were also obtained from the United States Department of the Interior. Mr. Leland Abel of the National Park Service assisted in this matter.

The following men were employed as laborers: Happy Jerry Begay, John Harry Blake, Albert H. Dele, Tom Dougi, Alex George, Tom Grey, George Klain, Jimmie Manygoats, Alvin Grass Tallman, Harry Tallman, Ben Whiterock. Gerald L. Hardy of Flagstaff served as assistant to the field archaeologist during the excavations, except for that of Ariz. I:3:1.

Out of the field, many individuals contributed toward the final publication of this report. The following college students worked in the laboratory washing and cataloging artifacts: Janice Callender, Charlotte Goodluck, Dennis Jobe, Jeff King, Dana Oswald, Ernie Schloss, Marilyn Smith, Craig Sweeney, Lyndsay Tunnell, and Carol Weed. Both Jobe and Weed aided in portions of the ground survey. Lyndon L. Hargrave made suggestions on ethnobiology; R. Roy Johnson identified the modern flora samples from the vicinity of the excavated sites and assisted in the writing of the section on flora.

Material remains and additional documentation for the survey and excavated sites are on file with the Black Mesa Archaeological Project.

INTRODUCTION TO SURVEY AND EXCAVATIONS

At the time of this writing, coal slurry is moving underground across northern Arizona in the Black Mesa Pipeline Company's pipeline. This fact, in conjunction with the publication of this report, signifies the conclusion of a joint undertaking by Black Mesa Pipeline Company and the Black Mesa Archaeological Project to recover before destruction any prehistoric and historic archaeological information to be found along the pipeline right-of-way. Where the sites encountered were large, the pipeline was rerouted to avoid disturbance of the remains. When buried sites were located in the exposed pipeline trench, the firm quickly approved estimated budgets for the necessary excavation.

Throughout the fieldwork, salvage archaeology methods were employed with emphasis on speed and economy of recovery. This objective was maintained during the entire project, without sacrificing the goals of our research. Significantly, no time loss resulted in the pipeline construction schedule due to the archaeological excavations.

The archaeological project extended over a 274-mile route from Peabody Coal Company's Black Mesa Mine on joint Navajo and Hopi tribal lands, to a point in Nevada across the Colorado River from Bullhead City, Arizona (Fig. 1). Upon completion of the fieldwork, fifty-eight sites had been recorded representing a variety of cultural components.

Six Kayenta Anasazi habitation sites from Basketmaker II through late Pueblo II (ranging from about A.D. 1 to 1100) were excavated. No sites of the Pueblo I period were excavated and Basketmaker III was best represented.

THE ENVIRONMENTAL SETTING

Physiography

This discussion of physiography is an attempt to give a general impression of the regions traversed by the pipeline right-of-way and to provide a setting for the individual site reports to follow.

The survey began at the coal preparation plant located on the interior upper portion of Black Mesa in northeastern Arizona, where at an elevation of approximately 6,500 feet the right-of-way abruptly enters Moenkopi Wash. The pipeline continues to the southwest through Dot Klish Canyon, paralleling the main water course for more than 18 miles (Fig. 1). Throughout this canyon system, above the alluvial floor, the Cretaceous Mesa Verde predominates, though arenaceous and argillaceous shale and coal deposits are pres-

ent. The canyons are cluttered with large slump boulders and blocks of sandstone.

Vegetation in the region is sparse and consists mainly of intermittent grass cover, small junipers, and tamarisk growing in isolated clumps along the wash bottom. The higher elevations along the canyon rim support more juniper, occasional piñons, and sagebrush. Along this stretch of Moenkopi Wash the canyon floor often becomes quite narrow before opening into short but comparatively wide side valleys. Vegetation on these valley floors consists of various grasses, yucca, buckhorn, prickly pear, and sagebrush. Occasional stunted juniper are also present. Where tributary washes enter these valleys, or where the main wash undergoes a meandering curve, there are floodplains of varying size and soil composition. Dry farming, given sufficient rainfall and wash runoff, should have been fairly rewarding. In all, thirteen sites were recorded within the environmental framework described above. Of these, five were of historic Navajo affinity and the remainder of the Kayenta Anasazi. One of the excavated sites, Ariz. D:10:1, a Dot Klish phase occupation, was adjacent to one of these large floodplains.

About 18 miles west of its beginning the pipeline ascends from Dot Klish Canyon and proceeds over one of the northwestern fingers of Black Mesa. This region is at a 5,900-foot elevation, and is characterized by rolling sandy hills. Farther west, large cliff-head sand dunes have been formed by the prevailing southwesterly winds. Vegetation consists of piñon and juniper on the larger stabilized dunes, with clumps of sagebrush, Mormon tea, and a general covering of short, scanty grasses. Two Kayenta Anasazi sites were discovered within this setting. Subsequent excavation of these sites revealed that Ariz. D:9:1 was assignable to the Lamoki phase, and that Ariz. D:9:2 was of Dot Klish phase affinity. Each site was situated at the head of a small arroyo where dry farming techniques could have been carried on immediately adja-

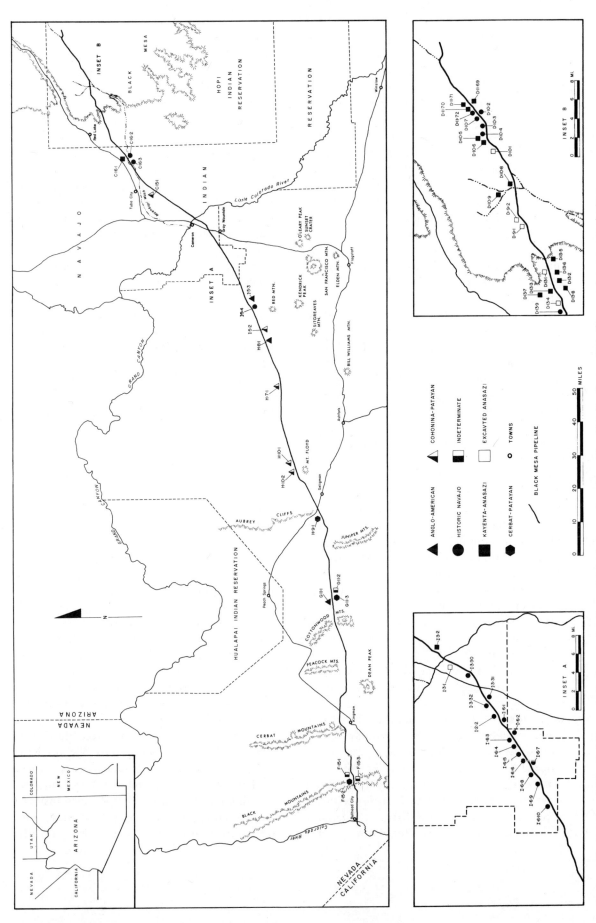

1. Location map of Black Mesa coal slurry pipeline right-of-way, showing site distribution, affiliation, and excavated sites

cent to the living area. This region appears to have been most often favored for habitation prehistorically on Black Mesa, and additional sites are probably near by.

Below the western escarpment of Black Mesa, the pipeline extends through a wide westward-sloping expanse of shifting and stabilized sand dunes. Occasional outcroppings of Navajo sandstone in a variety of shapes and forms have been exposed by the wind.

The vegetation here is characteristic of the grassland phase of the Upper Sonoran life zone. The pipeline descends in elevation from Black Mesa to Moenkopi Wash, a linear distance of approximately 15 miles. As a result, the juniper-covered talus slopes of the Mesa quickly give way to stunted shrubs and eventually to spacious grass-covered sand dunes.

Eight prehistoric sites and one historic Navajo structure were discovered adjacent to the pipeline in this stretch at a point where a modern spring now provides a source of water for Navajo needs. Two sites were excavated in this subarea: Ariz. D:13:1, assigned to a late Basketmaker II and early Basketmaker III period and Ariz. D:13:4, a probable Basketmaker II site.

The large number of prehistoric sites in this immediate area is an indication that this same spring produced water at some time in the past. With an adequate water supply and suitable locations for dry farming, the region was ideal for habitation; additional sites could undoubtedly have been located had the survey been expanded beyond the pipeline right-of-way.

South of an old uranium processing plant located on U.S. Highway 160, the pipeline recrosses Moenkopi Wash and ascends from the drainage over an expanse of desolate sand waste toward the escarpment of Newberry Terrace above the Little Colorado River. This section of the right-of-way covers a distance of over 13 miles, avoiding the sandstone cliffs which form the northern limits of the Moenkopi Plateau. Travel in this region is impossible by four-wheel-drive vehicle and slow by foot. Only two sites, both historic

Navajo habitations, were recorded in this section and both were located near Moenkopi Wash.

At the edge of the escarpment overlooking the Little Colorado River valley, a large prehistoric campsite was recorded. The environment is barren, with sparsely grass-covered sand hills extending in all directions. Although it may have been unfit for prolonged occupation, the site, Ariz. C:15:1, had been reused periodically since the Anasazi Basketmaker III horizon and into the Pueblo IV period. In the cliff face, large quantities of jasper and other hard variegated stones suitable for the manufacture of cutting tools are available. The windswept ground surface produced a large number of waste and utilized flakes, projectile points, knives, scrapers, sherds, and ground stone tools. People came to this spot to collect or mine the raw materials from along the escarpment. They returned to the campsite on the rim, where they reduced the raw material to finished products.

Beyond the escarpment, the right-of-way crosses the eroded Chinle formation of the western Painted Desert. The bleak terrain east of the Little Colorado River is characterized by sterile gray or reddish brown clay, often overlaid with patches of white caliche. Plant life is almost completely absent except along the river bottom. The pipeline crosses the river approximately four miles southeast of Cameron, Arizona. It was on the left bank of this river crossing that Ariz. I:13:1 was located and subsequently excavated. The pipeline also passed within view of a group of scattered ruins situated on several low mesas adjacent to the right bank of the Little Colorado River, both north and south of the right-of-way.

Reconnaissance of the line from the Little Colorado River to the western Navajo Reservation boundary, a distance of 16 miles, yielded no additional prehistoric remains, although data were recorded at thirteen historic Navajo sites. The region is now quite forlorn, consisting of small sand dunes partially stabilized by sparse sagebrush growth. The area was once occupied by a large Navajo population but as the region became unable to support the required number of sheep, people were forced to move elsewhere.

West of the Navajo Reservation the pipeline extends 184 miles across an expanse of ever-changing landscapes. It crosses old lava flows and around the extinct volcanoes north of Flagstaff and Williams. Along this section were recorded an Anglo "line-camp" of the 1930s, a recent Navajo piñon gathering camp, a recent sheepherding camp, and two isolated prehistoric Cohonina sites. Farther west the pipeline crosses U.S. Highway 66 at Seligman, continues over the Juniper Mountains, across an open grassland valley, over the Cottonwood Mountains, drops down the tortuous escarpment of the Aquarius Cliffs, passes south of the Peacock Mountains, through a Kingman suburb, over the Cerbat Mountains, across the Sacramento Valley, through Secret Pass at the top of the Black Mountains, down to the Colorado River within the city limits of Bullhead City, and into Nevada where the project teminates at the Mohave Power Project generating station.

Archaeological remains along this entire portion were sparse, consisting of a Cerbat Branch campsite along the eastern limits of the Juniper Mountains, and a historic Anglo-American homesteader's jacal ranch house, a Cerbat chipping station, and a lithic workshop farther west in the Cottonwood Mountains. These sites were all in juniper-piñon forests. In the vicinity of Secret Pass, high in the Black Mountains, a rockshelter of Cerbat occupation, an unclassified rockshelter site and a petroglyph panel were recorded.

Water Supply

It can be seen that a major portion of the area under consideration is typical of the semiarid Southwest, dependent for its moisture upon winter snows and summer rainstorms. There are no major streams in the entire region traversed by the pipeline right-of-way except the Little Colorado River and this can hardly be termed perennial. People living here were forced to seek other sources of water. After a violent summer thunderstorm large arid washes often turn into raging torrents for a short time. Then potholes and plunge pools located in the stream beds of the major drainages are filled, constituting a fairly reliable water supply for small groups of people. Additional water is furnished by springs and seeps in the region, but the supply from these sources is often meager and many are undependable in dry years. The Little Colorado carries large amounts of runoff for prolonged periods throughout the spring and late summer each year. Although this water is very silty, clearer water is often available in the residual pools formed as the river recedes. In both the Little Colorado River and along Moenkopi Wash, water can be obtained by digging shallow wells in the dry stream channel.

The scarcity of water is important when one remembers that in addition to domestic needs, the main concern of prehistoric farmers was to obtain enough soil moisture to begin planting and subsequent seasonal precipitation to mature the crop. Nonetheless, many prehistoric Anasazi sites have been recorded along the two ephemeral streams.

Climate

The diversity of topographical features along the pipeline results in a wide range of local climatic conditions, too detailed to include in this report. In general, the region is arid with pronounced fluctuation of temperatures and moisture. The eastern portion receives an annual average of less than 10 inches of precipitation, the central portion receives 15 to 20 inches, while the western section adjacent to the Colorado River receives less than 5 inches. Summer precipitation is in the form of local showers which often become torrential; storms can reach cloudburst proportions capable of deluging a small area with several inches of rain. At higher elevations, over 75 percent of the winter moisture falls in the form of snow while the lower areas usually receive rain. Drought conditions are often present in May and June and again in October and November. Throughout the year a high evaporation rate due to low humidity, high temperature, dry winds, and a preponderance of sunny days, contributes to the arid condition.

Temperature differences are the result of variation in elevation rather than latitude. Average summer temperatures fluctuate in the middle 90s below 500 feet, and the high 50s above 8,000 feet, corresponding to a decrease of about 1 degree Fahrenheit per 235 feet (Green and Sellers 1964:25). Thus, during the summer months, the regions between 7,000- and 9,000-foot elevations are between 25 and 30 degrees cooler than the surrounding desert valleys. The average daily temperatures are generally below 75 degrees, while in the afternoon it rarely exceeds 90 degrees. The higher mountain peaks occasionally experience readings below freezing. The lower elevations are quite warm during this period since the average daily maximum generally exceeds 90 degrees at elevations below 5,000 feet. Along the Lower Colorado River temperatures above 100 degrees in the midafternoon are normally reported. Record readings are above 120 degrees.

On the high mesas and mountain peaks, winters are often bitterly cold, particularly at elevations above 7,000 feet. Subfreezing temperatures are quite common from September to April. As might be expected, the coldest winter weather occurs after a heavy snowfall, when temperatures may drop 20 to 40 degrees. In most sections of the plateau clear, sunny days predominate.

Average wind speeds generally exceed 10 miles per hour, with the lightest winds experienced in late summer and fall. Because of local topographical variations, specific wind directions cannot be extrapolated, although field observations indicate a prevailing southwesterly wind. The wind creates numerous "dust devils," most of which are

scarcely more than whirling funnels of sand, though a few observed on the Navajo Reservation were powerful enough to damage crops.

Flora

The floral variation, from one end of the pipeline to the other, related to climate, is also quite noticeable. While all species characteristic of the various ecological niches need not be listed here, it is useful to note the range and variety of reported species utilized historically. The upper elevation at which individual species occur is determined by their ability to function at low temperatures. The lower limit is determined by the inability to resist drought. The extremes of climate rather than the daily means are usually the critical factors. The environmental and geographical separation of biotic communities in northern Arizona is not well defined and the borders of two separate floral communities often merge gradually, usually with no discernible line of demarcation.

The following description of the biotic communities was compiled from Nichol (1937), Kearney and Peebles (1951), and Lowe (1964).

Southwestern desert scrub. Southwestern desert scrub was the only biotic community encountered within the Lower Sonoran life zone. Two regions along the pipeline are of this type. The larger area is in the Lower Colorado River valley; the smaller in the Sacramento Valley situated between the Black and Cerbat mountains. This is one of the hottest and most arid deserts found in Arizona. The elevation ranges from 600 feet at the river to 3,500–4,000 feet on the two mountain slopes. Rainfall is irregular and total precipitation is between 3 and 11 inches per year.

Of the twenty-seven most common plant species characteristic of the southwestern desert scrub community, fourteen provided a source of food, nine served as raw materials, and one was used for medicine. The major food species are: banana yucca (*Yucca baccata*) and Mohave yucca (*Yucca schidigera*), buckhorn cholla (*opuntia acanthocarpa*), catclaw (*Acacia greggii*), desert saltbush (*Atriplex polycarpa*), fishhook cactus (*Mammillaria wilcoxii*), Joshua tree (*Yucca brevifolia*) mesquite (*Prosopis juliflora*), and netleaf hackberry (*Celtis reticulata*).

Great Basin desert scrub. In the vicinity of the Little Colorado River, between Tuba City and Leupp, the survey passed through a minor subdivision of Great Basin desert scrub. The region was originally named the "Painted Desert" by the geologist Newberry during Lieutenant Ives's exploration of the Colorado River in 1858 (Dellenbaugh 1932; McKee 1933).

This is the only actual desert biotic community located within the Upper Sonoran life zone. Elevation is from 3,000 to 6,000 feet, though primarily above 4,000 feet. Accordingly, it is referred to as "cool desert," "cold desert," or "semidesert." Precipitation is evenly distributed throughout the year, and averages between 7 and 12 inches.

The Great Basin desert scrub is a shrub and grass dominated desert in which the vegetation is of relatively low stature with a few species covering extensive areas of uniform relief (Lowe 1964:37). Trees are almost totally absent. Of the twenty-five most common plant forms fourteen are used for food and two serve medicinal purposes. The major food plants include: five species of dropseed grasses of which *Sporobolus interruptus* is the most common species; four-wing saltbush (*Altriplex canescens*), prickly pear (*Opuntia fragilis* and *Opuntia polyacantha*), Mormon tea (*Ephedra viridis*), pale lycium (*Lycium pallidum*), plateau yucca (*Yucca angustissima*), Utah serviceberry (*Amelanchier utahensis*), shad scale (*Atriplex confertifolia*), and whipple cholla (*Opuntia whipplei*).

Desert grassland. Located at the lower end of the Upper Sonoran life zone, the desert grassland community is best described as transitional between the desert and chaparral environment. Its lower limit is 3,500 to 4,000

feet with the best development at 4,000 to 5,000 feet. Most of the region receives 10 to 15 inches of precipitation per year.

The best example of this biotic community along the slurry line occurs near Kingman. The plant life is predominantly short grasses with scattered scrubs, yuccas, and cacti.

Nineteen species are characteristic of the desert grassland. Of these, six are of food value, and two are utilized for raw material. Food plants include the agave (*Agave utahensis*), bear grass (*Nolina microcarpa*), catclaw (*Acacia greggii*), mesquite (*Prosopis juliflora*), prickly pear (*Opuntia engelmannii*), and sand dropseed (*Sporobolus cryptandrus*).

Interior chaparral. Interior chaparral was encountered by the survey crew in the Hualapai and Cottonwood Mountain ranges. This biotic community is situated in the central portion of the Upper Sonoran life zone. Elevation is 3,500–4,000 to 6,500–7,000 feet. Precipitation ranges from 10 to 23 inches annually.

Interior chaparral is characterized by dense shrubby growth of uniform size. The dominant plant forms are scrub oak and manzanita. Twenty-three species are commonly present, of which five are edible. They are: catclaw (*Acacia greggii*), manzanita (*Arctostaphylos pungens*), red mahonia (*Berberis haematocarpa*), scrub oak (*Quercus turbinella*), and squawbush (*Rhus trilobata*). Four species provide raw materials; three others serve medicinal purposes.

Juniper-piñon woodland. Forming the upper limits of the Upper Sonoran life zone, the juniper-piñon woodland is essentially a desert zone, although it is not so arid or so hot as the Lower Sonoran desert. This biotic community covers the often flat-topped mesas and plateaus of the Navajo Reservation that are situated from an elevation of 5,500–5,800 to 7,000–7,200 feet. Precipitation is usually greatest in summer, with an annual average of between 12 and 20 inches. Typical plants are sagebrush, juniper, and piñon.

Thirty-four species are common throughout

these forests; twelve provide food, eleven are collected for raw materials, and four are used medically. Food species include: banana yucca (*Yucca baccata*), Colorado piñon (*Pinus edulis*), Gambel oak (*Quercus gambelii*), Indian ricegrass (*Oryzopsis hymenoides*), Mormon tea (*Ephedra viridis*), one-seed juniper (*Juniperus monosperma*), paintbrush (*Castilleja linariaefolia*), prickly pear (*Opuntia polyacantha*), sand dropseed (*Sporobolus cryptandrus*), serviceberry (*Amelanchier goldmanii*), scrub oak (*Quercus turbinella*), Utah juniper (*Juniperus osteosperma*). whipple cholla (*Opuntia whipplei*) and winter fat (*Eurotia lanata*).

Ponderosa pine forest. The ponderosa pine forest represents a transitional life zone, located mainly on the San Francisco Peaks and higher mountains. Elevation is ordinarily between 6,000–7,000 and 8,500–9,000 feet. The unmixed stands occur most commonly between 7,000 and 8,000 feet. Precipitation is 18 to 26 inches per year. Other dominant trees are Gambel's oak and New Mexico locust. Twenty-five plants are commonly found in this biotic community; of these, five plants are collected for medicine, five for food, and two others for raw materials.

The edible plants are: bracken fern (*Pteridium aquilinum*) which is poisonous until cooked, Canadian elder (*Sambucus coerulea*), Gambel oak, (*Quercus gambelii*), raspberry (*Rubus strigosus*), and wax currant (*Ribes cereum*).

The remaining biotic communities above 8,000 feet will be omitted from this report. As a direct result of high elevation, these ecological zones possess fewer species and, correspondingly, fewer edible plants. Accessibility, rather than the number of plants available, may have been the deciding factor in food collection at these altitudes.

The list of native or uncultivated plants that furnish food is long. Throughout the biotic communities described above, over sixty edible plants are present. Additional species grow in several biotic zones, and are therefore located within two separate communities, which adds thirty-seven other plants to those known to have been utilized for food.

Fauna

To the hypothetical prehistoric food supply provided by plants, one must add the list of animals whose remains have been recovered from the archaeological excavations which are discussed in Chapter 3. Many of these animals are present in the region today. Predatory mammals, such as the mountain lion, black bear, and timber wolf, are being exterminated, while the coyote and bobcat are still abundant. Mountain sheep, though few in number, are still hunted on a limited basis in Arizona, as are elk, deer, and prong-horned antelope.

There are a large number of birds. Major species include the golden eagle, red-tailed hawk, piñon jay, Clark crow, junco, nuthatch and meadowlark, wild turkey, Gambel's quail and mourning dove. A substantial number of great horned owls live on the large rodent population.

Rodents form the most conspicuous portion of the fauna, but are seldom seen as most of their activity is nocturnal. Species of this category are the black-tailed jackrabbit, Arizona cottontail, yellow-haired porcupine, pocket gopher, Kangaroo rat, and the Arizona pack rat. Of all the rodents, the squirrel family probably attracts the most attention. It includes the prairie dog, gray rock squirrel, big ground squirrel, Albert squirrel, and the chipmunk.

The prairie rattlesnake, Arizona bull snake, and the Great Basin striped racer are abundant. Large numbers of lizards and "horned toads" are found on the desert.

THE SURVEY

History and Methods

The archaeological survey of the 274-mile, 50-foot pipeline right-of-way was specifically coordinated with two phases of the construction schedule. First and most important, the initial 100 miles of the right-of-way was checked for cultural manifestations with a helicopter by Euler prior to all planned construction in 1967. A number of sites were easily spotted and landings at all suspected sites were made. Additional survey was accomplished in the same manner along several miles of proposed truck haulage roads. An area of approximately 100 feet on either side of the proposed pipeline path was also covered to prevent any possible destruction by heavy equipment during construction. The site survey was therefore intensive rather than extensive, being confined to the pipeline right-of-way. General site information was recorded in a format standardized by the Black Mesa Project (Gumerman 1970:13). In 1968, Euler and Gumerman completed the preliminary survey of the remaining 174 miles of the pipeline route, again by helicopter and before any construction had begun.

The company had the option to support the excavation of the endangered sites, or to reroute the pipeline to avoid them. Since the sites were all located in open areas in most cases, only slight realignments were necessary to move the line around them, and the firm chose to do so.

With the completion of the right-of-way clearance the excavation of the pipeline trench began, and the second portion of our survey was instigated by four-wheel-drive vehicles. Examination of the sides of the pipeline trench was an attempt to seek out any existing buried archaeological materials unobservable during the initial helicopter reconnaissance. The exposed trench was 3 feet wide and varied in depth from a minimum of 6 feet to as much as 15 feet where larger sand concentrations were penetrated. It should be noted that this revealed a number of sites not observable from aerial or ground surface investigation.

The combined helicopter and ground survey provided data on fifty-eight prehistoric and historic sites distributed across northern Arizona. Concentrations of prehistoric sites were discovered in Dot Klish Canyon, and in a region of vast sand dunes south of Red Lake Trading Post. West of U.S. Highway 89, a large number of historic Navajo sites were encountered. Five buried sites were located in the course of the ground survey.

Site Types

Almost the entire region has exhibited evidence of utilization by early inhabitants, though in a variety of ways at different times in the past. The majority are habitational remains although nonhabitational sites are represented by corrals and petroglyph panels.

An initial classification, for convenience in description, results in the following cultural category of sites: Anglo-American; Anasazi, Kayenta Branch; Cohonina Branch; Cerbat Branch; and an indeterminate category. Additional location, cultural affiliation, temporal placement, ceramics, and artifactual data of the survey sites can be found in Figure *1* and Tables 1 through 4.

Anglo-American Period

Temporary sheep camp. Ariz. H:8:1 consisted of a temporary sheepherding camp, attributed to the 1968 summer and fall grazing season. Two open-front ramadas, constructed by placing juniper branches over a lumber framework, formed three rooms. An associated woodpile, ash dump, and scattered cultural debris are present. Evidence for occupation by male shepherds consisted of the following: four decaying sheepskins left on the roof of a ramada, numerous sheep bones displaying cutting marks, lack of female associated items, and a preponderance of Gallo red wine bottles. The cultural affinity could possibly be traced to one of the Basque herding groups, who work for large sheep companies grazing flocks on the Coconino Plateau and at the base of the San Francisco Peaks each year.

Cattlemen's line-shack. Ariz. I:5:3 was once a cattleman's line-shack, with associated barbed wire corral. Two single-room lumber structures had been constructed. The main house or cabin had completely collapsed. The smaller unit, probably a storage structure, had suffered considerable damage resulting from the removal of material for possible re-use elsewhere. Traces of a faint road remain, heading northwest from the site. Presumably this road once joined Highway 180. Final abandonment of the line-shack was probably prior to 1940, judging from a thin surface scattering of cultural debris.

Homesteader's jacal cabin. Ariz. G:11:1 consisted of a homesteader's two-room jacal house (Fig. *2*), long shed, and associated corral. The house was constructed of vertical posts set short distances apart. To these were nailed stripped juniper branches forming a riblike frame to hold the adobe in place (Fig. *3*). Room 1 is rectangular, measuring 6.4 by 4.25 m. and had two windows and three doors. Adobe mortar held together a fireplace of shaped limestone slabs and blocks in the north wall. Room 2 is contiguous to the west wall of the main rooms. Nearly square, this room measured 4.2 by 3.7 m. Four doors and no windows opened into the room. Walls were generally 2.2 m. high, supporting a superstructure of poles, bark, and a covering of earth. The window and door frames were of lumber, as was the floor.

A small shed (3.5 by 2.5 m.) served a dual

2. *Ariz. G:11:1. Anglo homesteader's two-room jacal house*

3. *Ariz. G:11:1. Detail of jacal construction*

purpose, being utilized as both a storage facility and animal shelter. The structure was
constructed of pine logs notched at the corners. A large rectangular corral enclosed with
barbed wire is contiguous on the east side. A
smaller irregular-shaped corral area, damaged
by the initial right-of-way clearing, was constructed of closely aligned juniper posts
which were wired together.

Five different cattle brands, various initials,
and one man's name were carved or painted
on the house beams (Fig. 3). The lone name,
Buck Imus, is that of a Walapai Indian.
These markings could indicate that: a Walapai worked for the homesteader; a Walapai
group homesteaded; or various Walapais vis-

ited the site after its abandonment, leaving
their name, initials, and brands on the beams.
All situations are plausible, since the site is
located close to the present reservation.

It is unfortunate that dates were not also
placed on the beams. Consideration of the
cultural debris does, however, suggest an occupation five to ten years in length, placed
between 1900 and 1930. The nature of the
trash also reveals additional information.
Items usually associated with the presence of
children are noticeably absent, while items
of both adult male and female activities are
common. No item from the collection can be
directly associated with native Walapai material culture.

Historic Navajo Period

Twenty-six sites recorded during the survey are classified as post-1850 Navajo. The recent classification listed in Table 1 differentiates those sites which are still in use or were abandoned within the past ten years. The lack of Navajo sites from the earlier periods is probably due to the location of the project on the western edge of the reservation.

The sites can be further divided into single habitation units, multiple habitation units, and isolated corrals. All corrals were plotted, as they did not always occur in conjunction with occupational sites. Single unit sites include one hogan with associated trash; corrals may be absent. Two or more hogans, along with associated features, comprise the second type. Ramadas or shades were not encountered. Nonhabitational sites, other than the isolated corrals, consisted of petroglyph panels.

Mindeleff (1898), Hester (1962), and oth-

ers have adequately described Navajo architecture and there is no need to reiterate. However, three styles of hogans were represented and warrant brief discussion. The absence of sweat lodges was noted, but since these are generally constructed out of sight and often at some distance from the living area, it is highly possible that they were present outside the right-of-way.

Temporary piñon camp. At a temporary piñon gathering camp, Ariz. I:5:4, the main structure was a light wooden framework which supported a covering, similar to a wall tent. A small lean-to was also constructed by placing juniper branches against a piñon tree. Two boards nailed together on short legs formed a crude but serviceable table. Two fire pits were ringed with small stones and a scattering of recent trash was present. Temporal placement of the short Navajo occupation is approximately the fall of 1968.

Stone-wall hogans. The most common Navajo house type, although confined to the Cam-

1. CLASSIFICATION OF SURVEY SITES SHOWING TYPE, CULTURAL AFFINITY, AND TEMPORAL PLACEMENT

Site Types	Occurrence	Temporary Distribution or Phase *										
		His-toric	Recent	BM II	BM III	P I	P II	P III	P IV	Coconino	Medicine Valley	Hull
Anglo-American	3	1	2									
Navajo												
Single habitation	15	14	1									
Multiple habitation	3	2	1									
Corral †	7	3	4									
Petroglyph	3		3									
Total	23	19	9									
Kayenta Branch												
Masonry pueblo	3						2	3	1			
Pithouse village	14			1	10	7	3	1				
Sherd area	4				2	1	2	2	1			
Basketmaker II	1			1								
Total	22			2	13	10	8	4	1			
Cohonina Branch	4										1	3	2
Cerbat Branch	3											
Indeterminate	3											
Total	58	20	11	2	13	10	8	4	1	1	3	2

* Transitional sites are recorded in each phase.

† Five corrals were located at habitation sites.

eron area on the survey, was the stone-wall hogan. All thirteen stone hogans were circular with an entrance facing east. The earlier types tended to be somewhat smaller, with the walls now little more than foundations. Postoccupational use of these structures for construction material was suggested at several of the hogans, where portions of the walls had been removed. The masonry at these sites was dry laid, with all stone from local sources. None of the units had well-prepared stone blocks. The standing walls were either three or five courses high (75 to 100 cm.). The interior walls may have been plastered. These low walls acted as supports for the cribbed logs which formed the domed roof. Heavy winds and rain have swept away the covering of earth which must once have been a part of these houses. Only on the floor had fill accumulated, covering the floor features.

Cribbed-log hogans. The single clear-cut example of a cribbed-log hogan was Ariz. D:13:9. Basic construction consisted of horizontally placed logs, forming walls above shoulder height. A dome-shaped roof was formed of log layers of decreasing circumferences. A smoke vent slanted to the east. The entry was blocked with vertical logs indicating a burial in the hogan.

Surface indications of a raised ring of mud and bark located at Ariz. I:3:30 may represent an additional example of a cribbed-log hogan from which the timbers had been removed, possibly for reuse elsewhere. Surface trash was quite recent, and excavation of a similar feature at Toonerville, Arizona (Ward 1968:136) demonstrated the difficulty of classifying this type of site on the basis of surface indications.

Forked-stick hogans. Four forked-stick hogans were recorded at single habitation sites.

4. *Ariz. D:11:72. An example of a Navajo forked-stick hogan*

One example, located at Ariz. C:16:2, possessed a covered doorway or entrance passage. All were in a similar stage of preservation, with the earth covering removed from the interlocked, conically arranged logs (Fig. *4*).

Evidence for Anglo contact existed in the form of some glass and rusted metal fragments at two of these early sites.

Corrals. Six corrals were completely constructed of dry laid masonry on level ground. The seventh corral, Ariz. I:6:7, utilized the steep side of a Kaibab limestone ledge for one wall; the other walls were constructed of masonry. Walls were low, limiting their use to the confinement of sheep and goats. The outline of the corrals varied from circular to rectangular. In all instances, the entrances were blocked with several short logs.

Petroglyph panels. Other nonhabitational Navajo remains consisted of petroglyph panels (Figs. *5, 6*). At three locations numerous figures, initials, dates, words, and obscene phrases were pecked or incised into the soft

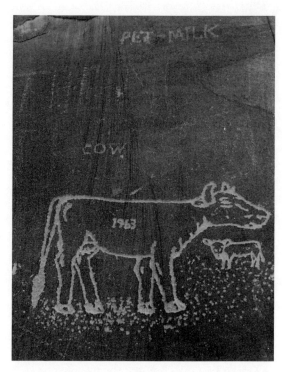

6. *Ariz. D:10:7. An example of recent Navajo petroglyph art*

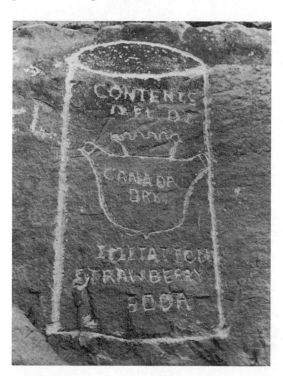

5. *Ariz. D:10:4. An example of recent Navajo petroglyph art*

Mesa Verde sandstone cliffs or on slump boulders located in Dot Klish Canyon. The three panels are in close proximity, and similar in subject matter and age. It seems safe to assume that they were made by the same person or persons over a comparatively short period. On the basis of the subject matter, it is obvious that the most likely creators of these panels were Navajo children who herd their families' flocks.

Prehistoric Period

Thirty-two locations of prehistoric remains were found along the pipeline right-of-way. The cultural categories are: Kayenta Anasazi, Cohonina, and Cerbat Branches. Three prehistoric sites lacking diagnostic artifacts were placed in an indeterminate category.

Kayenta Branch. Twenty-two separate locations of cultural remains have been assigned to the Kayenta Branch ranging from Basketmaker II through Pueblo IV, or from about A.D. 1 to 1300.

On surface evidence, it was possible to divide the Kayenta sites into masonry pueblos, pithouse villages, and sherd areas. Because jacal or ramada construction is prevalent on Black Mesa, but impossible to detect on surface survey, the possible presence of this type of construction could not be predicted. Excavation along the pipeline route and on Black Mesa (Gumerman 1970:17) has demonstrated that there is no temporal significance to the jacal form of architecture. Jacal units were found in all periods from possible Basketmaker II through early Pueblo III.

Masonry Pueblos. From surface evidence, three sites were distinguished by collapsed masonry walls, or by an outline of standing walls projecting from the surface. A depression located adjacent to the masonry was usually an indication of a subsurface kiva.

Pithouse Villages. Fifteen of the Kayenta sites were pithouse occupations. These sites were characterized by circular, basin-shaped depressions in direct association with accumulations of trash. Some had only large sherd concentrations and the presence of subsurface structures was assumed. This type of architectural village composition was the most common within the Anasazi area studied.

The dominance of pithouse sites is perhaps not unusual in light of the statement by Bliss (1960:10) that 80–90 percent of the population during the Pueblo period from A.D. 900 to 1200 in the area between Kayenta and Red Lake Trading Post were living in pithouses rather than masonry pueblos. The survey data reinforced this conclusion, although pithouses are relatively rare in the later phases on Black Mesa (Gumerman 1968; Gumerman, Westfall, and Weed 1972).

Sherd Areas. Four locations of concentrated ceramic fragments were classified as sherd areas. At these sites sherds were scattered about the surface with no evidence of depth and no deep organic staining of surface soils. Lack of architectural evidence further suggests that these remains represented campsites or small jacal structures.

Ariz. 1:3:2 is located between two mesas, adjacent to the east bank of the Little Colorado River, and probably represents solely trail breakage and not habitations. Both mesa tops contain remains of several sites, which have the same ceramic components as Ariz. I:3:2. Since the site is the easiest access to the river from the mesa tops, we assume that it is merely a result of trial breakage.

Ariz. C:15:1 represents a sherd area in which a large amount of lithic debris is present. The site is located at the edge of an escarpment overlooking the Little Colorado River Valley. Although the region is unfit for permanent occupation because of the absence of water and a good soil cover, ceramic evidence has shown that the campsite was reused periodically from the Basketmaker III into the Pueblo IV period. Artifacts in a totally mixed state were found in windswept areas. They included chipped and ground stone tools, ceramic fragments, and large quantities of variegated lithic chipping debris. The source of the material for the lithic assemblages was located along the escarpment where large quantities of jasper and other materials suitable for the manufacturing of hunting and cutting tools can be found.

We assume that over a number of centuries men came to collect or mine the raw materials from along the escarpment where they reduced this raw material into the finished product. These encampments were probably of short duration. However, the presence of ground stone tools brought to the site, suggests that some of the encampments were longer and women were most likely present.

Ariz. C:16:1 represents still another type of sherd area, with which only a few ceramic fragments or artifacts were associated. This type of site suggests one of the following situations: an accidental association due to some recent human activity, an isolated encampment, or a buried site eroding to the surface.

Cohonina Branch. Four sites represent the Cohonina Branch. They have little surface indications except for varying amounts of stone flakes, ceramic fragments, and some whole stone artifacts. The sites do not show any great span of time, and by themselves contribute little toward a better understanding of the Cohonina culture. It is, however, possible to make several generalizations.

On the basis of ceramic evidence the sites are temporally equivalent to the late Pueblo I and Pueblo II culture stages of the neighboring Anasazi. Evidence of contact with the Kayenta is recorded in the ceramic collections. Some ceramics also represent the Cerbat Branch.

The sites do suggest some form of seasonal or short occupation, probably encampments. There was evidence of much chipped stone, particularly at Ariz. H:10:1, a large site consisting of dense basalt and obsidian knapping debris.

Cerbat Branch. Three small sites belong to the Cerbat Branch. Ariz. F:15:2 is a rockshelter of good size with shallow fill. Although the rockshelter floor and talus slope produced little ceramic evidence, the smoke-blackened roof and walls do suggest repeated or prolonged occupation.

The majority of the ceramics are Tizon Brown Ware. Surface collections at two of these sites totaled only twenty-four sherds, but they do demonstrate contact with people of the Prescott Branch. Contact with prehistoric Mohave of the Amacava Branch is also hinted at by the presence of one sherd of Parker Red-on-Buff. Temporally the sites are comparable to Anasazi Pueblo II.

One small hunting camp, Ariz. G:11:3, was assigned to the Cerbat Branch on the basis of a characteristic side-notched projectile point. A small concentration of lithic waste was also present. Identification of a similar lithic concentration, Ariz. G:11:2, although identical in appearance, could not be accomplished since it lacked diagnostic artifacts.

Indeterminate. Three sites could not be assigned cultural affinity because of a lack of associated artifacts. Ariz. G:11:2, a small concentration of lithic material, has been mentioned above. Ariz. F:15:3 is a rockshelter lacking ceramic evidence. A projectile point

fragment was found on the talus in front of the shelter. The shape of the fragment is characteristic of the Pinto Basin forms, usually equated with the Desert Culture tradition. Much of the roof had fallen from the shelter leaving only isolated places which were still smoke-stained.

The remaining unclassified site is Ariz. F:15:11, a group of petroglyphs on a large outcrop of rhyolite. Geometric designs were pecked into the stone and diagnostic motifs or figures were absent.

Analysis of Survey Artifacts

Surface collections from the recorded survey sites yielded a wide range of historic and prehistoric implements and artifact types. Analysis has been with the intent of demonstrating cultural affiliation and temporal placement; the major categories are the Anglo-American Period, the Historic Navajo Period, and the Prehistoric Period. Subdivisions within the Prehistoric Period are Kayenta, Cohonina, and Cerbat.

Anglo-American Period

Three manifestations of Anglo-American origin were recorded; however, surface collections were not made at two sites because similar items are still in use. The only Anglo-American items collected are from Ariz. G:11:1, the homesteader's cabin in the western part of the survey.

Items gathered from the site are: twenty-four nails, including wire, square and horseshoe varieties; two wood screws; a spent .44 caliber cartridge; two buttons from men's Levi pants; a safety pin; a metal key from a sardine can, and a wire coat hook. Bottle fragments of purple, aqua, and clear glass were collected, as well as several fragments of porcelain and earthenware crockery.

Historic Navajo Period

Artifacts of a utilitarian nature were collected from the recorded Navajo sites. These are easily distinguishable as belonging within the Reservation Period of 1860 to the present (Hester 1962:62). This period of Navajo history is characterized by limited, though increasing Navajo-Anglo contact and the survey collections yielded ample evidence of this trend.

The collected objects were obtainable from Navajo Reservation trading posts and many can still be found for sale at these stores. Items represented are: numerous metal food containers, including the hole-in-the-top variety (Skinner 1967:113), smoking and chewing-tobacco cans, porcelain and earthenware utensil fragments, enamel pans, and a cast iron skillet fragment. The only items classifiable as tools are a teaspoon and a small stone with a prepared cutting edge. A floral design was stamped on the upper side of the spoon, with the trademark "Wm. A. Rogers silver-nickel" on the reverse. The stone knife was fashioned by chipping a brief cutting edge along one plane of a primary chert flake. Secondary flakes were removed by pressure retouching. The item was little used, and apparently discarded soon after manufacture. Articles of clothing such as overall fragments and shoes were observed but not collected. A metal toy truck was the only luxury item found.

Prehistoric Period

Manifestations of the Kayenta Branch are characterized by a distinct paucity of chipped stone artifacts and a larger number of ground stone implements. Conversely, ruins of the Cohonina are amply represented by implements of chipped obsidian, fine-grained basalt, and chert, yet ground stone is almost completely absent, suggesting a difference in ecological adaptation. However, a perusal of the stone artifact chart demonstrates that the presence or absence of both types of stone tools at various sites may depend, in part, on site locations with respect to sources of lithic material.

The terminology used here is similar to that of the first Black Mesa report (Gumerman 1968). Ground, chipped, and miscellaneous

forms of stone artifacts, including classifiable fragments, are shown in Table 2, while pieces not clearly recognizable as to type were classified as indeterminant.

Kayenta Branch. The majority of stone implements gathered at the Kayenta sites were for food-processing. The surveyed sites yielded a total of ten whole or identifiable *manos;* eight were fashioned from sandstone and two of conglomerate.

There were four one-hand manos. Three were bifacially ground, one unifacial. All grinding surfaces are convex, resulting from use in trough metates. The two whole specimens measure 9 and 10.2 cm. long, 8 and 7.6 cm. wide, and 4.2 and 4.3 cm. thick. Two-hand manos, represented by three fragments, were unifacially used in trough metates resulting in convex grinding surfaces. They range in width, from 11.2 to 11.6 cm.; and in thickness, from 2.6 to 4.7 cm. Three mano fragments could not be classified as either one or two-hand types. Their grinding surfaces are convex, with two fragments exhibiting bifacial use. The grinding surface of one fragment is slightly faceted.

One nearly complete basin *metate* was collected on the survey. The grinding surface had been made abrasive by pecking shortly before the implement was discarded. The specimen, of fine-grained sandstone, measures 28 cm. long, 31.2 cm. wide, 7.7 cm. thick. Five metate fragments appear to have come from one trough and four slab metates. They are constructed of sandstone and there is little evidence of use.

A *cylindrical abrader,* of dense siltstone, was also recovered (Fig. 7H). This specimen has opposing ground faces, while the blunted ends and sides display little work beyond the original shaping. It measures 6.8 cm. long, 1.5 cm. wide between nonutilized edges, and 9 mm. thick between the ground faces.

The Kayenta sites yielded only a few chipped stone artifacts. Two *projectile points* were found. Both were constructed by bifacial pressure retouching a primary percussion flake. One is the convex basal portion of

2. SITE SURVEY. LITHIC ARTIFACTS BY SITE, TYPE, AND CULTURAL AFFINITY

Artifact Type	Ariz. D:11:69	Ariz. D:11:70	Ariz. D:11:71	Ariz. D:10:5	Ariz. D:10:9	Ariz. D:13:3	Ariz. D:13:8	Ariz. C:15:1	Ariz. I:3:2	Ariz. I:5:2	Ariz. H:7:1	Ariz. H:10:1	Ariz. H:10:2	Ariz. H:9:1	Ariz. G:11:3	Ariz. F:15:2	Ariz. G:11:2	Ariz. F:15:3	Total
Manos																			
One-hand						2	1	1			1								5
Two-hand		1	1					1		1				1					5
Indeterminant								3											3
Metates																			
Basin	1																		1
Slab								4						1					5
Trough								1											1
Cylindrical Abrader				1															1
Projectile Points																			
Side-notched								1		1					1				3
Stemmed			1																1
Triangular													1						1
Indeterminant										1					1			1	3
Knives																			
Subrectangular								2		1		5							8
Triangular								4											4
Blanks												1							1
Indeterminant								1		2	1	4	2				1		10
Drill																	1		1
Scrapers																			
End								2	1										3
Side					1			5	3	1	4	22	8	1					45
Gravers								1											1
Choppers									1										1
Cores									1				1						2
Utilized Flakes								52	4	11	25	17	2			5			116
Waste Flakes	1							219	3	18	26	44	1			5			317
Hammerstones						1		2											3
Concretion								1											1
Total	2	1	2	1	1	3	1	300	13	36	57	93	15	3	2	10	1	1	542

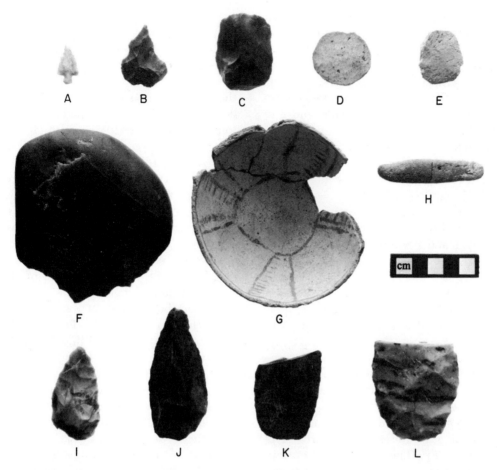

7. *Survey artifacts of Kayenta Anasazi affiliation: A, Ariz. D:11:71, stemmed projectile point; B, Ariz. C:15:1, drill; C, Ariz. C:15:1, end scraper; D, Ariz. D:13:3, Lino Gray worked sherd; E, Ariz. D:11:69, Lino Gray worked sherd; F, Ariz. I:3:1, chopper; G, Ariz. D:11:69, partially restored miniature Lino Black-on-gray vessel; H, Ariz. D:10:5, cylindrical abrader; I–L, Ariz. C:15:1, stone knives*

a small chert side-notched point; the other is a complete stemmed projectile point of white chert. The stem of the latter is narrower than the sides, and has a convex base (Fig. 7A). The dimensions are 25 cm. long, 1.4 cm wide, and 4.5 mm. thick.

Six *stone knives* were recovered from Ariz. C:15:1 (Figs. 7I–L), where they were probably made. They exhibit quite similar techniques of manufacture, percussion flaking followed by pressure retouching. One specimen lacked pressure retouching, but received similar surface scars during use (Fig. 7J). The specimens designated as "triangular"

actually vary from crescent to leaf-shaped; two are best described as subrectangular. Variegated chert was the raw material for all specimens. Whole implements range from 5.5 to 7.8 cm. long, 2 to 3.6 cm. maximum width, and 6 to 20 mm. thick.

One *drill*, presumably hand-held during use, was recovered (Fig. 7B). Reddish chert was pressure flaked to form a thin point with an expanding convex base. The dimensions are 38 cm. long, 2.9 cm. wide, 7 mm. thick.

Scrapers were common only at two Kayenta sites, both near sources of knapping material. Although produced primarily by percussion techniques (Fig. 7C), three scrapers exhibit cutting and scraping edges that were pressure retouched. Identification of scraper types was made on the basis of working edge location; nine side scrapers and three end scrapers were recorded. The measurements range from 3 to 6.4 cm. long, 2 to 5.8 cm. wide, and 2 to 22 mm. thick.

Variegated stone flakes that display use scars, smoothed edges, or both have been classified as *utilized flakes*. Many indicate use primarily in cutting activities.

Stone chips and knapping debris were collected from three sites, but primarily from Ariz. C:15:1 and Ariz. I:3:2, where raw material was close. None of these chips shows evidence of use. An absence of this type of material at other Kayenta sites indicates that most chipped stone implements were processed at specialized locations, such as at Ariz. C:15:1.

One irregular jasper flake, unifacially pressure flaked at one end, was probably utilized as a *graver*. The dimensions are 43 mm. long, 24 mm. wide, and 8 mm. thick.

One *chopper* was made by unifacial percussion flaking a fine-grained quartz river cobble (Fig. 7F). The specimen is oval in outline. It measures 10.5 cm long, 9.9 cm. wide, and 2.5 cm. thick.

One chert *core* was found. Several flakes had been removed, leaving the artifact oval in outline. The dimensions are 6.4 cm. long, 5.7 cm wide, and 2.7 cm. thick.

Rocks with battered surfaces showing repeated hammering, especially on the ends, have been classified as *hammerstones*. Three were collected; two of quartzite and one of jasper. The dimensions range from 7.2 to 8.4 cm. long, 4.8 to 7.5 cm. wide, and 3.5 to 4.8 cm. thick.

Ceramic Artifacts. On the survey 1,174 ceramic fragments were collected from sixteen Kayenta sites, excluding those sites which were excavated (Table 3). At several of these sites sherds were scarce, the collection representing nearly all of those present. At the larger sites, where enormous quantities were present, a representative sample was taken. Large collections of sherds were obtained from Ariz. C:15:1 and Ariz. I:3:2 in order to better assess the cultural affinity and temporal placement of these two manifestations. All of the sherds were sorted into the previously described wares and associated types (see Colton and Hargrave 1937; and Colton 1955; 1956). The decorated pottery is mainly Tusayan White Ware. Sherds possessing the characteristics of Tusayan White Ware, but lacking painted design were tabulated as unclassified as were those whose elements were either unusual or fragmentary for classification.

Varieties of Tusayan Gray Ware dominated the utility wares. Because of the impossibility of distinguishing sherds of Lino Gray from body sherds of Kana-a Gray these were classified as "Lino Tradition." Only the characteristic rim and unobliterated neck coil fragments were placed in the respective Lino Gray or Kana-a Gray varieties. The later period sites also yielded sherds that were unclassifiable or classifiable only to ware; they were simply recorded as Tusayan Gray Ware. Two sherds of Tallahogan Red, earlier often reported as Lino Red (Morris 1939:23; Brew 1946:294; Wendorf 1953:114), were gathered from the surface of Ariz. D:11:69, a Tallahogan phase manifestation. Additional examples of this type were recovered during the excavation of Ariz. D:13:1, D:9:2, and D:10:1. Tallahogan Red is discussed in greater detail in the Ariz. D:13:1 section of this report.

Relatively few sherd types which could be traced to an area other than the Kayenta were recognized. The presence of Deadmans Gray and Deadmans Black-on-gray indicated some contact with the Cohonina Branch to the west. Four sherds of San Juan Red Ware were collected from separate sites, fitting the type description of Abajo Red-on-orange. Whether these represent locally made vessels or trade pieces from the north is unknown.

One small partially restorable Lino Black-on-gray vessel was recovered from the surface of Ariz. D:11:69 (Fig. 7G). The vessel ap-

3. CERAMIC ANALYSIS OF THE UNEXCAVATED KAYENTA SITES

Ceramic Types	Ariz. D:11:69	Ariz. D:11:70	Ariz. D:11:71	Ariz. D:10:5	Ariz. D:10:6	Ariz. D:10:8	Ariz. D:10:9	Ariz. D:13:2	Ariz. D:13:3	Ariz. D:13:5	Ariz. D:13:6	Ariz. D:13:7	Ariz. D:13:8	Ariz. C:16:1	Ariz. C:15:1	Ariz. I:3:2	Total
Tusayan White Ware																	
Kana-a B/W	3	20	11	3			4		2	6		1			34		80
Black Mesa B/W	1		2			4		2		6	1	13				3	36
Sosi B/W							7										7
Dogozhi B/W						6	8					11				9	34
Flagstaff B/W						14	4									4	22
Tusayan B/W							31										31
Kayenta B/W						2	8										10
Unclassified	4	2	1	3		21	6			17		50 *			19	67	190
Tusayan Gray Ware																	
Lino Gray	4	6	5	1	25	1				1			13	4	7		67
Lino Tradition	12	27	21	11		2				5	8				48		134
Tallahogan Red	2																2
Lino F/G	2	3	6	8	2					1							21
Kana-a Gray	1	4	2	2						1	9				1		20
Coconino Gray										1							1
Tusayan Corr.						5		23		9		39			10	86	172
Moenkopi Corr.						15	1									19	35
Kiet Siel Gray						1	2										3
Tusayan Gray Ware						3	9			25		11				37	85
San Juan Red Ware																	
Abajo R/O		1	1			1				1							4
Tsegi Orange Ware																	
Tusayan B/R						2	2									1	5
Tusayan Poly.							7										7
Kayenta Poly.						1											1
Tsegi Orange Ware	2	2					4			1		6			2	30	47
Awatobi Yellow Ware																	
Jeddito Corr.															25		25
Jeddito Plain															59		59
San Francisco Mt. Gray Ware																	
Deadmans Gray															72	2	75
Deadmans B/G							1										1
Total	31	65	49	28	27	78	94	25	2	74	18	131	13	4	277	258	1174

a Includes one Shato B/W variety.

pears to be an early example of this type, as the design is exceedingly simple. The rim diameter is 10.6 cm.; body diameter, 9.3 cm.; height, 5.3 cm.; and the volume, 225 ml.

Six *worked sherds* were recovered from the Kayenta sites. Two are made from Lino Gray sherds (Fig. *7D–E*); the remaining four are fragments of Tusayan White Ware. Both of the Lino Gray examples, one each from Ariz. D:11:69 and D:13:3, are roughly circular measuring 3.3 and 3.7 cm. in diameter, respectively. The rest are too fragmented to determine the original shape, and appear to have been used for smoothing pottery.

One-half of a *ceramic ring* constructed from a flattened coil of Tusayan Gray Ware was found on the surface of Ariz. D:10:5, a Tallahogan phase site. The measurements are: outside diameter, 3.65 cm.; inside diameter, 1.5 cm.; width of coil, 1 cm.; and thickness of coil, 1.7 cm.

One undecorated fragment from a Tusayan White Ware *colander* collected at Ariz. D:10:9, a Toreva phase occupation, was the only recorded example of this style of ceramic treatment.

Cohonina Branch. The majority of stone tools gathered from the Cohonina sites were made for hunting and cutting purposes (Table 2).

Ground Stone Artifacts. Ground stone artifacts were sparse, consisting of only two *manos.*

One limestone one-hand mano has unifacial wear with the convex grinding surface resulted from use with a trough metate. The upper surface is unworked except for the original pecking to shape. The dimensions are 16 cm. long, 10 cm. wide, and 3.6 cm. thick. The second mano is of the two-hand type, constructed of vesicular basalt and has one convex grinding surface. The upper surface is unworked except for the original shaping. The dimensions are 19.5 cm. long, 9.5 cm. wide, and 5.3 cm. thick.

Chipped Stone Artifacts. Chipped stone implements and knapping debris were by far the most conspicuous elements of the Cohonina sites. The best workmanship is represented by percussion flaking, particularly in the large blade category. The chipped stone tools could have been multipurpose, although many appear to have been quickly and crudely fashioned to serve immediate needs. The majority of tools were fashioned of black obsidian, the exceptions being of fine-grained basalt and chert. Obsidian and basalt sources are common in the San Francisco volcanic field, while the chert is obtained from nodules eroding from the Kaibab limestone formation.

Three artifacts, including one unclassifiable tip portion, have been identified as *projectile points.* One specimen is a side-notched point (Fig. *8B*) with a slightly concave base. The artifact was pressure flaked from a primary flake of black obsidian. The tip is missing, as well as a portion of one side. The only complete measurement obtainable is that of thickness, 5 mm.

The second specimen is a long triangular point of black obsidian with convergent straight sides (Fig. *8F*). The secondary flaking indicates careful retouching. A portion of the convex base is missing. McGregor (1951: 111; 1967:89) characterizes this form as the most typical of the Cohonina culture.

The remaining projectile point is an unclassifiable tip section (Fig. *8G*). The fragment is representative of a large, heavy point, constructed by applying percussion and pressure flaking techniques to a thick black obsidian flake.

Sixteen stone *knives* are represented in the collection. Six speciments are listed as subrectangular knives (Table 2), although several are somewhat leaf-shaped. Four of these were constructed of black obsidian, the remaining two of fine-grained basalt and chert. Percussion knapping followed by pressure retouching was the method of manufacture. Two specimens (Fig. *8L–M*) have slight remnant tangs, indicating that these small knives were probably hafted. The dimensions are

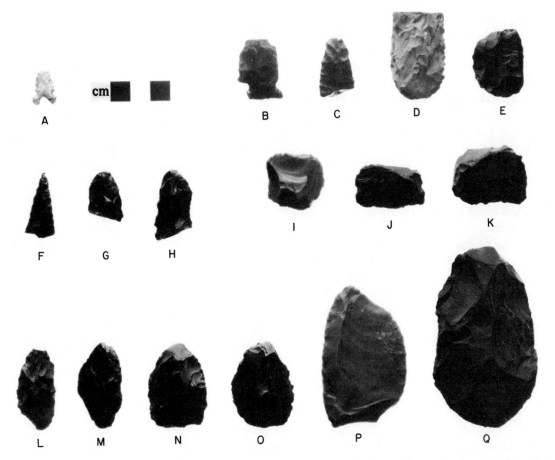

8. *Artifacts from Cerbat and Cohonina sites: A, Ariz. G:11:3, Cerbat side-notched projectile point; B–E, Ariz. I:5:2, projectile point and knife fragments; F–H, Ariz. H:10:2, projectile point and knife fragments; I–J, Ariz. H:10:1, side scrapers; K, Ariz. H:10:2, side scraper; L–P, Ariz. H:10:1, stone knives; Q, Ariz. H:10:1, knife blank*

3.9 to 6.4 cm. long, 1.9 to 4.2 cm. wide, and 6 mm. to 2 cm. thick. The chert knife (Fig. *8P*) was fashioned from a primary flake. The removal of a flake left a fluted scar across one side of the knife. This channel or flute renders the artifact ideal for hand use. The dimensions are 6.7 cm. long, 4.2 cm. wide, and 7 mm. thick.

One fine-grained black basalt artifact is representative of an unfinished knife. Although pounding scars are present, indicating secondary use as a chopping implement, the artifact is more characteristic of a knife blank (Fig. *8Q*). The blank was originally shaped

by percussion techniques, with use scars later resulting from its use as a blunt chopping or pounding tool. Its dimensions are 8.6 cm. long, 5.1 cm. wide, and 2.6 cm. thick.

Nine additional knife fragments were found; six are of black obsidian and three are of chert. Although they add little information, they do conform to production techniques described above.

Side *scrapers* were found at each Cohonina site. The scrapers are all rather heavy primary flakes with pressure retouching on one or more sides (Fig. *8I–K*). Of the thirty-five scrapers, twenty-seven were fashioned of black obsidian, five of black basalt, and three of pink chert. These scrapers range from subrectangular to oval, although most were irregular in form. The presence of secondary flaking, along one or more edges, differentiated the scrapers from the utilized knapping debris. Dimensions range from 3.4 to 6.4 cm. long, 2 to 4.2 cm. wide, and 3 mm. to 1.5 cm. thick.

One black obsidian *core* was recovered. The artifact is roughly circular with seven primary flakes removed to form a platform. Its dimensions are 3.8 to 4.9 cm. in diameter, and 2 cm. thick.

The knapping debris that displayed use scars, smoothed edges, or both, have been classified as *utilized flakes*. These artifacts were numerous, and many were utilized only once. *Waste flakes,* the knapping debris of stone tool manufacture, were also plentiful at Cohonina sites. None of these stone chips display evidence of use but are the debitage of tool manufacture. Obsidian, basalt, chert, and quartz in decreasing amounts were represented in the collection of utilized and waste flakes.

The lithic assemblage from the four recorded Cohonina sites shows considerable variation in both workmanship and form. Nevertheless, many of these tools would have been useful in skinning animals, preparing those skins, and butchering the meat.

Ceramic Artifacts. Ceramic remains were not as conspicuous a feature of the Cohonina sites as were the lithic tools. Ceramic fragments making up the various collections were predominantly San Francisco Mountain Gray Ware (Table 4) and were sorted according to the types described by Colton (1958). Deadmans Gray, a utility type of the Cohonina people, occurred at each site in larger numbers than any other type.

4. CERAMIC ANALYSIS OF THE UNEXCAVATED COHONINA AND CERBAT SITES

Ceramic Types	Cohonina			Cerbat			Total
	Ariz. I:5:2	Ariz. H:7:1	Ariz. H:10:2	Ariz. H:10:2	Ariz. H:9:1	Ariz. F:15:2	
San Francisco Mt. Gray Ware							
Floyd B/G	2						2
Deadmans Gray	89	5	29	78			201
Deadmans Fug. Red	19			8			27
Deadmans B/G	11		1	1			13
Tizon Brown Ware							
Cerbat Brown			3		8	11	22
Aquarius Brown				2			2
Prescott Gray Ware							
Aquarius Orange					2	1	3
Lower Colo. Buff Ware							
Parker R/Buff						1	1
Pyramid Gray						1	1
Tusayan Gray Ware							
Lino Gray					1		1
Tusayan Corr.	19						19
San Juan Red Ware							
Deadmans B/R	2						2
Unclassified	5						5
Tsegi Orange Ware							
Medicine B/R	2			1			3
Unclassified	2						2
Total	151	5	33	91	10	14	304

Only one worked sherd was recovered from the Cohonina sites; a large irregular sherd of Deadmans Fugitive Red.

The fragment, from Ariz. I:5:2, is 9.9 cm. long, 6.9 cm. wide, and 0.6 cm. thick.

When present, the best dating tools from surface collections are the intrusive sherds of known Kayenta manufacture. Because these sherds occur in low numbers at three of the sites, their temporal placement is not conclusive. The evidence does indicate that contact was well established with the Kayenta group, and that the area was occupied by the Cohonina during the period equivalent to the Kayenta Pueblo I-II periods (ca. A.D. 750–1100). The sites have been assigned to the various Cohonina cultural phases, described by Colton (1939; 1958) and McGregor (1951) as presented in Table 1. Assignment of phases, without excavation, rested solely on the ceramic components.

Cerbat Branch. A discussion of the artifact types from the Cerbat sites is of little value, as only sixteen items were collected (Table 2). For this reason, the individual artifacts are described without detailed comment except where special features merit attention.

Ground Stone Artifacts. A fragment of vesicular basalt has been classified as the remains of a *mano* with a flat grinding surface. Complete measurements cannot be given; however, the width is 9.2 cm. and the thickness is 4.2 cm.

One complete slab *milling stone* of vesicular basalt completes the collection of ground stone artifacts. Two sides and the top have been ground to form a subtriangular outline. The entire surface is flat and seems to have been used only slightly. This type of slab milling stone is recognized as representative of the historic and prehistoric (Cerbat) Walapai culture (Euler 1958:27). Its dimensions are 36.8 cm. long, 24 cm. wide, and 16.8 cm. thick.

Chipped Stone Artifacts. Two chipped stone artifacts have been classified as *projectile points*. The nearly complete specimen from Ariz. G:11:3 is a characteristic Cerbat

projectile point, fitting Euler's (1958:69, 147) descriptions. The chert projectile point is small, double side-notched, and triangular, with a deep concave base (Fig. *8A*). The dimensions are 1.7 cm. long (with tip missing), 1.2 cm. wide, and 2 mm. thick.

The other projectile point is represented by a body fragment of white chert. The artifact was pressure flaked. The width is 1.8 cm. and thickness, 5 mm.

One side *scraper* of gray basalt is triangular with a flat base. Edge flakes were removed along both sides by pressure retouch, with a slight tendency towards serration in some areas. The scrapers are 3.4 cm. long, 2.3 cm. wide, and 3 mm. thick.

Five *utilized flakes* and five *waste flakes* were collected from Ariz. F:15:2, although no other lithic artifacts could be located. The material consisted of chert (7), quartz (2), and basalt (1).

It is significant that Ariz. G:11:3 could be assigned to the Cerbat culture on the basis of the identified projectile point. The site was small, ill defined, and consisted of two damaged projectile points and a concentration of stone chips. Similar sites are reported for the Cohonina area (McGregor 1951:111) and are considered: to represent a prepottery occupation; workshops of protohistoric groups; or workshops of a pottery-making, house-building prehistoric group.

Ceramic Artifacts. Identification of the Cerbat sites rests solely on the geographical location and the dominance of Tizon Brown Ware. Sherd collections were small (Table 4), and were identified on the basis of the revised descriptions of Euler and Dobyns (1958). Only Cerbat Brown and Aquarius Brown were present. The presence of a few sherds of Prescott Gray Ware, indicating contacts with peoples of the Prescott Branch located to the south, enabled a placement of the occupations between A.D. 1000 and 1150. Both occupations were of short duration within this period.

The reason for the absence of ceramic material in large quantity is unknown. It may mean that few vessels were used, or that these were occupied for only a short time. Without excavation, the second hypothesis seems most likely.

Indeterminate. Two fragmentary lithic artifacts were collected from sites of unclassifiable cultural affinity. A *projectile point* fragment was found on the surface at Ariz. F:15:2, a nonceramic rockshelter occupation. The artifact was constructed of black basalt, possessing serrated parallel sides; the base and tip are both missing. Although the fragment is small, the general appearance suggests an original form characteristic of the Pinto complex of the Desert Culture. Patina on the artifact along with its presence in a nonceramic site suggests considerable antiquity. The measurable portions are: width, 1.3 cm. and thickness, 7 mm.

A fragment of a chert knife was found at Ariz. G:11:2, a small lithic workshop. This fragment, originally triangular, was probably broken during manufacture. The measurable portions are: width, 2.9 cm. and thickness, 7 mm.

In addition to the lithic artifact collected at Ariz. F:15:3, a number of normally perishable items were collected. All were fragmentary wooden specimens. Several fragments were smoothed round sticks, presumably *arrow shafts,* with one end ground to form a point. A *fire drill friction platform,* similar to one illustrated by Long (1966:14) from Glen Canyon, was among the collection.

SURVEY SUMMARY AND DISCUSSION

The survey section of this report is a summary of the data collected at fifty-eight sites distributed along the pipeline right-of-way. The sites were placed in cultural categories and when possible further described on the basis of site type, material culture, and temporal placement.

A portion of the area involved lies in northern Arizona within the modern Navajo Reservation. The Navajo remains recorded in the vicinity of Cameron warrant additional comment. The present occupation is sparse, except for the concentrations around Cameron and Buck Rogers Trading Post. The people now depend for the most part on wage work and various welfare programs, although a few small sheep and goat herds are maintained. The style of hogan has become the typical single-room frame house constructed of modern roofing material, siding, with glass windows. The only connection between this new house and the older traditional hogans is that the structure's entrance still faces east.

Overgrazing has destroyed much of the vegetation. This has resulted in nearly a complete abandonment of the region south of Cameron except for seasonal occupations by small herding groups late in summer after the "rainy season." This general depopulation is of fairly recent date, although some structures were certainly abandoned earlier than others. The small or single habitation sites represented occupations lasting through the summer grazing cycles, and the seasonal migrants returned to larger population centers during the winter. Apparently families either lived together in a group or in semi-isolation single habitational units, with nuclear families the general rule. Other than the two multiple habitation sites, consisting of two or more hogans and associated features, no evidence for extended families was recorded or observed. When the surrounding area could no longer support the required number of sheep, families were forced to move on, the area becoming totally abandoned. The exception is those Navajos living in the vicinity of Cameron and Buck Rogers Trading Post.

The study area was the prehistoric "homeland" of three recognized subcultures: the Kayenta, Cohonina, and Cerbat branches. As a result of various salvage archaeology programs conducted in northern Arizona and southern Utah over the past two decades, the Kayenta Anasazi have become the most studied prehistoric group in the Southwest. As Lindsay and Ambler (1963) have pointed out, these salvage programs are also responsible for revealing gaps in our knowledge of this culture. The information gained from the present project, and related work in the coal fields, has served to reduce the geographical void in Kayenta research.

The three sites of the Basketmaker III period that were excavated demonstrate an early habitational use of the western edge of Black Mesa and the region south of Red Lake Trading Post.

South of the Grand Canyon, between Flagstaff and the Colorado River, the survey recorded seven sites assigned to the prehistoric Cohonina and Cerbat branches. The sites are located west of the 112-degree meridian in an area Euler (1962) characterized as one of the most pressing regions for future research in Arizona archaeology. Although McGregor (1967) and Harrill (1968) have reported the results of their respective research in the area, little has taken place to change this evaluation. It is unfortunate that the number of these sites from the survey, and the artifacts gathered from them were too few to draw any new valid conclusions regarding these two manifestations.

The Cohonina Branch was first identified and named by Hargrave (1937,1938). Colton (1938,1945a) soon concluded that the Cohonina was a valid branch, and suggested that it be assigned to the Patayan Root. Recent work by McGregor (1951:134–42) mentioned a possible Cohonina and Havasupai relationship, which was later advanced and presented by Schwartz (1956a,1956b) and McGregor (1967) as a gradual evolution from the Cohonina prehistoric stage to the modern day Havasupai. However, this hypothesis has not been accepted by Dobyns (1956) or Euler (1958,1963) who have worked with the historic Walapai-Havasupai and prehistoric Cerbat remains. It is their contention that the Havasupai and Walapai culture is derived from the Cerbat Branch which moved eastward, eventually displacing the Cohonina, between A.D. 1150–1300. What happened to the Cohonina remains unknown as Euler (1963:84) has pointed out. Any study of the

interaction of cultures within this area must of necessity consider Schroeder's (1957,1960) Hakatayan concept, which at one time or another affected a number of Southwestern prehistoric cultures including: Amacava, Cerbat, Prescott and Cohonina branches, and the early Sinagua and Pioneer Hohokam (Euler 1963:83).

This brief account of the complex cultural relationships of the northwestern portion of Arizona demonstrates that much remains to be done if we are ever to reach a better understanding of the spatial, temporal, and cultural relationships between the Cohonina and Cerbat branches and the historic Havasupai and Walapai. Evidence of some trade relationship between the Kayenta, Cohonina, and Cerbat groups is recorded by ceramics. Limited contact between the Cohonina, Cerbat, and Prescott branches also existed. Without excavation the survey failed to produce detailed information on the interaction of these groups.

THE EXCAVATIONS

History and Methods

This section of the report deals with the results of salvage archaeological excavations conducted in connection with construction of the Black Mesa coal slurry pipeline. During the excavation of the pipeline trench, construction crews revealed five buried sites unobserved during the helicopter survey. The sites were all Kayenta Anasazi representing occupations ranging from possible Basketmaker II through Pueblo II (Lamoki phase).

The excavation techniques were oriented toward recovering the maximum amount of information with the least expenditure of time and money. Excavation was greatly facilitated by the use of heavy equipment in the removal of sand overburden and trenching-machine back dirt from the buried cultural deposits. Different circumstances necessitated the use of backhoes, bulldozers, and road graders. Skilled pipeline construction crews operated this equipment, removing large quantities of earth quickly with a minimum of danger to the hidden features. By these techniques we were able to discover and excavate a larger portion of each threatened site than would have been possible by hand labor.

Conventional archaeological techniques were used with Navajos hired as excavators. Subsurface features were discovered by digging trenches at regular intervals into sterile soil. Such trenching techniques were also employed to delimit the trash deposits and structures observed before excavation. All structures, because of a lack of observable stratigraphy, were excavated in two levels, fill and floor. The floor level consisted of the floor itself and the approximately 15 cm. of deposits above it. Walls and floors were, in general, cleared with trowels and whisk brooms; where practical, shovels were also utilized.

No tree-ring dates were derived from the forty-three dendrochronological specimens collected on this project. The samples were primarily from collapsed roofing debris found in various burned structures at Ariz. D:9:1 (9), Ariz. D:9:2 (20), and Ariz. D:10:1 (14). The specimens, submitted to the Laboratory of Tree-Ring Research, University of Arizona, Tucson, proved to be mostly juniper (*Juniperus* sp.); undatable due to the recurrence of missing or double rings, and compressed or erratic ring patterns (William J. Robinson, personal communication).

The following individual site reports are listed in temporal order, from oldest to the most recent, not in the order in which they were excavated.

Ariz. D:13:4

INTRODUCTION

Ariz. D:13:4 off the east edge of Black Mesa, has been assigned to the Basketmaker II cultural complex of the Kayenta Anasazi tradition, but with some reservations. This assignment depends essentially on negative evidence, including the absence of ceramics and pithouse architecture usually associated with later horizons of the Kayenta culture. It was unfortunate that we did not succeed in finding additional diagnostic artifactual evidence for reported Basketmaker II open sites (Eddy 1961; Gumerman 1966). If our temporal identification is correct, study of the site has broadened the picture of Anasazi Basketmaker II culture by the addition of a definite style of residential architecture—the jacal unit.

With reference to the Black Mesa pipeline, Ariz. D:13:4 is located at Station 1958 approximately 12 miles south of Red Lake Trading Post, Tonalea, Arizona (Fig. *1*).

The natural setting is in the Upper Sonoran life zone at an elevation of about 5,300 feet. The site lies upon deep eolian sand slopes situated between Black Mesa and Middle Mesa, a few miles to the east and west respectively. The entire valley floor slopes downward from the base of the two mesa escarpments, about 4 miles north of Moenkopi Wash.

This semiarid region is best described as consisting of stabilized sand dunes which support a desert grassland type of biotic community. Identified species include: Indian ricegrass (*Orysopsis lumenoides*), Indian wheat (*Plantago* sp.), Mormon tea (*Ephedra viridis*), narrow-leaf yucca (*Yucca angustissima*), sagebrush (*Artemesia* sp.), snakeweed (*Gutierrezia* sp.), prickly pear (*Opuntia* sp.), and cane cholla (*Opuntia* sp.). Substantial stands of juniper and piñon grow on Black Mesa and Middle Mesa at higher elevations nearby. A localized outcrop of Navajo sandstone is exposed about 100 meters south of the site. At certain times this formation may have supplied water which was trapped in small surface depressions.

No other sites were found near Ariz. D:13:4, although they may be similarly buried. No visible indications of prehistoric occupation were apparent on the present ground surface; however, exposed at a depth of 50 cm. in the wall of the pipe trench were two consolidated lenses of charcoal-stained sand. Careful examination of the trench back-dirt failed to locate any ceramics or stone tools, and a preceramic site was anticipated.

The site was excavated between July 25 and 30, 1969, requiring twenty-two man-days to complete. Excavation was begun by digging trenches parallel to the pipe trench. Trenching was used to delimit Structure 1 and to search for additional features. Excavation affirmed the nonceramic character.

ARCHITECTURE

Structure 1 (Figure 9)

Type of Structure. Subrectangular jacal dwelling; four contiguous domestic surface rooms. Interior rooms irregular in outline.

Dimensions. East-West, 7.3 m.; North-South, 4.4 m. Average depth of floor below present ground surface, 50 cm. Floor on old occupation surface.

Walls. Jacal. Dwelling divided into four rooms by three partitions. Pattern consisting of eighty-six postholes delineating all walls and entries. Distance between wall support posts varied only slightly. Plastered with daub as indicated by clay in fill. Height unknown. Depth of posts below old occupation surface, 6 to 20 cm.; diameter, 9 to 18 cm.

Entrances. One exterior entryway and three interior passageways indicated by wall openings. Openings through partitions gave access to all rooms. Openings range from 45 to 78 cm. in width.

Floor. Well preserved; packed red orange sand, 5 cm. thick. Easily followed with trowel.

Hearth. Circular, 55 cm. in diameter; 15 cm. deep. Basin-shaped in cross section. Walls of baked sand. No ash in fill.

Storage Pits. 1. Circular. Vertical walls perpendicular to flat bottom. No evidence of plaster. Diameter, 55 cm.; depth, 15 cm. 2. Oval. Basin-shaped in cross section. No evidence of plaster. Length, 35 cm.; width, 25 cm.; and depth, 15 cm.

Roof. 5 cm. layer of darker stained, often clayey, reddish brown compacted sand now resting on the floor. No discernible pattern of timbers remained.

Fill. Overburden of 80 cm. of windblown sand. Occasional charcoal flecks and daub fragments near floor.

Material Culture. Three fragments from one slab metate, one combination hammerstone-handchopper, one chert waste flake, all near the floor.

ARCHITECTURAL SUMMARY

In spite of extensive testing only one architectural feature was located at Ariz. D:13:4. The floor and its details were easily defined, but doubt remained as to the form and method of construction of the superstructure. Jacal architecture implies a certain technique of roofing, which the excavation failed to substantiate completely. Residual roofing material was directly superimposed on the floor. No samples of natural wood were recovered. In similar structures of comparable age, Fenenga and Wendorf (1956:208) have reported that only burned fragments of clay daub demonstrated that structures were once present. Since the structure at Ariz. D:13:4 had not burned, the daub decomposed much more readily. The well-preserved floor with associated artifacts clearly demonstrates the presence of a jacal dwelling.

REFUSE

The only refuse located was the charcoal-stained concentrations of sand. Such areas were easily recognized, as they contrasted sharply with the surrounding sterile sand.

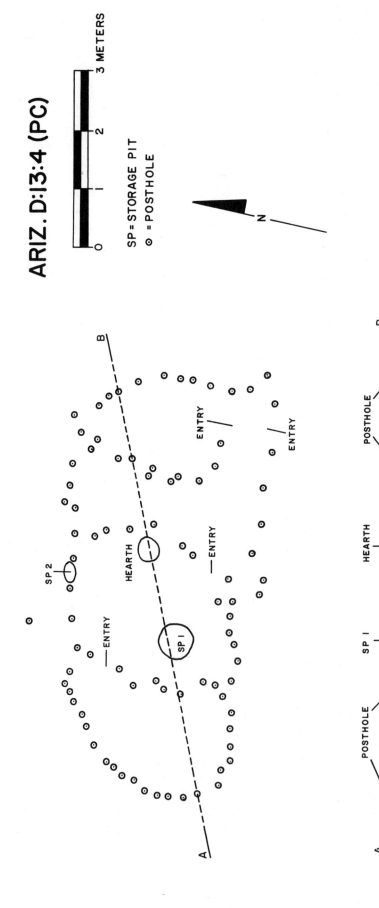

ARIZ. D:13:4 (PC)

3 METERS

SP = STORAGE PIT
⊙ = POSTHOLE

N

B

ENTRY

ENTRY

SP 2

HEARTH

ENTRY

SP 1

ENTRY

A

B

POSTHOLE

HEARTH

SP 1

POSTHOLE

A

9. Ariz. D:13:4. Plan and profile of jacal dwelling

Two concentrations of ash-stained sand were located 15 meters apart in front of the dwelling, where ash taken from the hearth had been dumped. These deposits were excavated in 10 cm. levels and all soil was screened. The deposits were void of cultural material, and were never more than 40 cm. thick. Samples of this charcoal-stained soil were submitted to the Geochronology Laboratory at the University of Arizona in hopes that a carbon-14 date could be obtained. Utilizing the flotation method, enough carbon could not be reclaimed to assure accuracy in dating.

OTHER EXCAVATIONS

Fourteen test trenches, 1 meter wide and totaling 92 meters in length, were dug to slightly below the old occupational level (ranging from 40 to 80 cm. below the present ground surface) in search of associated features or artifacts. In this manner the entire site area within the fifty foot right-of-way was tested.

ARTIFACTS

Artifacts were rare at the site. All items collected were associated with the jacal dwelling, except a single waste flake found in a test trench nearby. The artifacts are shown in Figure *10*.

Ground Stone Artifacts

Ground stone artifacts (Fig. *10B*) were represented by three *metate* fragments, pre-

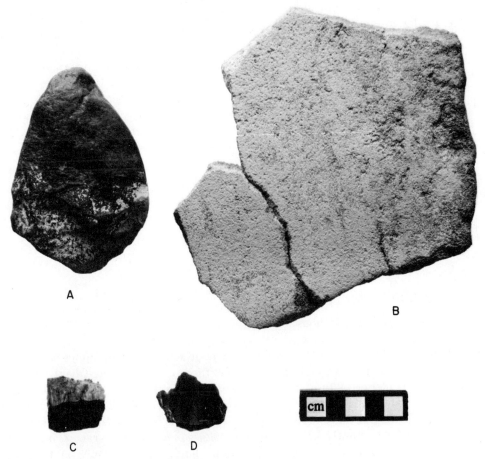

10. *Ariz. D:13:4. Ground and chipped stone artifacts*

sumably from the same flat or slab metate. The only meaningful measurement is thickness—1.8 to 3.3 cm.

Chipped Stone Artifacts

There were three chipped stone artifacts (Fig. *10A*). A combination *hammerstone-handchopper* was fashioned from a quartz river cobble by removing several primary flakes from one end using the percussion technique. A heavy coating of patina covering these knapping scars attests to the age of the tool. Evidence of battering, owing to secondary use as a hammerstone, is also present. The measurements are 9.7 cm. long, 6.4 cm. wide, and 5.2 cm. thick.

One *scraper* (Fig. *10C*) of variegated chert indicates limited use along one edge. Patina is present on the surface, but not along the worked edge. Its dimensions are 2.9 cm. long, 2.8 cm. wide, and 1.2 cm. thick.

The remaining chipped stone artifact was a gray chert *waste flake* (Fig. *10D*). The item was a result of percussion flaking, and with no evidence of pressure retouch or utilization.

SUMMARY AND DISCUSSION

Ariz. D:13:4 has provided evidence for a probable Basketmaker II occupation at an open site. The architectural remains excavated are unique for an open site of a non-ceramic character, differing from those recorded at open sites of similar antiquity by Fenenga and Wendorf (1956), Eddy (1961), and Gumerman (1966). Nor does the site conform to previously described patterns of the Basketmaker II culture of the San Juan area, the Navajo Reservoir District in New Mexico, or the one Lolomai phase site excavated on Black Mesa (see Karlstrom, Gumerman, and Euler, this volume). The site in all probability represents a local variant of the Basketmaker II culture so well documented from the caves of the San Juan area (Roberts 1929; Amsden 1949; Lockett and Hargrave 1953; Morris and Burgh 1954; Lockett and Lindsay 1968).

The dwelling was built with a minimum of effort, giving short-term shelter to a small group. The lack of datable material necessitates a guess date of between A.D. 1 and 500. The most important information derived from Ariz. D:13:4 is: 1. that sites of this type do exist, and 2. that the previously unrecorded presence of jacal architecture is a probable trait of the Basketmaker II tradition.

Ariz. D:13:1

INTRODUCTION

Ariz. D:13:1 is a Dot Klish phase site, occupied at the time ceramic technology was being introduced to the Kayenta Anasazi. Dates for the ceramic Basketmaker III component are about A.D. 500 or 600 to 700.

The site is located approximately three miles east of Ariz. D:13:4, at Station 1808 on the Black Mesa pipeline, slightly below the western escarpment of Black Mesa (Fig. *1*).

The setting is similar to that previously described for Ariz. D:13:4, the major difference being its proximity to Black Mesa. Here also, the immediate environment is characterized by large stabilized sand dunes occurring at an elevation of 5,580 feet. Characteristic plant species identified include: Indian ricegrass (*Orysopsis hymenoides*), Mormon tea (*Ephedra viridis*), narrow-leaf yucca (*Yucca angustissima*), grama grass (*Bouteloua sp.*), cane cholla (*Opuntia* sp.), and prickly pear

5. ARIZ. D:13:1. CERAMIC ANALYSIS

Ceramic Types	Surface	Structure			Broadside				Test Trenches	Total
		1 Fill	2 Fill	3 Fill	1	3	4	5		
Tusayan Gray Ware										
Lino Gray	3	8	18	6	48	21	90	16	18	228
Lino Smudged	6	2	8	4	34	5	28	2	29	118
Tallahogan Red			3			3				6
Total	9	10	29	10	82	29	118	18	47	352

(*Opuntia* sp.). Stands of juniper and Colorado piñon (*Pinus edulis*) grow on nearby Black Mesa, with occasional stunted junipers growing at the base of the escarpment.

Located one-half mile north of the site is a seep spring, which now provides water for Navajo herds. Nearby are eight prehistoric settlements ranging temporally from Basketmaker III (Dot Klish phase) into Pueblo II (Lamoki phase), which probably indicates that this same water source was available prehistorically. Small plots of land suitable for dry-farming techniques, combined with an adequate water supply enabled the early inhabitants of the region to remain in the region over a span of several hundred years.

Visible indications of a prehistoric occupation were lacking on the present ground surface but the pipe trench bisected a subterranean dwelling. Examination of the trench back-dirt exposed sherds of Lino Gray suggesting a Dot Klish phase occupation. Later excavation and artifactual analysis affirmed this.

Ariz. D:13:1 was excavated between July 14 and 25, 1969, requiring fifty-three man-days to complete. Excavation was begun by digging test trenches parallel to both sides of the pipe trench. Where buried structures were encountered, Broadsides were established to delimit features and collect associated artifacts from the overburden. In Table 5, Broadside 1 is asociated with Structure 1; Broadside 3 with Structure 2; Broadside 4 with Structure 4; Broadside 5 with Structure 5.

ARCHITECTURE

Structure 1 (Figure *11*)

Type of Structure. Circular pithouse.

Dimensions. Diameter, 3 m. Average depth of floor from present ground surface, 1.2 m.; from old occupation surface, 80 cm.

Walls. Formed by unplastered sides of original pit excavated into consolidated orange sand. Vertical.

Entrance. Probably through roof.

Ventilator. Opens into pithouse through southeast wall, 8 cm. above floor level. Circular in cross section. Diameter of room opening, 40 cm. Horizontal section of shaft, 1.6 m. Unlined. Diameter of opening at old ground surface, 55 cm.

Floor. Bisected by pipe trench. Native orange sand packed by use. Even. Wall-floor juncture at right angles.

Hearth. Destroyed by pipe trench. Burned sandstone slabs, recovered from trench back-dirt, suggest slab-lined hearth.

Posthole. Single primary roof support on floor, near east wall. Depth below floor, 20 cm.; diameter, 14 cm.

Roof. Polygonal framework or domed roof suggested by nine primary support posts spaced around perimeter of subterranean dwelling. Depth of posts below old occupation surface, 15 to 17 cm.; diameter, 15 to 16 cm. Covered with daub.

Fill. Orange sand containing charcoal flecks, wind- and water-deposited. Trash de-

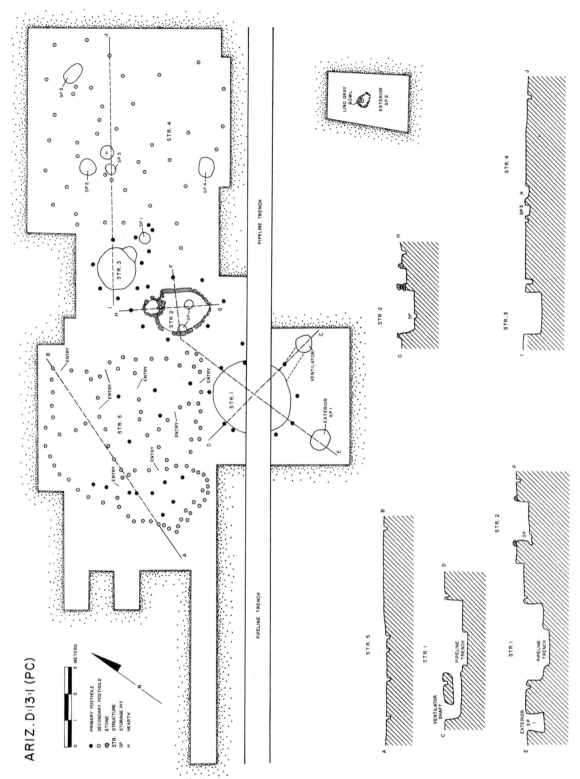

ARIZ. D:13:1 (PC)

PRIMARY POSTHOLE
SECONDARY POSTHOLE
STONE
STR. STRUCTURE
SP STORAGE PIT
H HEARTH

11. *Ariz. D:13:1. Architectural plan and profiles*

posited after dwelling had been allowed to stand abandoned for some time. Debris consisted mostly of organic trash and a few sherds.

Material Culture. From the fill: restorable Lino Black-on-gray bowl, bone awl fragment, end scraper, slab metate fragment, trough metate fragment, one-hand mano, indeterminant mano fragment, and three hammerstones. Also from the fill is an unworked piece of gypsum crystal and one fossil mollusk shell (*Gryphgea* sp.) .

Structure 2 (Figure *11*)

Type of Structure. Oval subsurface storage room.

Dimensions. East-West, 1.9 m.; North-South, 2.6 m. Average depth of floor from present ground surface, 85 cm.; from old occupation surface, 70 cm.

Walls. Portion below old occupation surface formed by unplastered sides of original pit excavated into native consolidated orange sand. Section above old ground surface constructed of sandstone masonry. Sandstone pieces are unprepared and vary greatly in size. Wall averages two courses in height, and one stone in width; maximum height of standing wall is 20 cm. Average width is 15 cm.

Entrance. Probably through roof.

Floor. Even, native orange sand packed by use. Wall-floor juncture is at right angles.

Storage Pit. Additional storage area or recess in west wall. Floor is flat; located 10 cm. below room floor. Diameter at floor level, 35 cm.; height, 30 cm. May have held large olla.

Miscellaneous Hole. Possibly pot rest. Slight depression in center of floor, presumably for holding round-bottomed containers. Diameter, 50 cm.; depth, 7 cm.

Storage Bin. Bonded circular masonry feature, constructed on old ground surface, contiguous to north end of storage pit. Masonry similar to that described above; smaller stone. Floor flat; located 30 cm. below top of

masonry and 10 cm. below old occupation surface. Diameter, 60 cm. Fill consisted of orange sand with charcoal flecks.

Roof. Quadrilateral arrangement of primary roof supports suggests a rectangular plate on which horizontal timbers rested. Covered with daub. Nine primary roof supports, set away from masonry wall; depth below old occupation surface 13 to 45 cm. Diameter, 12 to 15 cm.

Fill. Wind- and water-deposited orange sand containing charcoal flecks and sherds. Layer of roofing daub, 5 to 15 cm. thick, located 35 cm. above floor indicates structure abandoned for short period before roof collapsed.

Material Culture. A single waste flake in fill.

Structure 3 (Figure *11*)

Type of Structure. Circular subsurface storage room.

Dimensions. East-West, 1.45 m.; North-South, 1.38 m. Average depth of floor from present ground surface, 1.3 m.; from old occupation surface, 65 cm.

Walls. Formed by unplastered sides of original pit excavated into consolidated orange sand. Vertical. Wall-floor juncture at right angles.

Entrance: Covered passageway or entry through east wall; evidenced by posthole pattern and step cut into wall. Step located 33 cm. above floor; width, 68 cm.; depth, 16 cm.

Floor. Native orange sand packed by use. Wall-floor juncture at right angles.

Roof. Quadrilateral arrangement of primary roof supports suggests a rectangular plate on which horizontal timbers were supported. Covered with daub. Eight primary posts set around perimeter of pit; depth below old occupation surface, 18 to 32 cm. Diameter, 13 to 16 cm.

Fill. Orange sand, wind- and water-deposited, containing charcoal flecks and a few sherds. Layer of roofing daub fragments, 6 cm. thick located 27 cm. above floor, demonstrates that the storage room was abandoned for some time before roof collapsed.

Material Culture. Only a few sherds in fill.

Structure 4 (Figure *11*)

Type of Structure. Summer shade or ramada. Work area.

Dimensions. East-West, 7.1 m.; North-South, 6.9 m. Average depth of floor below present ground surface, 85 cm.; originally constructed on old ground surface.

Walls. No evidence. Were probably not enclosed.

Floor. Even native orange sand packed by use. Varying amounts of charcoal worked into floor.

Hearth. Circular, 55 cm. in diameter; 20 cm. deep. Basin-shaped in cross section. Walls of baked sand. Some gray wood ash in sandy fill. Located in north central portion of structure.

Storage Pits. 1. Circular, 45 cm. in diameter; 15 cm. deep. Vertical walls. Floor flat; curves up to meet walls. Wind deposited orange sand with charcoal flecks constituted fill. Located along west wall near entrance to structure 3. 2. Circular, 40 cm. in diameter; 30 cm. deep. Walls vertical. Floor flat; curves up to meet walls. Fill consisted of orange sand with charcoal flecks. Located 40 cm. northwest of hearth. 3. Circular, 40 cm. in diameter; 20 cm. deep. Walls vertical. Floor flat, but slopes down to east; curves up to meet walls. Fill of orange sand with charcoal flecks. Located 20 cm. west of hearth. 4. Circular, 60 cm. in diameter; 20 cm. deep. Walls vertical. Floor flat; curves up to meet walls. Fill of orange sand with charcoal flecks. Located near south wall in center of structure. 5. Oval, 80 cm. in length; 60 cm. wide: 30 cm. deep. Basin-shaped in cross section. Fill of orange sand with charcoal flecks. Located in northeast portion of ramada.

Postholes. Forty-three roof supports. Depth below floor, 11 to 22 cm.; diameter, 10 to 30 cm.

Roof. Probably perishable material resting on ridge poles.

Fill. Overburden of 85 cm. of windblown orange sand. Occasional charcoal flecks increasing in concentration near floor. Few sherds and stone artifacts were collected in broadside provenience.

Material Culture. Sherds and waste flakes in Broadside 4.

Structure 5 (Figure *11*)

Type of Structure. Circular jacal dwelling; six contiguous domestic surface rooms. Interior rooms irregular in outline.

Dimensions. East-West, 6.7 m.; North-South; 6.53 m. Average of floor depth below present ground surface, 80 cm.; constructed on old occupation surface.

Walls. Jacal. Dwelling divided into six rooms by partitions. Pattern consisting of eighty-nine postholes indicated all walls and entries. Distance between wall support posts varied. Walls were covered with clay. Thickness varied from 15 to 20 cm. Height unknown. Depth of posts beneath old occupation surface, 9 to 40 cm. Diameter, 10 to 16 cm.

Entrance. Three exterior entrances and five interior passageways indicated by wall openings with packed floors. Exterior doorways placed on the leeward side of the predominating southwesterly winds. Openings through interior partitions gave access to all sections of dwelling. Openings range between 55 and 70 cm. wide.

Floor. Similar to other floors at the site.

Postholes. Fourteen interior primary roof supports were located. Depth below floor. 10 to 27 cm.; diameter, 11 to 14 cm.

Roof. Possibly perishable material resting on walls and daubed.

Fill. Overburden of 80 cm. of windblown orange sand and charcoal flecks. Charcoal flecks extend 22 cm. above floor, while fragmented daub pieces are located on the floor. Sherds and occasional artifacts collected from Broadside 5.

Material Culture. Items collected in Broadside 5.

Extramural Storage Pits (Figure *12*)

1. Located 1.2 m. south of Structure 1. Circular, diameter 75 cm. Average depth of floor below present ground surface, 1.15 m.; below old occupation surface, 75 cm. Walls vertical, or nearly so. Sides of original pit unplastered. Floor flat, curves up to meet walls. No evidence of roofing. Wind- and water-deposited orange sand containing charcoal flecks constituted the fill. 2. Located 10 m. east of Structure 1. Circular pit lined with vertical sandstone slabs. This slab-lined storage pit could have been sealed to deter rodents. Walls vertical; two slabs high. Maximum height above old occupation surface, 23 cm. Diameter, 50 cm. Average depth of floor below old occupation surface, 20 cm.; from present ground surface, 55 cm. Fine orange sand, wind- and water-deposited, with occasional charcoal flecks. Material culture: a complete Lino Gray bowl.

ARCHITECTURAL SUMMARY

Ariz. D:13:1 appears to have no distinguishable village pattern unless the orientation of Structures 3 and 5 to the east, is considered evidence of an attempt at village planning. If so, the settlement faced east with the dwellings on the western limit, with storage rooms, work area, and trash extending east.

Structure 1 served as a subterranean dwelling and was later utilized as a trash pit. The lack of a hearth in Structure 5 suggests that the occupation was of short duration or only seasonal. Occupation on a more permanent basis was indicated by the presence of two subsurface storage rooms, Structures 2 and 3. These same storage rooms, along with two extramural storage pits, appear to front the dwellings on the east. Structure 4 was a ramada or summer shade under which the inhabitants conducted daily activities. No clear

indications of different construction periods exist except that Structure 3 may have been added after the ramada was built. There is no evidence of considerable time lapse, however, and they appear to have been purposely built in proximity.

REFUSE

Well-defined refuse areas were not found at Ariz. D:13:1. Rather, the trash consisted mainly of sherds scattered east of the ramada work area. Some trash, mainly organic, had been deposited in the pithouse. The lack of trash depth implies that the site occupation was of short duration.

OTHER EXCAVATIONS

Fourteen test trenches, 1 meter wide and totaling 120 meters in length, were dug to slightly below the old occupation surface (ranging from 40 cm. to 1 m. below the present ground surface). Thus the area within the 50-foot right-of-way adjacent to the excavated structures was tested.

ARTIFACTS

Back dirt collections from the pipeline construction and excavations at the site yielded thirty-seven identifiable stone artifacts.

Ground Stone Artifacts

Nine ground stone artifacts were collected, six of a food processing type and three of personal adornment.

Three *mano* fragments were found from one indeterminate and two one-hand manos. The sandstone manos were unifacially ground on trough or basin metates creating convex grinding faces. One of the fragments represents a circular one-hand mano; diameter, 8.7 cm.; thickness, 4.2 cm. The remaining fragments are from subrectangular manos. Width varies from 8.2 to 11.2 cm.

One trough *metate* and two slab metate

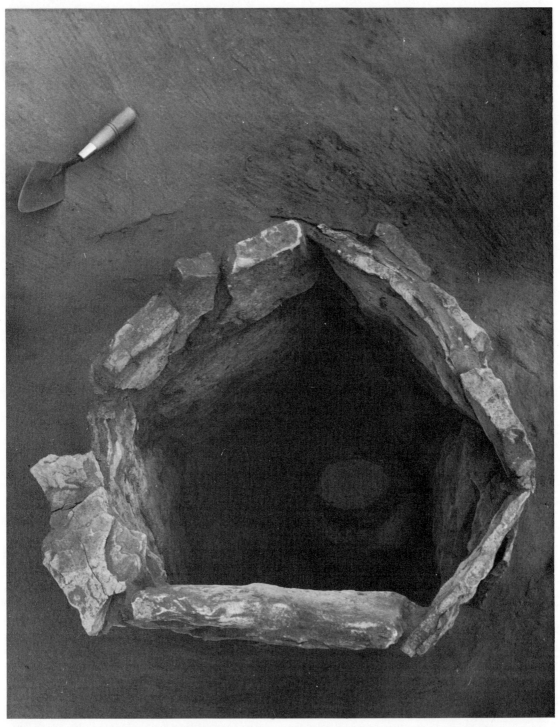

12. *Ariz. D:13:1. Extramural Storage Pit 2; Lino Gray seed bowl in situ. Trowel points north*

fragments were excavated. They were made of fine-grained sandstone with only the trough specimen, which was open at one end, exhibiting much use. Measurements are valueless.

Three items of personal adornment were ground from thin veinlets of pink calcite. A *stone disc* was probably intended for a pendant. This disc is nearly subrectangular with ground edges. Length, 2.8 cm.; width, 2.6 cm.; thickness, 5 mm. Two fragments of similar ground calcite were from unfinished pendants which may have been broken during construction. The larger fragment has a groove 2 mm. wide, ground into one face. Thicknesses of the two pieces are 3 and 7 mm.

Chipped Stone Artifacts

Chipped stone artifacts were rare. An end *scraper* was unifacially pressure flaked from an irregular percussion flake of jasper with a length, 3.9 cm.; width, 3.5 cm.; thickness, 8 mm.

Three *utilized flakes* and twelve *waste flakes* constituted the knapping debris collected. The utilized flakes are identifiable by small-use scars or flakes removed along one or more edges. Stone types consisted of chert (8) and chalcedony (7).

Six *hammerstones* were excavated. All are oval or round quartzite stream cobbles, probably obtained from Moenkopi Wash or the Little Colorado River. Size ranges from: length, 5 to 10.9 cm.; width, 8.7 to 5 cm.; thickness, 7.2 to 3 cm.

Unworked *minerals* and *pigment* brought to the site by the prehistoric inhabitants include: *calcite* (2), *gypsum* (2), *hematite* (1), and *limonite* (1), all small irregular unmodified pieces.

Ceramic Artifacts

The ceramic component of Ariz. D:13:1 can be assigned to the Dot Klish phase of the Kayenta Anasazi tradition. Although only 352 sherds were collected, they were found to be homogeneous and in accordance with types recognized for the Basketmaker III period (Colton and Hargrave 1937; Colton 1955). By applying the published dates (Breternitz 1966:83) for the ceramic type and its varieties recognized, it becomes possible to date the ceramic component as occurring between A.D. 575 and 620. This period falls within the era generally accepted as Basketmaker III in northern Arizona (Jennings 1966:33; Lindsay et al., 1968:3).

Lino Gray and two recognized varieties of this type, Lino Smudged and Tallahogan Red, were the only ceramics recovered (Table 5), except for a restorable bowl of Lino Black-on-gray. Lino Smudged is identical to Lino Gray except that the interiors have been smudged and lightly polished. Only bowl fragments were represented in the collection. Only sherds which possessed signs of polishing were identified as Lino Smudged to exclude fragments which may have been accidentally blackened. The blackened sherds lacking evidence of polishing were then classified as ordinary Lino Gray. Similar sherds have been reported from Shabik'eschee Village (Roberts 1929:117), Kiatuthlanna (Roberts 1931:117), Allentown (Roberts 1940:48), the Bear Ruin (Haury 1940:84), Jeddito 264 (Daifuku 1961:50), and from the Petrified Forest (Wendorf 1953:114).

Tallahogan Red, previously known as Lino Red (Wendorf 1953:114), was represented by six sherds. Tallahogan Red can best be described as having a Lino-type paste with an overall red paint (Brew 1946:294). The paint or red slip is fired on the vessel, instead of the fugitive red applied as a wash after the pot had been fired. At Jeddito 264, Daifuku (1961:48) found examples of Tallahogan Red in enough quantity to name and describe the type. Identical sherds have been reported from the Southwest by Guernsey (1931:91), Morris (1939:23), Brew (1946:294), and Wendorf (1953:114).

Lino Gray and its varieties are assigned to Tusayan Gray Ware. Lino Gray was the dominant type, comprising 64.7 percent of the total collection, while Lino Smudged was 35.5 percent and Tallahogan Red, 1.8 percent.

No worked or drilled sherds were recovered. Only twenty-five rim sherds and one lug handle were present, suggesting that very few vessels are represented in the sherd sample.

Two restorable vessels were recovered during the excavations (Fig. *13*). The largest is a Lino Gray seed bowl from extramural Storage Pit 2. The bowl possesses a carbon coating, resulting from use over an open fire. The rim diameter is 9.2 cm.; maximum diameter, 19.1 cm.; height, 16.5 cm.; volume, 2,750 ml.

The second vessel is a Lino Black-on-gray bowl from the pithouse fill. The interior of the bowl is decorated in typical Lino Black-on-gray fashion, with design elements located on the interior walls. The motif is repeated twice on opposing sides and consists of large pendant triangles filled with black dots. The four triangles are suspended from an encircling black line which is drawn just below the rim. Further decoration consists of a light red wash applied after firing to the exterior surface. The Lino Black-on-gray bowl is uniformly shaped with the exterior surface roughly finished. Rim diameter, 17.6 cm.; height, 9.3. cm.; volume, 1250 ml. No other sherds characteristic of either painting or a wash were found.

Bone Artifact

A badly weathered bone *awl* fragment of the split-bone variety, was found in the pithouse fill. It was originally ground smooth with a point at one end; no articular surface remains and the faunal species is unknown.

NONARTIFACTUAL MATERIALS

Shell

Four fossil mollusk shells (*Gryphaea* sp.) were found during excavation on the surface (1); in the pithouse fill (1); and in test trench 8 (2). The fossils are of Cretaceous origin (Jurrassic-Eocene period) and were probably fresh water species. The inhabitants collected the fossil shells elsewhere, returning them to the site. They are unworked.

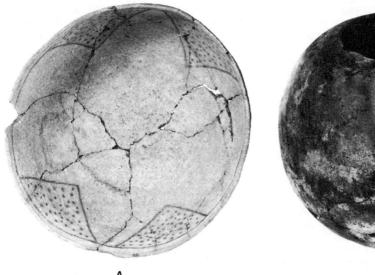

A   B

13. *Ariz. D:13:1. Ceramic vessels: A, Lino Black-on-gray bowl; diameter, 17.6 cm.; B, Lino Gray seed bowl*

FLORAL MATERIALS

Three charred corncobs were found in the fill of Structure 3, a subsurface storage room. These specimens have been submitted for analysis to Dr. Hugh Cutler of the Missouri Botanical Garden.

SUMMARY AND DISCUSSION

Ariz. D:13:1, the fourth site excavated along the Black Mesa pipeline, has provided data on the Dot Klish phase. The paucity of ceramic fragments, the small number of individual vessels represented, and the presence of only one ceramic type suggests that the knowledge of ceramic technology was of recent introduction. Stratigraphic evidence from the pithouse contributes additional support to the theory that ceramics were a late introduction. The trash deposited consisted mainly of organic material, discarded stone artifacts and ceramic fragments. These sherds and one restorable Lino Black-on-gray bowl were found near the surface of this trash accumulation.

Ariz. D:9:2

INTRODUCTION

Ariz. D:9:2 is another Dot Klish phase site, consisting of three pithouses and two extramural storage pits of Kayenta affiliation. Relative ceramic dating would place the settlement's occupation between approximately A.D. 500 and 700.

The settlement is located on Black Mesa, at Station 1620, approximately four and one-half miles east of the western escarpment (Fig. 1) at an elevation of 5,900 feet. It overlooks a small open valley surrounded by a heavy growth of juniper and Colorado piñon (*Pinus edulis*). Other plants characteristic of the local environment include: aster (*Aster hirtifolius*), actinea (*Hymenoxys* sp.), Indian ricegrass (*Orysopsis hymenoides*), Mormon tea (*Ephedra viridis*), Spurge (*Euphorbia* sp.), snakeweed (*Gutierrezia* sp.), milkweed (*Asclepias* sp.), narrow-leaf Yucca (*Yucca angustissima*), prickly pear (*Opuntia* sp.), and cane cholla (*Opuntia sp.*). Agricultural land is available on the valley floor, or along small arroyos which pass near the site and eventually enter the valley.

6. ARIZ. D:9:2. CERAMIC ANALYSIS

Ceramic Types	Sur-face	Structure 1 Fill	Structure 1 Floor	Structure 2 Fill	Structure 2 Floor	Structure 3 Fill	Structure 3 Floor	Storage Pit 2 Fill	Broadside 1	Broadside 2	Test Trenches	Construction Back Dirt	Total
Tusayan Gray Ware													
Lino B/G				1		3				2	10	1	17
Lino Gray	8	103	9	31	4	95	7	2	69	139	120	55	642
Lino Fugitive Red		3		11		8				2			24
Lino Smudged	1	20	4	27	5	121	12	16	30	44	64	10	354
Tallahogan Red				4									4
Tusayan Corr.	5											5	10
Tsegi Orange Ware													
Tusayan Poly.	1												1
Total	15	126	13	74	9	227	19	18	99	187	194	71	1,052

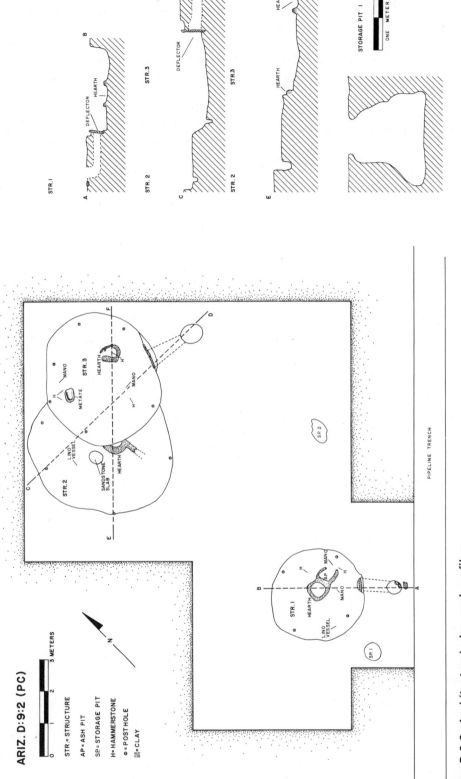

ARIZ. D:9:2 (PC)

0 1 2 3 METERS

STR.=STRUCTURE
AP=ASH PIT
SP=STORAGE PIT
H=HAMMERSTONE
⊙=POSTHOLE
▦=CLAY

N

STR.I
STR.2
STR.3
MANO
METATE
HEARTH
LINO VESSEL
SANDSTONE SLAB

STR.I
HEARTH
MANO
LINO VESSEL
SP.I
SP.2

PIPELINE TRENCH

STR.I
DEFLECTOR
HEARTH
A B

STR.3

STR.2
DEFLECTOR
C D

STR.3

STR.2
HEARTH
HEARTH
E F

STORAGE PIT I
ONE METER

14. *Ariz. D:9:2. Architectural plan and profiles*

This site was excavated between June 18 and 23, 1969, being completed on July 1, 1969. The break in the excavation became necessary with the discovery and immediate need to excavate Ariz. D:10:1. Prior to excavation, the only evidence for past human occupation was charcoal-stained sand and a few Lino Gray sherds in the construction back dirt. Excavation was begun by digging trenches parallel to the pipe trench. Where buried structures were encountered, broadsides were established to delimit features and collect associated artifacts from the overburden. In Table 6, Broadside 1 is associated with Structure 1; Broadside 2 with Structures 2 and 3.

ARCHITECTURE

Structure 1 (Figures *14, 15*)

Type of Structure. Oval pithouse.

Dimensions. East-West, 3.05 m.; North-South, 2.9 m. Average depth of floor below present ground surface, 1.19 m.; from old occupation surface, 66 cm.

Walls. Lower portion formed by unplastered sides of original pit excavated into consolidated orange sand. Vertical. Burned. Upper portion of perishable material extending above old ground surface. Poles probably utilized as leaners and daubed.

15. *Ariz. D:9:2. Structure 1, excavated Dot Klish phase pithouse*

Entrance. Through roof or wall.

Ventilator. Opens into pithouse through east wall, 15 cm. above floor. Circular in cross section. Diameter of opening, 30 cm. Clay ring outlines opening; slot in bottom of ring held damper. Slot length, 36 cm.; width, 4 cm.; depth, 3 cm. Horizontal portion of shaft, 1.38 m. Unlined. Opening at old occupation surface rimmed with small unshaped sandstone pieces. Oval. East-West, 50 cm.; North-South, 40 cm.

Damper. Subrectangular sandstone slab covered ventilator opening. Slab shaped by chipping. Length, 39 cm.; width, 34 cm.; thickness, 3 cm.

Floor. Poorly preserved. Sterile orange sand packed by use. Burned. Even. Wall-floor juncture at right angles.

Hearth. Circular, 50 cm. in diameter; 11 cm. deep. Basin-shaped in cross section. Walls of baked clay. White wood ash in fill. Clay collar 12 to 13 cm. high, 10 cm. wide outlines hearth. Approximately in center of dwelling.

Ash Pit. Rectangular depression contiguous to east side of hearth. Length, 40 cm.; width, 30 cm.; depth, 15 cm. Rimmed north and south with clay ridges. Height of ridge, 12 to 13 cm.; width, 10 cm. Small amount of white wood ash in fill.

Postholes. Four-post primary roof support pattern. Depth in floor, 13 to 22 cm.; diameter, 14 to 18 cm.

Roof. Quadrangular arrangement of roof support posts suggests a rectangular plate on which horizontal timbers rested. Covered with daub.

Fill. Wind- and water-deposited orange sand containing charcoal flecks; fine and loosely consolidated to a depth of 27 cm. above floor. Remaining fill of burned roofing material, sherds, and artifacts. Additional trash may have been deposited for short period after roof collapsed.

Material Culture. A projectile point, hammerstone, and partially restorable Lino Gray and Forestdale Smudged bowls in fill; unworked piece of hematite, utilized flake, pebble pounder, one-hand mano, indeterminate mano fragment, partially restorable Lino Gray jar and neck from Lino Fugitive Red narrow-mouth jar on floor.

Structure 2 (Figures *14, 16*)

Type of Structure. Oval pithouse.

Dimensions. Estimated East-West, 3.9 m.; North-South, 4.6 m. Average depth of floor below present ground surface, 1.06 m.; from old occupation surface, 26 cm.

Walls. Lowest 26 cm. formed by unplastered sides of original pit excavated into consolidated sterile orange sand. Upper portion of perishable material extending above old occupation surface. Poles probably utilized as leaners and daubed.

Entrance. Probably through roof.

Ventilator. No evidence. Probably destroyed by construction of superimposed Structure 3.

Floor. Poorly preserved. Native orange sand packed by use. Even. Wall-floor juncture at right angles.

Hearth. Partially destroyed by Structure 3. Circular, 40 cm. in diameter; 15 cm. deep. Basin-shaped in cross section. Walls of baked clay. White wood ash in fill. Clay collar, 12 cm. high and 21 cm., wide surrounds hearth. Located south of dwelling center.

Wing Wall. Clay collar surrounding hearth extends south, probably to the wall, although part of ridge eroded away and is untraceable. Maximum height, 13 cm.; width, 17 cm.

Postholes. Four posts of roof support pattern remaining. Depth below floor, 19 to 26 cm.; diameter, 14 to 18 cm.

Roof. Quadrangular arrangement of roof support posts suggests a rectangular plate on which horizontal timbers were placed. Covered with daub.

Fill. Wind-deposited fine orange sand, loosely consolidated, containing heavy charcoal flecking, sherds, and other artifacts.

Material Culture. Unworked piece of gypsum, one-hand mano, handchopper fragment, end scraper, *Olivella* shell bead, partial Lino Black-on-gray bowl, and six waste flakes. A

16. *Ariz. D:9:2. Structures 2 and 3, excavated superimposed Dot Klish phase pithouses*

partially restored Lino Black-on-gray bowl on floor.

Structure 3 (Figures *14, 16*)

Type of Structure. Oval pithouse.

Dimensions. East-West, 4.15 m.; North-South, 3.8 m. Average depth of floor below present ground surface, 1.4 m.; from old occupation surface, 60 cm.

Walls. Lower portion formed by unplastered sides of pit excavated into native orange sand. Wall slopes outward at surface. Burned. Upper portion of perishable material extending above old occupation surface. Poles probably utilized as leaners and daubed.

Entrance. Probably through roof.

Ventilator. Opens into pithouse through east wall, 10 cm. above floor level. Rectangular in cross section. Wall opening, 50 cm. high; width, 36 cm. Horizontal portion of shaft, 1.75 m. Unlined. Opening at old occupation surface elongated oval; length, 72 cm.; width, 63 cm. Opening once covered by sandstone slab; found in shaft fill. Length, 55 cm.; width, 41 cm.; thickness, 2 cm. The interior opening was sealed, prior to final abandonment. Two large sandstone slabs placed vertically and plastered in place to block flow of air.

Floor. Poorly preserved. Native orange sand packed by use. Burned. Slightly concave or basin-shaped. Wall-floor juncture at right angles.

Hearth. Subrectangular, 48 cm. in length; 40 cm. wide; 11 cm deep. Clay ridge outlines south and west sides. Height of ridge, 13 cm.; width varies from 12 to 16 cm. Two vertical sandstone slabs enclose east side. White wood ash and small pieces of juniper charcoal in fill. Located east of dwelling center.

Postholes. Six post primary roof support pattern. Depth below floor, 14 to 38 cm.; diameter, 12 to 19 cm.

Roof. Quadrilateral arrangement of roof support posts suggests a rectangular plate on which horizontal timbers were placed. Covered with daub.

Fill. Wind- and water-deposited fine orange sand, loosely consolidated, containing occasional charcoal flecks to a depth of 66 cm. Underlying 19 cm. layer of burned red roofing daub and charred juniper beams and poles. Sherds and other artifacts interspersed.

Material Culture. Sandstone maul, waste flake, and three trough metate fragments in fill. Ventilator fill contained partial Lino Black-on-gray bowl. Charred bow fragment, partial Lino Black-on-gray bowl, one-hand mano, two-hand mano, indeterminate mano fragment, five hammerstones, and five charred basketry fragments on floor.

Extramural Storage Pits

1. Located 75 cm. south of Structure 1. Bell-shaped in cross section. Diameter of surface opening, 55 cm. Walls unplastered side of original pit excavated into native orange sand. Depth of floor below present ground surface, 1.34 m.; from old occupation surface, 1.09 m. Even. Curves up to meet walls. Wind- and water-deposited orange sand fill containing charcoal flakes and disintegrating sandstone slabs. Slabs may be remnants of cover. 2. Located 3.4 m. northeast of Structure 1. Irregular oval outline. Basin-shaped in cross section. Length, 80 cm.; width, 47 cm.; depth, 46 cm. Average depth of floor below present ground surface, 90 cm.; from old occupation surface, 50 cm. No evidence of

plaster. Fill of wind- and water-deposited orange sand containing charcoal flecks and a few sherds.

ARCHITECTURAL SUMMARY

Three Dot Klish phase pithouses were excavated. The village orientation appears to have been toward the southeast. A different construction period is represented by the superimposed pithouse. Though additional dwellings were anticipated, extensive trenching failed to locate any.

Structures 1 and 3 were occupied when they burned. The three pithouses differed mainly in size, ranging from approximately 3 to 4.6 m. in diameter.

Both extramural storage pits were simply unprepared subsurface pits dug into consolidated sand. The larger bell-shaped pit may have been sealed to deter rodents.

REFUSE

A trash midden could not be located at Ariz. D:9:2, although extensive test trenching was carried out in search of additional features. Some scattered trash was found around the excavated dwellings consisting mostly of ceramic fragments and organically stained soil.

The cultural deposits in Structure 1 were screened to increase artifact recovery on the theory that additional trash may have been deposited in the smaller pithouse after a fire rendered it uninhabitable.

OTHER EXCAVATIONS

Five test trenches, 1 m. wide and totaling 96 m. in length, were dug to slightly below the old occupation surface (ranging from 40 to 53 cm. below the present ground surface) testing the regions adjacent to the excavated structures.

ARTIFACTS

Forty-five stone artifacts were recovered from all proveniences.

Ground Stone Artifacts

Twelve ground stone artifacts are of the food processing type. Three whole one-hand *manos* were found; two fragments were identified as portions of one-hand manos. Four of these are sandstone; the other quartzite. One specimen has pounding scars resulting from secondary use as a hammerstone. Particles of pigment (hematite and limonite) still adhere to the grinding surface of another.

Three manos are ground on two convex faces; the rest on one. The dimensions of the two subrectangular one-hand manos are: length, 15.4 and 16.7 cm.; width, 8.3 and 10.7 cm.; thickness, 3.4 and 5.3 cm., respectively. The two oval one-hand manos measure: length, 7.1 and 8.9 cm.; width, 5.9 and 7.8 cm.; thickness, 4.5 and 3.8 cm.

There are two examples of two-hand manos. Both are sandstone, with subrectangular outlines. One has a single convex ground face, the other two. Traces of hematite are present on the grinding surface of one specimen. The whole specimen measures: length, 19 cm.; width, 10.7 cm.; thickness, 4.6 cm.

One indeterminate fragment from a subrectangular sandstone mano with two convex grinding surfaces retains traces of hematite on one surface.

One complete trough *metate* of Mesa Verde sandstone, the grinding surface an enclosed shallow trough, was found protruding from a dune. A slab of sandstone had been chipped and pecked to shape a subrectangular block 31 cm. long, 25.5 cm. wide, and 9.5 cm. thick. One face contained a trough 20 cm. long, 15 cm. wide, and 1.2 cm. deep. Three trough metate fragments from Structure 3 from separate metates. The fragments are of Mesa Verde sandstone and show considerable use. Hematite stains remain on one.

Chipped Stone Artifacts

Chipped stone artifacts were again rare. A *projectile point,* with the tip and base missing, was percussion flaked from a primary basalt flake. Pressure retouching scars are evident along both edges. The width is 2.3 cm.; thickness, 6 mm.

A *scraper* of chert lacking evidence of use was located. A working edge at one end was created by unifacial pressure flaking. The length is 2.3 cm.; width, 1.9 cm.; thickness, 3 mm.

Three *utilized flakes* and twelve *waste flakes* were excavated. Stone types are chert (14) and jasper (1).

A Mesa Verde sandstone *maul* was prepared for hafting by pecking a shallow encircling groove. The artifact is rectangular in shape with a transverse cross section somewhat D-shaped. Both ends are flat and all edges were pecked. The length is 17.8 cm.; width, 11.3 cm.; and thickness, 7.3 cm.

Miscellaneous Stone Artifacts

Ten rocks showing pounding scars are classified as *hammerstones.* Seven of the hammerstones are quartzite, the remaining ones from chert nodules. One hematite-stained hammerstone was used to crush pigment. The outlines are oval or irregular and are between 5.5 and 10.5 cm. long, 4.9 and 8.5 cm. wide, and 2.7 and 5.6 cm. thick.

One additional quartzite hammerstone is better described as a *pebble pounder* or *pecking stone* because of its small size. Held by the fingers it could not have been wielded with great force. The length is 5.1 cm.; width, 4.8 cm.; and thickness, 4.2 cm.

One *handchopper* fragment was found which is bifacially percussion flaked chert.

Two pieces of *gypsum* were excavated. The largest was ground along three edges forming a square. One face was partially ground. The function of this artifact is unknown. The length is 9.6 cm.; width, 9.1 cm.; and thickness, 11 cm. The second piece of gypsum is an unworked irregular fragment that is transparent.

A piece of unworked *hematite* was excavated. Use of hematite was indicated by its presence on ground stone artifacts and a hammerstone.

Ceramic Artifacts

All of the 1,052 ceramic fragments from Ariz. D:9:2 (Table 6), except for eleven intrusive sherds of later Anasazi origin, can be classified as Lino Gray or one of its recognized varieties. The occupation of Ariz. D:9:2, on the basis of this ceramic evidence, is clearly assignable to the Dot Klish phase of the Kayenta Anasazi tradition.

Lino Gray was the dominant ceramic type, comprising 61.7 percent of the collection. Lino Smudged occurred with great frequency at 34 percent, followed by Lino Fugitive Red at 2.3 percent, Lino Black-on-gray at 1.6 percent, and Tallahogan Red at 0.4 percent.

The ceramic types recovered differ in no significant aspect from the same types found at Ariz. D:13:1. The only consistent variation is the yellowish cast on a small number of sherds. Seventeen sherds of Lino Gray, which represents at least four separate vessels, have this characteristic. This discoloration on a single Lino Black-on-gray sherd caused the usually black design to become a yellowish orange color creating a "ghost" pattern. Gumerman (1970:24) attributes this phenomenon to an overfiring, perhaps due to the use of coal as a source of fuel.

Sherds from later Pueblo periods (Lamoki

and Toreva phases), such as Tusayan Corrugated and Tusayan Polychrome were found scattered randomly on the surface in disturbed soil. These chronologically later sherds are considered intrusives.

Forty-four rim sherds and two handles were represented in the ceramic collection, while no drilled or worked sherds could be associated with the occupation. One intrusive *worked sherd* of Tusayan Polychrome was collected from the surface. The sherd had been ground circular, forming a disc 2.8 cm. in diameter and 4 mm. thick.

Six ceramic vessels excavated were partial or partially restorable. One partial Lino Black-on-gray bowl (Fig. *17A*) was excavated from the fill of Structure 2. The vessel appears to be an early example of this type, as the design is elementary and poorly controlled. The rim diameter is 16 cm. and height, 5.5 cm. Another partial Lino Black-on-gray bowl (Fig. *17B*), which also possessed an exterior iron oxide wash, was taken from in the ventilator fill of Structure 3. The vessel is clearly of Dot Klish phase origin, while the design element is well controlled tending toward the later Dinnebito phase Kana-a Black-on-white design. The rim diameter is 16 cm. and height, 8 cm.

From the floor of Structure 1 was excavated the restorable neck portion of a Fugitive Red narrow-mouth jar.

Inverted on the floor of Structure 1 (Fig.

17. *Ariz. D:9:2. Ceramic vessel fragments:* A, B, *partial Lino Black-on-gray bowls*

15) was a partially restorable Lino Gray jar, with a rim diameter of 10.2 cm. and maximum body diameter of 18 cm.

A partially restorable Lino Gray bowl was recovered from the fill of Structure 1 with a rim diameter of 18 cm. and a height of 8.8 cm.

The most interesting vessel represented was a partially restorable Forestdale Smudged bowl. The presence of this intrusive type indicates contact to the southeast during the Dot Klish phase. Six sherds of this type were found in Structure 2 fitting together to form the portion collected. No other sherds of this type were found at this or any of the other Dot Klish phase sites. The interior and exterior are highly smudged and polished. The rim diameter is 16.8 cm. and the height, 9.8 cm.

Basketry

Six charred basket fragments were excavated from the floor of Structure 3. The small pieces were found together and appear to represent the same basket (Fig. *18*). Following Morris and Burgh's (1941) terminology, the fragments can be classified as examples of the simple stitch, uninterlocked, two-rod-and-bundle, bunched variety. The rods are small twigs with the bark intact; the bundles are finely split yucca leaves. The splints are of narrow-leaf yucca. There are six coils and thirteen stitches in 3 cm. with no evidence of pitch.

Shell

One olivella (*Olivella biplicata*) shell bead was excavated from Structure 2 fill. The bead is whole, except for grinding at one end. The length is 1.8 cm. and the width is 1.1 cm.

Wood

One fragment of worked wood was found on the floor of Structure 3. This charred juniper fragment is the notched tip from a bow. A groove, 3 mm. wide and 2 mm. deep, encircles three sides approximately 1.5 cm. from the rounded end. The cross section is somewhat cylindrical and the ventral surface flattened.

FLORAL MATERIALS

Thirty charred corncobs were represented by whole and fragmented specimens. These were excavated from the floors of Structures 1 (23) and 3 (7). What appears to be a bunch of charred corn silk came from the fill of Structure 2.

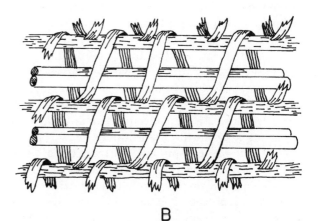

A   **B**

18. *Ariz. D:9:2. Drawing of basket fragment from Structure 3 floor: A, actual fragment; length, 4.1 cm.; B, diagrammatic view of simple stitch, uninterlocked, two-rod-and-bundle, bunched method of construction*

SUMMARY AND DISCUSSION

Ariz. D:9:2 contained the only undisturbed Dot Klish phase pithouses excavated on this project. The subterranean dwellings are circular, or nearly so, and lack antechambers. Architecturally the antechambers had been replaced by ventilators, and entry was now effected through a smoke hole in the roof. Only one dwelling possessed evidence of the characteristic wing or interior partition wall, which has commonly been reported for pithouses of comparable age.

The settlement was probably occupied on a seasonal basis by a small farming community which practiced a form of sand dune agriculture (Hack 1942a:26). The archaeological investigation demonstrated, through the finding of a number of charred corncobs, that the prehistoric inhabitants were farmers, probably supplementing their crops to some extent by the harvesting of wild plant foods and hunting.

Contact with peoples to the southeast is indicated by the presence of a Forestdale Smudged container.

Dot Klish Village, Ariz. D:10:1

INTRODUCTION

Dot Klish Village, located in Dot Klish Canyon on Black Mesa (Fig. 1), was occupied by peoples of the Kayenta Anasazi tradition in the Basketmaker III period. This is the site for which the Dot Klish phase was named. The village (Figs. 19, 20) was constructed atop a large knoll on the right bank of Moenkopi Wash, which drains much of the northern half of Black Mesa. The settlement is at Station 772 along the pipeline, approximately 17 miles downstream from the coal preparation plant. At this point the wash makes two large meandering curves in a deeply eroded channel, first to the south and then to the west, creating two extensive floodplains, the agricultural potential of which is apparent. Water could have been obtained on a yearlong basis by collecting runoff and by digging holes in the wash bottom.

Near the site, canyon walls of the Mesa Verde formation range from 50 to 200 feet in height. The canyon floor is cluttered with slump boulders from the walls and is easily accessible from many points along the rim. Large stabilized and shifting sand dunes are present in the immediate vicinity.

The elevation is 6,100 feet and the vegetation at the site is typically Upper Sonoran.

Wolfberry (*Lycium pallidum*), Utah serviceberry (*Amelanchier utahensis*), shad scale (*Atriplex confertifolia*), four-wing saltbush (*Atriplex canescens*), Russian thistle (*Salsola kali*), prickly pear (*Opuntia* sp.) and cane cholla (*Opuntia* sp.) grow on the valley floor. Juniper (*Juniperus* sp.), Colorado piñon (*Pinus edulis*), and sagebrush (*Artemesia tridentata*) grow along the higher elevations of the canyon rim. A substantial growth of salt cedar or tamarisk is present along the wash bank.

During the excavation of Ariz. D:9:2, a bulldozer, widening one of the numerous haul road crossings of Moenkopi Wash, uncovered some cultural debris at Ariz. D:10:1. Immediate inspection confirmed the presence of an archaeological site, and all pipeline work in the vicinity was suspended. Excavation began June 24, 1969, and lasted until June 29, requiring thirty-nine man-days to complete.

At Dot Klish Village a slab-lined storage cist and a small trash midden had already been destroyed; however, the main portion of the settlement had escaped damage by being buried by the construction backdirt. Excavation was begun by clearing the disturbed soil and collecting artifacts from a provenience listed as "Construction Back Dirt." To collect

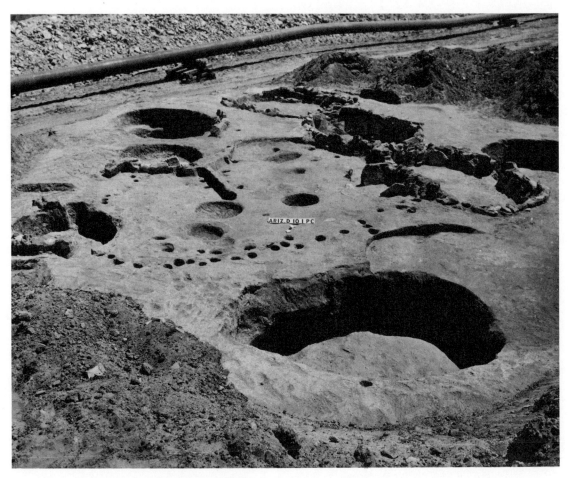

19. *Ariz. D:10:1. View of Dot Klish Village*

artifacts from the natural overburden, Broadside 1 was established.

As the excavation progressed, important architectural data that had been absent at the two previously excavated sites of comparable Dot Klish phase age were uncovered.

ARCHITECTURE

Structure 1 (Figures *19, 20*)

Type of Structure. Circular, slab-lined, storage cist.

Dimensions. Unknown. Major portion of cist destroyed by construction equipment. Estimated diameter, 2 m. Average depth of floor from present ground surface, 85 cm.; from old occupation surface, 80 cm.

Walls. Vertical sandstone slabs, averaging 55 cm. in length, held in place by adobe plaster. Slabs originally covered with clay plaster.

Entrance. Opening in roof.

Floor. Adobe plaster. Wall-floor juncture at right angles.

Roof. Poles resting on occupation surface; covered with daub. Probable slab cover for opening.

Fill. Upper 20 cm. of wind-deposited brown sand containing many charcoal flecks and much white wood ash. Remaining fill: fewer charcoal flecks, no ash, some sherds, and fragments of roofing daub.

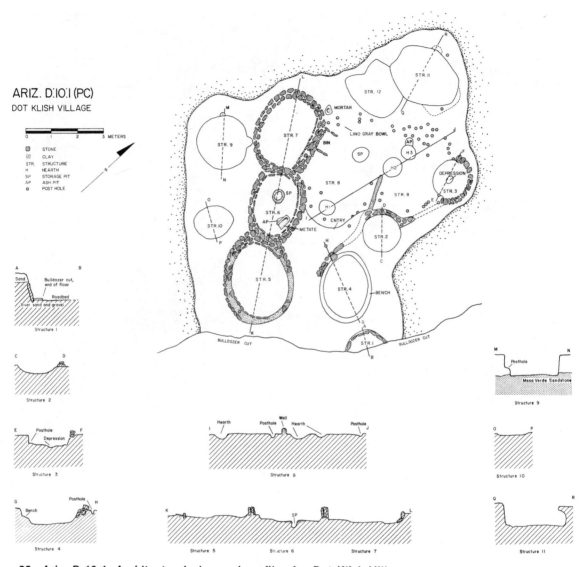

20. *Ariz. D:10:1. Architectural plan and profiles for Dot Klish Village*

Material Culture. Two-hand mano fragment from fill.

Structure 2 (Figures 19, 20, 21)

Type of Structure. Circular storage cist.

Dimensions. East-West, 1.56 m.; North-South, 1.3 m. Average depth of floor from present ground surface, 57 cm.; from old occupation surface, 50 cm.

Walls. Clay-plastered sides of original pit excavated into consolidated brown sand. Basin-shaped.

Floor. Adobe plastered. Basin-shaped.

Roof. No evidence. Probably long poles resting on occupation surface and covered with daub.

Fill. Upper 11 cm. of wind-deposited brown sand mixed with some sherds and charcoal flecks; lower 14 cm. had little charcoal

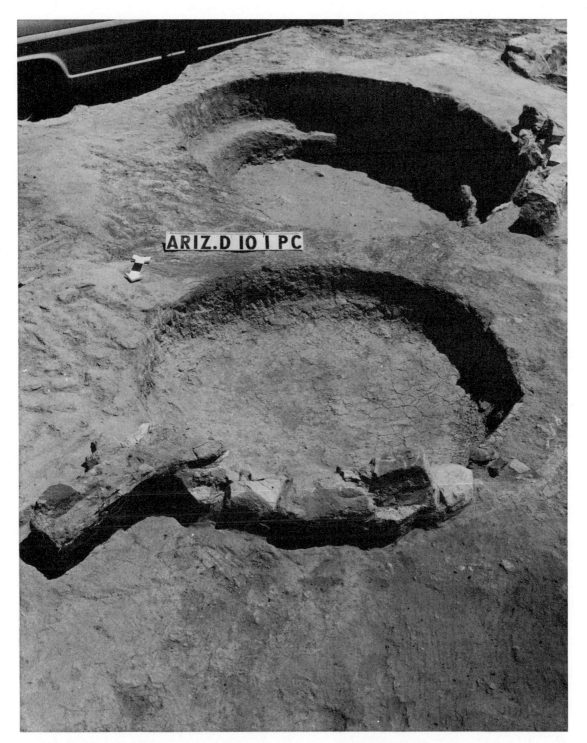

21. *Ariz. D:10:1. Structures 2 and 4, excavated storage cists; Structure 4 in background*

flecking. Floor contained recent rodent nest and animal bones.

Material Culture. Partial Lino Black-on-gray bowl, side scraper, fragment of worked sandstone, utilized flake, waste flake, and seven unworked pieces of gypsum in fill.

Structure 3 (Figures *19, 20*)

Type of Structure. Circular storage cist.
Dimensions. East-West, 1.36 m.; North-South, 1.4 m. Average depth of floor from present ground surface, 46 cm.; from old occupation surface, 40 cm.
Walls. Clay-plastered vertical sides of original pit excavated into consolidated brown sand.
Floor. Clay plastered. Uneven with central depression. Wall-floor juncture at right angles.
Roof. No evidence. Later enclosed by Structure 8.
Fill. Wind-deposited brown sand with charcoal flecking, sherds, and stone artifacts. Some root disturbance.
Material Culture. Two-hand mano fragment, two utilized flakes, and a waste flake from fill. One-hand mano on floor.

Structure 4 (Figures *19, 20, 21*)

Type of Structure. Oval storage cist.
Dimensions. East-West, 2.8 m.; North-South, 2.05 m. Average depth of floor from present ground surface, 55 cm.; from old occupation surface, 50 cm.
Walls. Clay-plastered vertical sides of original pit excavated into consolidated brown sand. Sandstone slab plastered in wall on west side.
Bench. Constructed by leaving natural soil in place. Clay plastered. Height averages 20 cm. above floor; width averages 13 cm. Approximately three-fourths of the original bench remains; the southern section had crumbled away.
Floor. Poorly preserved. Clay plastered. Even. Floor juncture curves up to meet walls.

Fill. Wind-deposited brown sand containing charcoal flecks, masonry remnants, sherds, and other artifacts.
Material Culture. From fill: discoidal scraper, two utilized flakes, waste flake, sandstone vessel cover, clay vessel cover seal, bone awl, bone-fleshing tool, and a concretion used to store hematite. Slab metate fragment and hammerstone on floor.

Structure 5 (Figures *19, 20, 22*)

Type of Structure. Oval surface dwelling or storage room.
Dimensions. East-West, 2.83 m.; North-South, 3.47 m. Average depth of floor from present ground surface, 60 cm.; from old occupation surface, 51 cm.
Walls. Section of wall below old occupation surface formed of minimally shaped sandstone slabs and plastered sides of original pit dug into native brown sand. Outlining this wall but above the old ground surface, was a remnant masonry wall constructed on a clay footing. The adobe base ranged in height from 10 to 16 cm. Standing masonry portions are one to three courses high and average two stones wide; a large section of the eastern wall had collapsed. Construction material consisted of irregular sandstone boulders and slabs, which were not well fitted together, held in place by copious amounts of clay. Both sections of the masonry wall were plastered on the interior. The upper wall abuts Structure 6 on the north end, attaining its maximum standing height at this point, 51 cm. above the floor; above the old occupational surface, 13 cm. Width varies between 20 and 42 cm.
Entrance. Probably through roof.
Floor. Poorly preserved. Plastered. Uneven. Curves up to meet walls.
Postholes. Four primary roof supports were set in the masonry wall. Depth below the top of the wall 20 to 30 cm. Diameter, 13 to 15 cm.
Roof. Quadrilateral arrangement of roof supports suggests a rectangular plate on

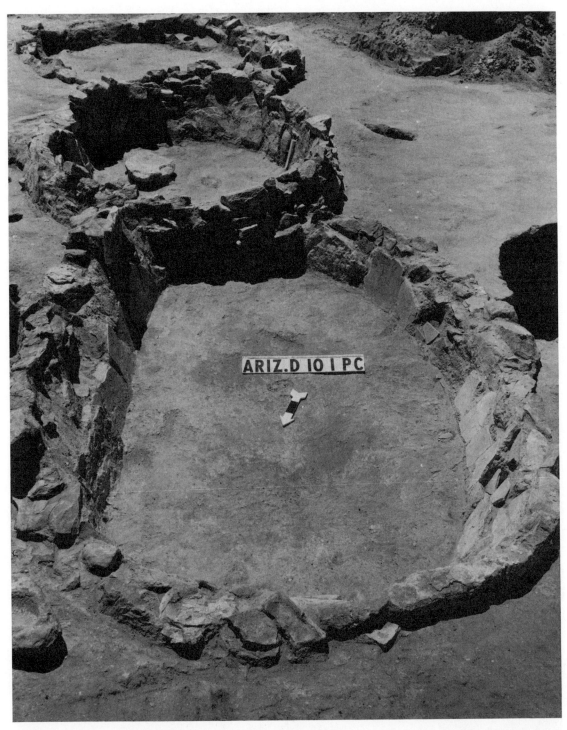

22. *Ariz. D:10:1. Contiguous slab and masonry room block at Dot Klish Village; Structures 5 through 7 from top to bottom*

which horizontal timbers were placed. Probably covered with daub.

Fill. Wind-deposited brown sand containing charcoal flecks, masonry rubble, plaster and daub fragments, and sherds.

Material Culture. Partial Lino Black-on-gray bowl, and hammerstone from fill. Two-hand mano fragment removed from masonry wall after excavation.

Structure 6 (Figures 22, 23, 24)

Type of Structure. Oval surface dwelling or storage room.

Dimensions. East-West, 2.3 m.; North-South, 3.05 m. Average depth of floor from present ground surface, 65 cm.; from old occupation surface, 58 cm.

Walls. Similar to Structure 5 in method of construction; although better constructed. Section of wall below old ground surface slab-lined (Fig. 23). Outlining this slab wall, built upon a prepared clay footing placed on the old occupation surface, was a horizontal masonry wall of irregular sandstone blocks and slabs (Fig. 24). Standing portions were three to five courses high and averaged one stone wide. The south and north walls are abutted by Structures 5 and 7 respectively. Maximum wall height above floor, 60 cm.; above old occupation surface, 36 cm. Width varies from 20 to 50 cm.

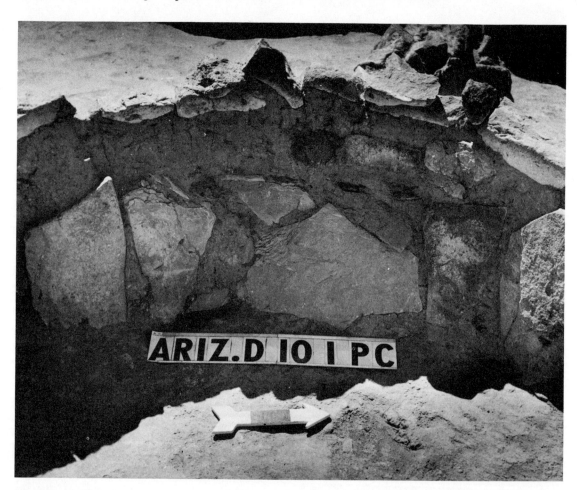

23. *Ariz. D:10:1. Structure 6, interior masonry detail; slab-lined section in west wall below old occupation surface*

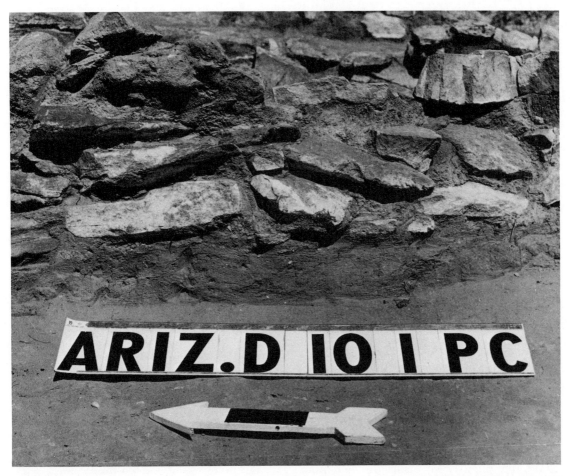

24. *Ariz. D:10:1. Structure 6, exterior masonry detail; section in west wall constructed above old occupation surface*

Entrance. Probably through roof.

Floor. Well preserved. Plastered. Even. Curves up to meet walls.

Ashpit. Shallow depression 60 cm. in diameter near southeast wall. Walls are only slightly baked indicating little use. Depth, approximately 2 cm. Full of white wood ash.

Storage Pit. Circular. Vertical walls perpendicular to flat bottom. Plastered. Diameter, 28 cm.; depth, 30 cm. Plaster collar 10 cm. high and 10 cm. wide surrounds opening.

Postholes. No evidence. Posts may have rested on masonry walls.

Roof. No evidence. Probably roof of hori-zontal crossbeams, covered with daub, resting on perishable upper walls.

Fill. Wind-deposited brown sand containing charcoal flecks, masonry rubble, plaster fragments, sherds, and artifacts.

Material Culture. Sandstone maul fragment, utilized flake, waste flake, and two un-worked pieces of limonite in fill. Slab metate fragment and two-hand mano blank removed from masonry wall. Trough metate on floor.

Structure 7 (Figures 19, 20, 22)

Type of Structure. Subrectangular surface dwelling or storage room.

Dimensions. East-West, 1.8 m.; North-South, 2.6 m. Average depth of floor from present ground surface, 85 cm.; from old occupation surface, 70 cm.

Walls. Similar to Structures 5 and 6 in method of construction. Standing portions one to five courses high. Maximum height above floor, 70 cm.; above old occupation surface, 46 cm. Width varies from 27 to 38 cm.

Entrance. Through roof.

Floor. Well preserved. Plastered. Uneven. Curves up to meet walls.

Postholes. No evidence.

Roof. No evidence, except daub fragments. Probably horizontal crossbeams resting on perishable upper walls and daubed.

Fill. Wind-deposited brown sand containing charcoal flecks, masonry rubble, plaster and daub fragments, sherds, and one stone artifact.

Material Culture. Two-hand mano fragment in fill.

Structure 8 (Figures 19, 20)

Type of Structure. Jacal dwelling.

Dimensions. East-West. 6.5 m.; North-South, 4.6 m. Average depth of floor from present ground surface, 68 cm.; originally constructed on old ground surface.

Walls. Jacal. North wall indicated by irregular posthole pattern, perhaps due to the need for repairs or additional roof support. East wall and portion of south wall set on masonry footing. Footing extends southward to Structure 4, suggesting wing wall for protecting entry. Masonry constructed of unshaped sandstone boulders. Height average 25 cm. above floor level; average width, 20 cm. West wall composed of the east walls of Structures 6 and 7. Partition wall, indicated by adobe footing and four postholes, extended from south wall. Length of partition, 1.38 m.

Entrance. Doorway possibly indicated by break in posthole pattern in western portion of south wall. At this point, the wing wall in association with the placement of Structures 5 and 6 offers considerable protection against wind blowing in either direction through the canyon.

Floor. Well preserved. Plastered. Even.

Hearths. 1. Circular. Basin-shaped; walls of baked sand. White wood ash in fill. Diameter, 55 cm.; depth, 19.5 cm. 2. Circular. Basin-shaped; walls of baked sand. White wood ash in fill. Diameter, 70 cm.; depth, 24 cm. 3. Circular with contiguous ashpit. Basin-shaped. Walls of baked sand. White wood ash in fill. Diameter, 50 cm.; depth, 17.5 cm.

Ashpit. Subrectangular. Contiguous to north side of Hearth 3. Walls of baked sand. White wood ash in fill. Length, 32 cm.; width, 29 cm.; depth, 5 cm.

Storage Pit. Oval. Near center of room. Walls vertical. Floor flat; curves up to meet walls. Length, 70 cm.; width, 55 cm.; depth, 33 cm.

Storage Bin. Formed by two short masonry walls projecting from exterior wall of Structure 7. Walls formed by two vertical sandstone slabs; held in place by clay mortar. The slabs are placed approximately 10 cm. below the plastered floor. Length of walls, 55 cm.; height, 48 cm.

Postholes. Forty-six postholes were excavated while searching for details of wall construction. Depth below floor, 8 to 17 cm. Diameter, 10 to 17 cm.

Roof. Burned juniper beams suggest center pole or poles extended from west to east wall, supported in the center by the partition wall, with horizontal poles placed in a north-south direction. Covered with daub.

Fill. Burned roofing beams, charcoal, wind-deposited brown sand, and sherds.

Material Culture. Partial Lino Black-on-gray bowl, two waste flakes, and hammerstone on floor.

Structure 9 (Figures 19, 20)

Type of Structure. Circular storage cist.

Dimensions. East-West, 2.4 m.; North-South, 2.1 m. Average depth below present ground surface, 1.5 m.; from old occupation surface, 80 cm.

Walls. Unplastered sides of original pit excavated into native brown sand. Vertical.

Entrance. Evidenced by small circular portion cut from east wall to floor. Length, 25 cm.; width, 42 cm.

Floor. Dug to bedrock; disintegrating Wepo sandstone. Even, or nearly so. Floor-wall juncture at right angles.

Posthole. Unassociated posthole in north wall. Predates structure; partially destroyed when subterranean cist was built. Depth, 49 cm.; diameter, 27 cm.

Roof. No evidence. May have been horizontal poles resting on ground surface or vertical posts set on the bedrock supporting a perishable superstructure.

Fill. Wind-deposited brown sand containing charcoal flecks along with some sherds.

Material Culture. Bone awl in fill.

Structure 10 (Figures 19, 20)

Type of Structure. Plaster-mixing cist.
Dimensions. East-West, 1.9 m.; North-South, 1.6 m. Average depth below present ground surface, 56 cm.; from old ground surface, 6 cm.

Walls. Plastered sides of original pit excavated into native brown sand. Basin-shaped.

Floor. Plastered bottom of pit. Basin-shaped.

Fill. Wind-deposited brown sand containing charcoal flecks and sherds.

Material Culture. Sherds.

Structure 11 (Figures 19, 20)

Type of Structure. Oval storage cist.
Dimensions. East-West, 2.65 m.; North-South, 2.1 m. Average depth below present ground surface, 96 cm.; from old ground surface, 87 cm.

Walls. Plastered vertical sides of original pit excavated into brown sand. Portions of the wall are undercut creating additional stor-

age area at floor level. The undercut located in the north wall is 60 cm. high, 45 cm. wide, and dug 27 cm. into the wall; a larger one in the east wall is 53 cm. high, 1.5 m. wide, and dug into the wall between 20 and 60 cm.

Entrance. Probably through roof.

Floor. Bottom of original pit. Plastered. Even. Curves up to meet walls.

Postholes. Two primary roof support posts located on original surface near wall. Depth below old occupation surface, 16 to 18 cm.; diameter, 14 to 15 cm.

Roof. Two roof support posts suggest a quadrilateral arrangement upon which a rectangular plate of horizontal timbers was placed. Covered with daub.

Fill. Layer of wind-deposited brown sand containing roofing daub fragments on floor; followed by trash deposits due to use of storage cist as dumping pit.

Material Culture. Two two-hand manos, two-hand mano blank, three two-hand mano fragments, one-hand mano, three hammerstones, ball of clay, bone awl fragment, and two pieces of unworked gypsum in fill.

Structure 12 (Figures 19, 20)

Type of Structure. Surface dwelling or storage room.
Dimensions. Accurate measurements cannot be determined due to erosion and superimposed Structure 11. Room appears to have been circular, with a diameter of less than 3 m. Average depth of floor below the present ground surface, 15 cm.; originally constructed on surface.

Walls. Perishable material; evidenced by burned poles on floor. Covered with daub.

Floor. Burned clay. Eroded on north side. Eastern portion destroyed by construction of Structure 11.

Roof. Perishable material covered with daub evidenced by burned beams and daub in fill.

Fill. Remnants of burned roofing material and wind-deposited brown sand.

Material Culture. None.

ARCHITECTURAL SUMMARY

The settlement pattern for Dot Klish Village cannot be fully determined because the entire site was not excavated. The layout of the cleared segment suggests single surface dwelling and surrounding rooms and subterranean cists for storage of food. It is very likely, however, that there are pithouses somewhere on the knoll because of the large number of storage facilities. The basic architectural form of the storage rooms and cists duplicates that of other sites of comparable age (Gladwin 1945:11–19; Daifuku 1961: 30–34; Carlson 1963:22–26). The units described by these authors are generally small, contiguous rooms varying in shape from circular to subrectangular and were used for the storage of foodstuffs. The storage function of many of the rooms was reinforced by the fact that while some of the rooms were large enough to have served as work areas or dwellings, the lack of compacted floors suggests this was not their primary function. At Ariz. D: 10:1, however, plastered floors were encountered in the three contiguous rooms, Structures 5 through 7. Of course, this may have been done to protect the contents from the harmful effects of ground moisture rather than for any domiciliary need. Structure 6 was the only room, except the jacal dwelling, showing any evidence for use as a workroom or domicile. This room had a shallow ashpit and metate on the floor. Fires were built or hot coals had been placed directly on the floor and subsequent cleanings created a shallow depression.

The walls of Structures 5 and 7 clearly are overcut by those of Structure 6, demonstrating that the three rooms were not constructed as a single unit and that Structure 6 was built first. It could not be determined if Structures 5 and 7 were added at the same or at separate times.

Structure 1 was the only "typical" Basketmaker III slab-lined storage cist excavated. The floor of this cist had been dug through the sand deposits into a loosely consolidated layer of gravel, which forced the prehistoric builders to utilize vertical slabs to maintain walls and avoid slumpage.

Structures 2, 3, 4, 9, and 11 were subsurface storage cists of varying shapes and sizes. Except for the walls of Structure 9, which are unplastered, all walls are the plastered sides of the original excavation. An extensive search for postholes along the narrow bench of Structure 4 gave no clue to the intended function of this feature. The excavation into the walls of Structure 11 was probably an attempt to increase storage space.

Within Structure 8, a jacal dwelling, most of the daily household tasks were probably conducted. It was here that the family meals were cooked and individuals took shelter during bad weather.

Structure 10 appears to have been a shallow plaster mixing pit; probably utilized during the construction of the masonry surface rooms.

Structure 12 was represented by portions of a burned floor. Erosion together with the construction of a later cist had destroyed much of the evidence; it was impossible to determine the function of this surface room. However, the ratio of storage rooms to dwellings suggests that Structure 12 was the latter.

The quality of masonry, although generally crude, must be considered far superior to that of others reported for this same stage and time period.

REFUSE

Undoubtedly, Structure 11 served as the major trash dump area after it was abandoned.

A small concentration of trash, disturbed by the construction equipment, was originally placed east of Structure 1 at the southeastern limits of the settlement. The disturbed trash consisted mainly of organically stained soils bearing sherds, stone artifacts, charcoal fragments and flecks. No evidence of interments could be seen. The possibility also exists that the original trash deposits were larger than now indicated, and that the wash has carried away much of the evidence as it has undermined the bank in the years since deposition.

ARTIFACTS

Ground Stone Artifacts

Twenty-five ground stone artifacts are in the collection from Dot Klish Village.

A complete trough *metate* was found covering a portion of the ashpit in Structure 6. The metate was fashioned from a large block of Wepo sandstone, with the trough open at one end. The shallow grinding surface is concave and measures in length, 29 cm.; width, 25 cm.; and depth, 3.5 cm. The dorsal surface and exterior sides are unworked. The overall measurements are: length, 49.5 cm.; width, 39 cm.; and thickness, 13.5 cm. Two trough metate fragments were excavated from the fill of Structure 11. Both are of sandstone and were little used.

Three slab metate fragments were excavated; one each from Structures 4, 6, and 11. All are sandstone; the fragment from Structure 4 has traces of hematite on the dorsal surface.

A *mortar* was excavated from the old occupation surface near the north end of Structure 7 (Fig. *22*). A depression 18 cm. in diameter and 16 cm. deep had been pecked into an unmodified block of Wepo sandstone. The depression is basin-shaped and had been roughened just prior to discard. The overall measurements are: length, 28.5 cm.; width, 32 cm.; and thickness, 11.5 cm.

Two whole one-hand *manos* were excavated, one each from Structures 4 and 11. Both are of sandstone; the latter has one convex grinding face, the former, which is burned, has two. The dimensions are: length, 12.5 and 14.2 cm.; width, 9.2 and 8 cm.; and thickness, 4.1 and 6.7 cm., respectively.

Two-hand manos were represented by two whole specimens and six fragments. Four are constructed of fine-grained sandstone and four of coarse-grained. The manos represented were all subrectangular with one convex grinding face with one exception. The exception is also subrectangular, but is wedge-shaped in cross section with two convex grinding faces converging at one edge. Two of the fragments have thumb and finger grooves, and a third has hematite stains on the grinding surface. The complete specimens were excavated from the fill of Structure 11. The two-hand mano measurements are: length, 20.1 and 21.7 cm.; width, 10.6 and 11.4 cm.; and thickness, 9.3 and 4.4 cm., respectively.

One large and bulky two-hand mano is better classified as a *mano blank*. The subrectangular specimen of coarse-grained sandstone has been pecked to shape and shows no evidence of use. Thumb and finger grooves are present. The artifact was found plastered into the west wall of Structure 6. Its dimensions are: length, 22.7 cm.; width, 12.7 cm.; and thickness, 5.7 cm.

The proximal portion of a sandstone *maul* was recovered from Structure 6. The original artifact was broken along the full-groove, perhaps as the groove was being made. The artifact shows no evidence of use. Its dimensions are: width, 8.7 cm.; and thickness, 7.4 cm.

A sandstone *disc* was found in Broadside 1. Both faces are ground flat; the edge is convex. A small chip is missing along the edge. Its diameter is 3.15 cm., and thickness, 4 mm.

A sandstone slab excavated from Structure 4 is believed to represent a *vessel cover*, although one face shows evidence of abrasion. The circular slab was shaped by chipping from one face. Its maximum diameter is 26.2 cm. and its thickness, 1.7 cm.

Recovered from the disturbed trash midden was an artifact best described as a *sharpening stone*. The object is an unmodified piece of Wepo sandstone upon which there are remnants of six parallel grooves. The grooves extend from one edge toward the center and are the probable result of shaping and sharpening bone awls; they could not have been used for smoothing arrow shafts since the grooves do not extend across the stone. The grooves are U-shaped in cross section and range in length from 9 to 14. cm.; width, 3 to 9 mm.; depth, 3 to 5 mm. The sandstone piece measures in length, 31 cm.; width, 31 cm.; and thickness, 11 cm.

Chipped Stone Artifacts

Chipped stone artifacts were extremely rare at Dot Klish Village. A *discoidal scraper* had been fashioned from a piece of chert by the percussion technique, followed by pressure retouching to create a working edge around three-fourths of the artifact. The working edge displays considerable use. Its dimensions are: length, 4.7 cm.; width, 4.6 cm.; and thickness, 1.2 cm.

Half of the stone chips and flakes recovered show signs of having been used for cutting and scraping. Seven *utilized flakes* were recognized; six are of chert, one of jasper.

Flakes or chips lacking secondary modification were considered *waste flakes*. Seven examples were found, six of chert, one of jasper. In addition, ten pieces of unworked gypsum were found.

Miscellaneous Stone Artifacts

Eight *hammerstones* fashioned of quartzite (5), conglomerate (1), petrified wood (1), and goethite (1) were recovered. All specimens display one or more battered surface, usually on the ends and along broken or projecting edges. The hammerstones are 6.25 to 11 cm. in length; 5 to 12.1 cm. in width; and 2.85 to 8.3 cm. in thickness.

A hollow goethite *concretion*, forming a small bowllike object, was utilized to store ground hematite. The entire surface of the bowl is stained with pigment. The oval bowl is 3.5 cm. long; 2.3 cm. wide; and 2 cm. deep. The concretion's exterior measurements are 4.6 cm. long; 3.4 cm. wide; and 2 cm. thick.

Two pieces of *pigment* were recovered. Both are irregular unmodified pieces of *limo-*

nite from Structure 6. The dimensions are: length, 4.5 and 11 cm.; width, 3 and 7 cm.; and thickness, 6 mm. and 4.5 cm.

Ceramic Artifacts

The 1,446 sherds excavated from Dot Klish Village can be classified under Tusayan Gray Ware, as Lino Gray or one of its recognized varieties (Table 7). There can be no doubt about the assignment of Ariz. D:10:1 to the Basketmaker III phase (or Dot Klish phase) of the Kayenta Anasazi tradition.

Lino Smudged (45 percent) predominated over Lino Gray (40 percent) in contrast to the previous sites reported on this project; scarcer varieties include Lino Fugitive Red (9 percent), Lino Black-on-gray (4 percent), and Tallahogan Red (2 percent). These types are identical to those already discussed in detail for Ariz. D:13:1 and Ariz. D:9:2. The only consistent variation was again the yellowish cast on some Lino Gray sherds. Thirteen of these sherds representing one vessel, were excavated from the floor of Structure 8. It has been hypothesized that this discoloration results from an overfiring due to the use of coal as fuel (Gumerman, Westfall, and Weed 1972).

No drilled or worked sherds were encountered; sixty-four rim sherds and three handle fragments were present. Three partial Lino Black-on-gray vessels are pictured with sherds of this type and Tallahogan Red in Figure 25. The rim diameter of A is 19.3 cm.; of B, 19 cm.; and of C, 13.8 cm. The three partial vessels are early examples of this type as the designs are elementary and poorly controlled. Design elements consist of pendant triangles with or without interior dots, concentric triangles, and irregular lines used to form crude treelike motifs.

Bone Artifacts

Four implements fashioned from animal bone were found at Dot Klish Village (Fig. 26).

A *fleshing tool* (Fig. 26A) was in the fill of

7. ARIZ. D:10:1, DOT KLISH VILLAGE. CERAMIC ANALYSIS

Ceramic Types	Surface	1 Fill	1 Floor	2 Floor	3 Fill	3 Floor	4 Fill	4 Floor	5 Fill	5 Floor	6 Fill	6 Floor	7 Floor	8 Floor	9 Fill	9 Floor	10 Floor	11 Fill	Broadside 1	Construction Back Dirt	Total
Tusayan Gray Ware																					
Lino B/G	9	2		3	1		1		2		1		1	5	9	2		4	3	9	52
Lino Gray	169	5		26	5	1	33		58	4	20	18	6	26	21	6	5	23	64	77	566
Lino Fugitive Red	1		7	18	1		5	5	1	3	3	1	10	13	19	1	4		22	23	138
Lino Smudged	10	18		39	3		68	19	17	4	69	21	10	35	75	17	2	97	88	68	660
Tallahogan Red					5						1				3	1		8	3	9	30
Total	189	25	7	86	15	1	107	24	78	11	94	40	27	79	127	27	11	132	180	186	1,446

25. *Ariz. D:10:1. Ceramic vessel fragments aad type sherds from Dot Klish Village:* A–C, *partial Lino Black-on-gray bowls;* D–I, *Lino Black-on-gray sherds;* J–N, *Tallahogan Red sherds*

Structure 4. The tool was made from a split long bone with the entire articular surface removed. The proximal end and edges are rounded and ground smooth. The distal or tip portion is as wide as the shaft, worn at a slight angle to the shaft, and has been smoothed down until the leveled edge is quite thin and sharp. The tool would have been ideal for smoothing, rubbing, or scraping activities. The artifact is 10.7 cm. long; width averages 1.2 cm.; and thickness averages 5 mm.

Two *awls* (Figs. *26B, C*) were found; one each from the fill of Structures 4 and 9. The former is of the split-bone variety. The articular end is nearly gone from having been ground flat. The tip portion is stubby; only 16 mm. from the tip does the pronounced taper begin. The edges were also ground. The awl demonstrates considerable use and was probably resharpened many times thereby reducing its overall length. In its present state its measurements are: length, 8.8 cm.; width, between 1.3 and 1.6 cm.; base width, 2 cm.; thickness, between 3 and 6 mm.; and base thickness, between 7 and 9 mm.

The second awl was made by breaking or cutting a long bone shaft in two and grinding a tapered point at the broken end. Constant resharpening of the point has left practically nothing but the articular end which formed the handle on this specimen. In its present state its measurements are: length, 5.9 cm.; maximum width, 1.8 cm.; and maximum thickness, 1.2 cm.

The tip portion of a split bone awl was recovered from the fill of Structure 11. The point was tapered back 1.7 cm. from the tip. The edges had been ground as had the shaft.

Clay Artifacts

Three unfired artifacts of clay were recovered. A clay *vessel cover,* or perhaps more accurately a seal, made of gray clay was found in the fill of Structure 4. The plug is circular in plan view, with the upper and lower surfaces convex and uneven. The edge is beveled along the lower half and is smooth from contact with a ceramic vessel. A portion of the seal is missing. The diameter was originally 9

A   B   C

cm

26. *Ariz. D:10:1. Bone artifacts from Dot Klish Village:* A, *fleshing tool;* B, C, *bone awls*

cm.; maximum thickness, 5.7 cm.; and width of beveled edge, 2.6 cm.

Two small lumps of clay are believed to have been balls of potter's clay. The smaller one was found in the construction back dirt; it was nearly round with a diameter of 2.7 cm. The larger lump is amorphous in shape and was found in the fill of Structure 11. Its length is 4.7 cm.; width, 4.1 cm.; and thickness, 3.3 cm. There are no impressions on these clay balls.

FLORAL MATERIALS

A total of ten charred corncobs was found. The small cobs were excavated from the fill of Structure 4 (3), Structure 9 (2), and Structure 11 (5). These specimens have been submitted to Dr. Hugh Cutler of the Missouri Botanical Garden for analysis.

SUMMARY AND DISCUSSION

Dot Klish Village, the third site excavated on this project, introduces additional data for the Basketmaker III period of the Anasazi or Dot Klish phase of Black Mesa.

The arrangement of excavated structures and cists consists of a surface dwelling and surrounding surface and subterranean storage rooms. Without further excavation there is no way to tell if this pattern holds true for the entire village. The contiguous masonry storage rooms, one of which showed evidence of habitational use, furnish additional substantiation of the hypothesis that such rooms were eventually to develop into the multi-roomed pueblos of the later periods. Although by most standards the quality of masonry found at Dot Klish Village must be considered crude, it is far superior to that of others reported for this phase.

The presence of two large floodplains, coupled with a year-round water supply, would seem to have created an ideal situation for prolonged occupation, although there are indications from the ceramic count and trash that the occupation was not long. The ratio of storage facilities to dwellings indicates that other unexcavated dwellings probably exist at the site.

Ariz. I:3:1

INTRODUCTION

Ariz. I:3:1 is a Pueblo II archaeological site located on the west bank of the Little Colorado River, at Station 3858 + 67, approximately 4 miles east of Buck Rogers Trading Post, Cameron, Arizona (Fig. 1). The village was occupied year round by inhabitants of the Kayenta Anasazi tradition near the border of the Anasazi area. The initial occupation began around A.D. 950 and lasted until the eruption of Sunset Crater, a large cinder cone, located 35 miles south of the site, which erupted near the end of the Pueblo II period between A.D. 1064 and 1067 (Smiley 1958:186; Breternitz 1967:72).

The village was constructed upon a Moenkopi sandstone terrace which is capped by 5 feet or less of Shinarump Conglomerate, intermixed sand and quartzite pebbles. The terrace remnant is narrow, between 50 and 75 meters wide; it drops off abruptly for 50 feet in a steep sand and boulder strewn slope to the floodplain of the Little Colorado River. Beyond the terrace, the land surface rises toward Gray Mountain, located 10 miles to the west. Short distances east and west of the village, two intermittent gully drainages cut deep into the terrace to reach the floodplain.

Vegetation in the region is sparse, except along the riverbank, and is characteristic of the Southwestern Desert scrub biotic community of the Lower Sonoran Life Zone. Species identified from the sand and gravel covered bench include: cliff rose (*Cowania mexicana*), Mormon tea (*Ephedra viridis*), narrow-leaf yucca (*Yucca angustissima*), rabbit bush (*Chrysothamnus* sp.), shad scale saltbush (*Atriplex confertifolia*), skunkbush or squawbush (*Rhus trilobata*), snakeweed (*Gutierrezia sarothrae*), spurge (*Euphorbia* sp.), three-on-grass (*Aristida* sp.), prickly pear (*Opuntia* sp.), wild buckwheat (*Eriogonum* sp.), and a variety of short papus stickweed or wire lettuce (*Stephanomeria* sp.). On the river floodplain, at an elevation of

8. ARIZ. I:3:1. CERAMIC ANALYSIS

Ceramic Types	Sur-face	Structure 1 Fill	Structure 1 Floor	Structure 2 Fill	Room 2 Fill	Room 2 Floor	Room 3 Floor	Structure 3 Fill	Structure 4 Rm. 1 Floor	Structure 5 Floor	Broadside 1	Broadside 2	Broadside 3	Broadside 4	Test Trenches	Total
Tusayan White Ware																
Kana-a B/W	42	1							6	9	1	9			64	132
Black Mesa B/W	51		3			16	17	4	3	33	1	27	7		187	349
Sosi B/W	2					1				2					3	8
Dogoszhi B/W										1					10	11
Unclassified B/W	59					7	4		4	22		46		5	209	356
Tusayan White Ware	60	2	1	1		13	7	3	2	52	2	23	8	8	134	316
Tusayan Gray Ware																
Lino B/G										2					2	4
Lino Gray	2									9			1		7	19
Kana-a Gray	35		5		1	17	2	1	2	17		12	4	5	164	263
Coconino Gray	26		1							8		14	2		77	131
Honani Tooled															5	5
Tusayan Corr.	7										2				2	11
Moenkopi Corr.															2	2
Tusayan Gray Ware	129	4	18	5	1	66	5	2	5	45	2	66	6	6	472	832
San Francisco Mt. Gray Ware																
Deadmans Gray	28			5		23		1	5	32		21	1	17	93	226
Deadmans Fugitive Red	3								2	18	1	20	1		44	89
Tsegi Orange Ware																
Medicine B/R	3			2		7			5	2					4	21
Tusayan B/R	17			2		9	19		3	1		5			56	113
Tsegi Orange Ware	17					41	2		5			3	2	1	43	115
San Juan Red Ware																
Deadmans B/R	4	1		1			2			1		3			8	20
San Juan Red Ware	9									1					7	17
Totals	494	8	28	17	2	200	58	11	42	255	9	249	32	42	1,593	3,040

4,240 feet, are salt cedar or tamarisk (*Tamarix* sp.) thickets, cocklebur (*Xanthium saccharatum*), Drummond goldweed (*Haplopappus Drummondii*), and sedge (*Cyperus* sp.).

Dry farming is not currently practiced by the Navajo along the floodplain in the vicinity of the site, but could have been carried on immediately adjacent to the village. If not, the unentrenched intermittent mesa-top drainages would have been suitable for small garden plots. Perhaps both terrain types were utilized.

The site was originally recognized by Euler during the helicopter reconnaissance of the pipeline right-of-way on July 28, 1967. Surface indications of past human occupation consisted of an L-shaped mound, associated depression, scattered ceramic fragments, and knapping debris. Subsequent heavy equipment damage destroyed the mound and masked the depression. Excavation began on September 29, 1969, and lasted until October 10, 1969, requiring forty-nine man-days. Parallel trenches were first excavated to locate the features buried by the disturbed soil. Broadsides were established once structures were encountered to remove the disturbed overburden and collect artifacts. In Table 8, Broadside 1 is associated with Structure 1, Broadside 2 with Structure 5, Broadside 3 with Structure 2 and 3, Broadside 4 with Structure 4.

ARCHITECTURE

Structure 1 (Figures 27, 28, 29)

Type of Structure. Rectangular pithouse.
Dimensions. East-West, 3.85 m.; North-South, 4.1 m. Average depth of floor below present ground surface, 1.66 m.; from old occupation surface, undeterminable.
Walls. Lower walls dug into bedrock through a shallow capping of sand and gravel. Lowest portion, 68 to 86 cm. high, unplastered sandstone sides of original pit excavated into bedrock. Vertical, but rough along

east wall where difficulties in fracturing the bedrock were encountered. Upper portion through layers of sand and gravel, 78 to 83 cm. above bedrock, must have been reinforced with perishable material to eliminate slumpage. Reinforced wall probably extended short distance above old occupation surface, supporting superstructure. Base of upper wall rested on bedrock.
Entrance. Through opening in northeast corner of north wall. Single step dug 50 cm. back into bedrock with a width of 110 cm. and depth of 50 cm.
Floor. Plastered bedrock. Basin-shaped. Curves up to meet walls.
Roof. Perishable superstructure supported by walls. Daubed and covered with earth.
Fill. See Figures 27 and 28. On floor, 30 to 58 cm. of wall and roofing debris (daub fragments containing sand and some small pebbles). Resting on roofing debris, 13 to 25 cm. of black volcanic ash attributed to the eruption of Sunset Crater. Above the ash was a maximum of 1 m. of wind and water-deposited river silt, sand, charcoal flecks, and intermixed small pebbles.
Material Culture. An olivella shell bead and side scraper from fill.

Structure 2 (Figures 27, 30)

Type of Structure. Three-room pueblo; storage facility.

Room 1

Type of Room. Rectangular surface storage room.
Dimensions. East-West, 1.5 m.; North-South, 2.4 m. Average depth of floor below present ground surface, 20 cm.; constructed on old occupation surface.
Walls. Upper walls of perishable materials, daubed and resting on masonry footing. Masonry portion two courses high, one course wide, and constructed of shaped rectangular sandstone slabs. Slabs ranged from 25 to 67 cm. in length, 17 to 20 cm. in width, and 3 to 5 cm. in thickness. Highest masonry remnant

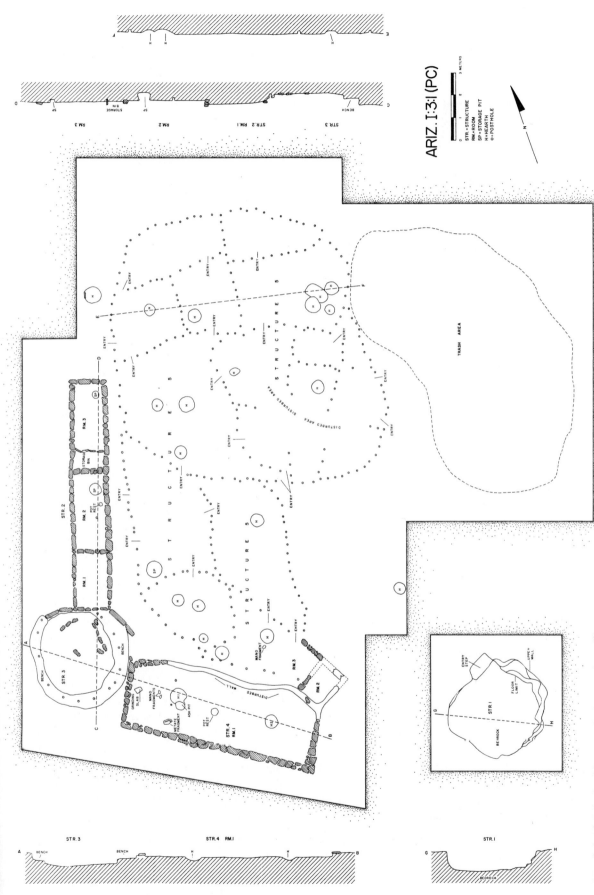

27. *Ariz. I:3:1. Architectural plan and profiles*

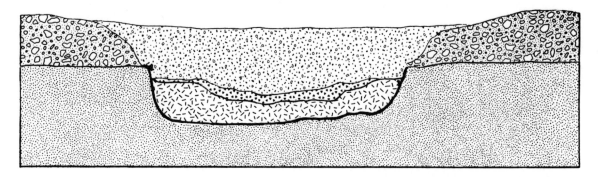

MOENKOPI SANDSTONE

SHINARUMP CONGLOMERATE

SILT, SAND, & PEBBLES

BLACK VOLCANIC CINDERS

WALL & ROOFING DEBRIS

28. *Ariz. I:3:1. Profile of fill in Structure 1*

ARIZ. I:3:I (PC)

PROFILE
PITHOUSE I

METERS

12 cm. above old occupation surface; lowest, 2 cm. Footing placed directly on old occupation surface.

Entrance. No evidence. Probably through roof.

Floor. Plastered old occupation surface which slopes downward along south wall. Well preserved.

Roof. Perishable material resting on vertical walls. Daubed.

Fill. Wind- and water-deposited river silt, sand, daub fragments, charcoal flecks, and small pebbles.

Material Culture. Sherds in fill.

Room 2

Type of Room. Rectangular surface storage room.

Dimensions. East-West, 1.35 m.; North-South, 3.4 m. Average depth of floor below present ground surface, 35 cm.; constructed on old occupation surface.

Walls. Similar to Room 1 in construction detail. Upper walls of perishable material, daubed, resting on masonry footing. Footing eight courses high, of which six were laid below the old occupation surface along the sides of the excavated pit. The masonry is a single course wide, and consists of prepared Moenkopi sandstone slabs. Highest standing wall above the floor, 28 cm.; above the old occupation surface, 8 cm. Width, 19 to 26 cm.

Entrance. No evidence. Probably through roof.

Floor. Bottom of rectangular pit excavated 25 cm. below old ground surface to level the floor. Plastered. Even. Well preserved.

Storage Pit. Oval. Located near northeast corner of room. East-West, 56 cm.; North-South, 43 cm.; 30 cm. deep. Vertical walls. Floor flat; curves up to meet walls. Wind-deposited river silt, sand, charcoal flecks, and artifacts constituted the fill.

Miscellaneous Hole. Slight depression in

29. *Ariz. I:3:1. Close-up of stratigraphy in Structure 1:* A, *plastered bedrock floor;* B, *collapsed roofing debris;* C, *black volcanic cinders attributed to eruption of Sunset Crater;* D, *wind- and water-deposited river silt and sand*

center of room along east wall, presumably for holding round bottomed containers. Basin-shaped in cross section. Diameter, 12 cm.; depth, 4 cm.

Posthole. Single posthole located southeast of room center. Function unknown. Depth below floor, 7 cm.; diameter, 10 cm.

Roof. Perishable material resting on vertical walls. Daubed.

Fill. Wind- and water-deposited river silt, sand, daub fragments, charcoal flecks, and small pebbles. Intermixed were a few sherds and artifacts.

Material Culture. Three projectile points from the storage pit fill. Partially restorable

Kana-a Gray jar, hammerstone, and small amount of ground hematite and limonite on floor.

Room 3

Type of Room. Rectangular surface storage room.

Dimensions. East-West, 1.26 cm.; North-South, 3.65 m. Average depth of floor below present ground surface, 28 cm.; constructed on old occupation surface.

Walls. Similar to Rooms 1 and 2 in construction detail. Upper walls of perishable materials, daubed, resting on masonry footing. Footing five courses high, of which three

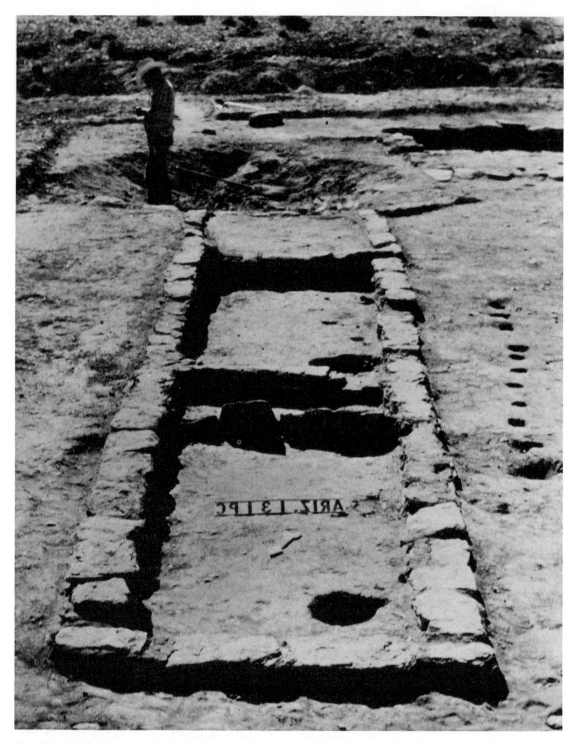

30. *Ariz. I:3:1. Structure 2; from the top: Rooms 1, 2, and 3*

courses were laid below the old occupation surface along the side of a pit excavated to level the floor. The masonry is a single course wide and consists of prepared Moenkopi sandstone slabs. Highest point of wall above the floor, 24 cm.; above the old occupation surface, 12 cm. Width, 20 to 27 cm.

Entrance. No evidence. Probably through roof.

Floor. Bottom of rectangular pit excavated 15 cm. below old ground surface to level floor. Plastered. Well preserved.

Storage Pit. Circular. Located in northeast corner of room. Diameter, 30 cm.; depth, 12 cm. Vertical walls. Floor flat but curves up to meet walls. Wind-deposited river silt, sand, and daub fragments.

Storage Bin. Created by partition wall of five vertical sandstone slabs setting off south end of room. Top of wall averages 19 cm. above floor. East-West, 130 cm.; North-South, 75 cm.

Roof. Perishable material resting on vertical walls. Daubed.

Fill. Wind- and water-deposited river silt, sand, charcoal flecks, daub fragments, and small pebbles.

Material Culture. Partially restorable Kana-a Gray jar and hand chopper from floor of storage bin. Fragment of a ground stone disc from room floor.

Structure 3 (Figure 27)

Type of Structure. Oval pithouse.

Dimensions. East-West, 4.15 m.; North-South, 4.35 m. Average depth of floor below present ground surface, 55 cm.; from old occupation surface, 33 cm.

Walls. Upper walls of perishable material, daubed, with support posts set in bench. Lower walls plastered sides of original pit excavated into highly consolidated gravel deposits. Vertical, or nearly so. Two short masonry footings extended east and west from the south end of Structure 2. Footing constructed on old occupation surface. Both foot-

ings are constructed of a single course of prepared Moenkopi sandstone slabs, two in length and one in width. Additional slabs removed from the fill suggests footing originally extended further around the east side. Highest point of wall above old occupation surface, 12 cm.; width, 20 cm. Height of plastered wall below old occupation surface averaged 33 cm.

Bench. Constructed by leaving natural soil in place. Patches of plaster present similar to that found on wall. Height varies from 15 to 20 cm. above the floor; width varies between 40 and 90 cm. Fourteen wall and roof support posts located on bench.

Entrance. Break in posthole pattern in wall on northwest side, in area of masonry footing, may indicate entry at ground level. This area protected from prevailing southwesterly wind.

Floor. Plastered bottom of original pit excavated into highly consolidated gravel. Ten prepared Moenkopi sandstone slabs plastered in floor. Even, or nearly so; curves up slightly to meet walls.

Postholes. Fourteen wall and roof supports located along bench. Depth below surface of bench, 9 to 15 cm.; diameter, 10 to 19 cm.

Roof. Perishable materials resting on vertical walls. Daubed. Probably gabled.

Fill. On floor, 1 cm. thick layer of black volcanic ash attributed to the eruption of Sunset Crater. Resting on the cinders, 5 to 10 cm. of clean wind-deposited sand and river silt, followed by 12 to 18 cm. of wall and roofing debris consisting mainly of daub fragments, sand, river silt, charcoal flecks, and some small pebbles. Above roofing debris, 39 to 51 cm. of wind- and water-deposited river silt, sand, and charcoal flecks. Few sherds intermixed.

Material Culture. Few sherds in fill.

Structure 4 (Figure 27)

Type of Structure. Three-room pueblo; surface dwelling and storage facility.

Room 1

Type of Room. Rectangular surface dwelling.

Dimensions. East-West, 8.37 m.; North-South, 2.83 m. Average depth of floor below present ground surface, 35 cm.; constructed on old occupation surface.

Walls. Upper walls of perishable materials, daubed, and resting on masonry footing. Masonry along north wall largely destroyed by construction equipment. Footing five courses high, one course wide, and constructed of prepared and unprepared Moenkopi sandstone slabs. Set on the old ground surface. Majority of slabs in upper and lower course prepared, while middle courses consisted of thin unshaped slabs set in copious amounts of brown mortar. Size of slabs varies considerably. Footing width averages from 19 to 42 cm. Highest masonry remnant 18 cm. above old occupation surface; lowest, 14 cm. Highest point above floor, 30 cm.; lowest, 21 cm.

Entrance. No evidence.

Floor. Plastered bottom of rectangular pit excavated to make floor horizontal. Poorly preserved. Even, or nearly so; curves up to meet walls.

Hearths. 1. Circular with contiguous ashpit; diameter, 79 cm.; depth, 15 cm. Basin-shaped in cross section. Walls of baked clay plaster. Some white wood ash in fill. 2. Circular, 55 cm. in diameter; 13 cm. deep. Basin-shaped in cross section. Walls of baked clay plaster. White wood ash in fill.

Ashpit. Circular, contiguous to south side of Hearth 1. Diameter, 40 cm.; depth, 12 cm. Basin-shaped in cross section. Walls of baked clay plaster. White wood ash constituted all of fill.

Postholes. Two postholes near Hearth 1 suggest additional roof support. Depth below floor, 9 and 16 cm.; diameter, 10 and 14 cm., respectively.

Miscellaneous Hole. Plastered depression, presumably for holding round bottomed containers. Basin-shaped in cross section. Diameter, 32 cm.; depth, 9 cm.

Roof. Perishable materials resting on vertical walls. Daubed.

Fill. In eastern half of room on floor only, unmeasurable scattering of black volcanic ash cinders attributed to the eruption of Sunset Crater. Remaining fill, 35 cm. of wall and roofing debris consisting mainly of daub fragments, river silt, and sand. Other materials intermixed in the fill were charcoal flecks and small pebbles.

Material Culture. Disc shell bead, knife blade, one-hand mano fragment, grinding slab, basin metate fragment, and hammerstone on floor.

Room 2

Type of Room. Rectangular surface storage room.

Dimensions. East-West, 1.05 m.; North-South, 1.55 m. Average depth of floor below present ground surface, 30 to 35 cm.; constructed on old occupation surface.

Walls. Upper walls of perishable materials, daubed, resting on masonry footing. Footing constructed of single course of prepared masonry slabs plastered on to old ground surface. Footing disturbed by construction equipment. Highest remaining portion, 12 cm. above floor; lowest, 8 cm. Width varies from 19 to 26 cm.

Entrance. No evidence.

Floor. Plastered occupation surface. Even. Poorly preserved due to construction equipment damage.

Roof. Perishable materials, daubed, resting on vertical walls.

Fill. Consisted of daub fragments, river silt, sand, and small pebbles.

Material Culture. None.

Room 3

Type of Room. Rectangular surface storage room. Indicated by masonry footing or wing wall extending from Room 2. This area was later included as a part of jacal room in

Structure 5. Room disturbed by construction equipment.

Dimensions. Estimated East-West, 1.2 m.; North-South, 1.87 m. Average depth of floor below present ground surface, 30 to 33 cm.; constructed on old occupation surface.

Walls. Probably identical to Room 2. Length of footing or wing wall, 1.28 m.

Entrance. No evidence for original room.

Floor. Plastered old occupation surface. Originally even. Poorly preserved due to construction equipment damage.

Roof. Perishable materials, daubed, resting on vertical walls.

Fill. Consisted of daub fragments, river silt, sand, and some small pebbles.

Material Culture. None.

Structure 5 (Figure 27)

Type of Structure. Jacal multiroomed dwelling.

Dimensions. Structure originally consisted of circular multiroomed unit measuring: East-West, 11.5 m.; North-South, 12 m. Four-room annex later constructed contiguous to south wall: East-West, 7 m.; North-South, 8.5 m. Depth of floor below present ground surface varies from 15 to 20 cm.; constructed on old occupation surface.

Walls. Jacal. Circular pattern consisting of 102 postholes indicated exterior walls of original structure. Dwelling divided by partition walls into a number of rooms with square, rectangular, or irregular outlines. Exact number of rooms unknown due to construction equipment disturbance; number of rooms totaled between eleven and thirteen. Distance between posts varied little. Six posts along one portion of an interior partition wall had been set in plaster. Holes slightly larger than the post diameters had been dug into consolidated sand and gravel, the posts put in place and the remaining space filled with plaster. Excess plaster was then removed, leaving a clay ring around the posts above the floor level. No other postholes evidenced

this additional stabilization. Walls were daubed with a mixture of river silt and sand. Thickness varied from 18 to 22 cm. Height unknown. Depth of posts below old occupation surface, 10 to 21 cm.; diameter, 11 to 22 cm.

A later addition of four large rooms with irregular outlines, was evidenced by an exterior wall pattern of fifty-four postholes contiguous to the south wall of the main multiroomed unit. The method of construction is identical to that described for the main unit, except for the portion of Structure 4 incorporated.

Entrances. Exterior entrances and interior passageways were indicated by wall openings with packed floors. These openings gave easy access to all sections of the dwelling. Openings ranged between 49 and 80 cm. in width.

Floor. Poorly preserved because of shallow overburden and construction equipment damage. No evidence of plaster. Probably even.

Hearths. Seventeen hearths were excavated within Structure 5. Sixteen were circular; diameters ranged from 40 to 69 cm. Depth ranged from 5 to 20 cm. All were basin-shaped in cross section, with baked plastered walls. The other hearth was subrectangular, with a round bottom. The walls were baked clay plaster. Length, 100 cm.; width, 57 cm.; depth, 23 cm. All hearths contained traces of white wood ash.

Storage Pit. Circular, 70 cm. in diameter; 42 cm. deep. Walls vertical. Floor flat; curves up to meet walls.

Roof. Perishable materials, daubed, resting on vertical walls.

Fill. Wind- and water-deposited river silt, sand, small pebbles, daub fragments, and charcoal flecks.

Material Culture. Two-hand mano fragment, knife, and worked sherd from floor.

Extramural Hearths. 1. Located north of Structure 2 and west of Structure 5. Circular; 72 cm. in diameter; 19 cm. deep. Vertical sandstone slab plastered on west side. Basin-shaped in cross section, with walls of burned sand and gravel. White wood ash in fill. 2. Located halfway between Structures 1 and 5. Circular; 55 cm. in diameter; 14 cm. deep. Basin-shaped in cross section. Walls of burned sand and gravel. White wood ash in fill.

ARCHITECTURAL SUMMARY

Ariz. I:3:1 meets the requirements set forth by Reed (1956:11) for a unidirectional or front-oriented village, in that a definite orientation of the settlement's major components was arranged on a northwest-southeast axis.

Structure 1, a pithouse, was constructed well into the underlying bedrock, and roofed; it may never have been utilized. Excavation into the bedrock, though requiring considerable effort, was facilitated by the tendency of the Moenkopi sandstone to scale or break off in sheets of 1 to 3 cm. in thickness. More consolidated sections of bedrock encountered along the east wall were left in place. Here the face of the rock was often dressed by pecking until a smooth surface was obtained. The floor was similarly treated, receiving a coating of clay plaster to level off the remaining irregularities. The vertical roof supports rested on the bedrock, either on the floor or at the bedrock surface, without any attempt being made to carve special holes for them. A perishable superstructure was then constructed and daubed with a mixture of river silt and clay. This was in turn covered with earth, which contained a number of small pebbles. Apparently all of the superstructures at Ariz. I:3:1 received this final coating of earth, as small pebbles were always found resting on the fallen roofing daub fragments. The pithouse had fallen into disuse, and was allowed to collapse prior to the village's final abandonment. This was evidenced by the presence of volcanic ash resting on the fallen roofing debris.

Examination of the wall abutments and bondings of Structure 2 yielded evidence concerning the growth of this storage pueblo. Rooms 2 and 3 were constructed first, with the dividing wall abutting the exterior wall on both sides. Later, Room 1 and Structure 3 were added, perhaps at the same time.

Structure 3 was labeled a pithouse for ease of description, although the circular shape and lack of floor features seem to indicate that it may have been used for storage. Other than the presence of a bench, presumably constructed to receive the roof support posts, only the bare essentials in construction features are present, precluding the structure's use as a ceremonial room or kiva.

Structure 5, a large multiroomed jacal dwelling, was built in two separate construction phases. The main unit was circular or nearly so, consisting of eleven to thirteen rooms. The dwelling was built after the site had been occupied for some time, as the east wall had been constructed in order to avoid previously deposited trash. Lacking dendrochronological evidence, there is no way to assess the time lapse between construction phases. The second phase consisted of the addition of four rooms at the south end of the main unit and probably represents the last construction undertaken at the settlement. Both sections of Structure 5 were divided by jacal partition walls, creating rooms with square, rectangular or irregular outlines. Three basic types of rooms seem to be present: habitation rooms, storage rooms, and rooms which probably served a combination of these needs. Habitation rooms possessed one or more hearths, while storage rooms lacked floor features, except for a single storage pit in one room. It seems to have been a frequent practice to abandon a hearth or heating pit, fill it with earth, and construct another, sometimes at a distance from the original or sometimes superimposed over a portion of it. An extreme example of this is the four hearths traceable in one room. Only one of these seems to have been functional at any given time. Some of the hearths appear to have been extramural and filled with earth as the jacal unit or annex was built.

The six posts which had their bases set in plaster represent a construction trait heretofore unrecorded in jacal architecture excavated either on Black Mesa or along the slurry pipeline. It is readily apparent that this special treatment provided added support.

REFUSE

A trash area at Ariz. I:3:1, was found concentrated where the east wall of the main unit of Structure 5 had been constructed to avoid it (Figure 27). Originally the trash had been higher, and probably somewhat less extensive in periphery. The trash was shallow due to wind erosion, measuring only 22 cm. at its deepest point. During the excavation, no perishable items or bones were encountered, and only a few pieces of charcoal, sherds, broken artifacts, and humus-stained soil were present to indicate the limits of the trash deposits. On a northwest-southeast axis the trash extended 14 m.; on a southwest-northeast axis it extended 6.5 m. Since the deposits were shallow, and mixed because of wind erosion, the trash was not excavated by stratigraphic levels, but rather was totally excavated by a series of parallel test trenches 1 m. wide.

Other small areas of sheet trash, consisting mainly of pottery fragments, were located and excavated near the structures.

OTHER EXCAVATIONS

Twenty test trenches, 1 m. wide and totaling 158 m. in length, were dug to slightly below the old occupation surface, ranging between 8 to 46 cm. below the present ground surface. These trenches were laid out to test the regions adjacent to the excavated structures, and to test the trash midden.

ARTIFACTS

Ground Stone Artifacts

Ground stone artifacts were rare at Ariz. I:3:1, perhaps indicating that these tools were not abandoned with the site.

A single sandstone one-hand *mano* frag-

ment was excavated from Structure 4. The fragment represents a subrectangular mano, with one convex grinding surface and a width of 7.5 cm. and thickness of 3.6 cm.

Two two-hand mano fragments were excavated, one from the annex of Structure 5 and one from the trash midden. Both fragments represent subrectangular sandstone manos. Both are wedge shaped, the former with two convex grinding surfaces converging at one edge, the latter with one. The widths are 10.5 and 10 cm. and thickness, 3.5 and 3 cm.

A sandstone basin *metate* fragment was found in Structure 4. The exterior surface was shaped by pecking and the grinding surface had been roughened prior to the artifact being discarded.

A complete sandstone *grinding slab* was excavated from Structure 4. The flat slab is rectangular, and evidences little use. The edges are exfoliated. The length is 28 cm.; width, 16.5 cm.; and thickness, 4.8 cm.

A small stone *disc* was found on the surface. The artifact is complete (Fig. 31S), and was formed by grinding the edge of a thin piece of brown sandstone; the two faces are unworked and flat. Its diameter is 3.5 cm. and thickness, 7 mm. A fragment from a similar disc was found in Structure 2. The artifact was ground from a thin piece of yellowish mudstone. Both faces are worked. Remnants of a biconical hole are near the center. The thickness is 5 mm.

Chipped Stone Artifacts

The chipped stone artifacts from Ariz. I:3:1 were not only numerous, when compared to similar artifacts from the other excavated sites, but also represent a larger range of tool types. The stone material utilized indicates that considerable use was made of the gravel capping (Shinarump Conglomerate) on the terrace. The stone tools were manufactured from various forms of cryptocrystalline quartz, with variegated chert and jasper predominating.

Three complete *projectile points* were exca-

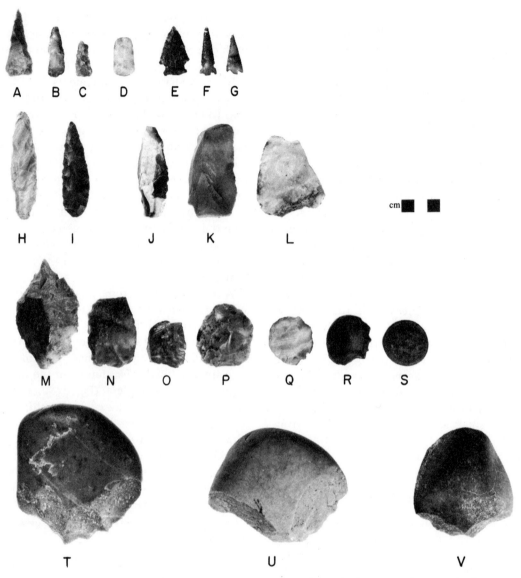

31. *Ariz. 1:3:1. Stone artifacts: A–C, drills; D, pendant; E–G, triangular notched pro-jectile points; H–L, knives; M, combination scraper-graver; N–R, scrapers; S, ground sandstone disc; T–V, choppers*

vated from the storage pit in Room 2, Struc-ture 2. The artifacts are triangular notched points differing mainly in the number and location of the notches (Fig. *31E–G*) ; two are elongated. The largest point (Fig. *31F*), was pressure flaked bifacially from a primary flake of red jasper. The triangular form was altered by notching the two sides near the

base, producing barbs almost as long as the base. The tips of both barbs are damaged, and the base is slightly concave. The point was well-made and measures in length, 3.8 cm.; width, 2.4 cm.; and thickness, 0.5 cm. The largest elongated triangular point (Fig. *31F*) was bifically pressure flaked from a thin piece of chert. The point was well made and possesses both double side and basal notches. Its length is 3.8 cm.; width, 1.1 cm.; and thickness, 0.3 cm. The smaller example (Fig. *31G*) was pressure flaked from a piece of quartzite. The artifact is well made and possesses two basal notches. Its length is 3.1 cm.; width, 1.3 cm.; and thickness, 0.4 cm.

Drills (Fig. *31A–C*) are represented by four classifiable specimens and one unclassifiable tip portion recovered from the trash midden. The largest example (Fig. *31A*) was formed by pressure retouching a thick primary flake of chert. The edges are steep, while the expanded base is nearly flat, being separated from the shaft by distinct shoulders. The polished ground surface extending 7 mm. from the tip of the tool indicates use for drilling. The length of the drill is 5.2 cm.; shoulder length, 1.65 cm.; width, 2.1 cm.; and thickness, 1 cm. The second example (Fig. *31B*) is triangular with a convex base. The tip portion is missing. The implement was bifacially pressure flaked from a piece of quartzite, and is plano-convex in cross section. Its length is 4 cm.; width, 1.3 cm.; and thickness, 0.4 to 0.9 cm. The third example (Fig. *31C*) is slightly curved and may have been utilized as a small knife. The tool was bifacially pressure flaked from a thin piece of quartzite. The base is flat and separated from the curving shaft by distinct shoulders. The tip portion is missing. The estimated length is 3.6 cm.; shoulder length, 1.5 cm.; width, 1.3 cm.; and thickness, 0.4 cm. The basal portion of the fourth example is convex. The drill was bifacially pressure flaked from a thin piece of chert with a width of 1.5 cm. and thickness of 0.4 cm. The unclassifiable tip portion represents a drill bifacially pressure flaked from chert. The fragment shows very slight use near the tip.

Stone *knives* were represented by five complete specimens and five fragments. The complete specimens can be divided into three types on the basis of shape (Fig. *31H–L*): oval or leaf-shaped, rectangular, and irregular.

Oval knives were represented by three spec-

imens in Figure *31:H, I,* and *J*. Knife *H* was bifacially flaked from a piece of chert; pressure retouching along both edges is evident. Both ends are blunt and the artifact is plano-convex in cross section. The tool was found in the trash midden. Its measurements are: length, 8.1 cm.; width, 2 cm.; and thickness, 1.6 cm. The second knife (Fig. *31I*) of chert, is lenticular in cross section and was bifacially flaked with only a few locations along the edge requiring pressure retouching. The knife was excavated from the floor of Room 1, Structure 4, and its measurements are: length, 7.3 cm.; width, 2.1 cm.; and thickness, 0.8 cm. The third oval knife (Fig. *31J*) was crudely fashioned from a thick piece of quartzite. The knife possesses two blunt ends and is plano-convex in cross section. The edges are steeply percussion flaked. Tiny use scars are present. The implement was excavated from the trash midden and measures 7 cm. long, 2.5 cm. wide, and 1.3 cm. thick. The only rectangular knife consists of a large chert flake which was utilized along one edge for cutting. Marginal retouching and use scars are present along the working edge. The base is flat; cortex remains on both ends. The proximal surface evidences scars of four primary flakes which were removed prior to the striking of the flake forming the tool. The knife was excavated from the trash midden and measures 7.1 cm. long; 2.6 cm. wide; and 1.7 cm. thick. The remaining complete knife (Fig. *31L*) is irregular in outline. The artifact is a large flake struck from a quartzite cobble which evidences limited use along one edge. The implement was found on one of the jacal room floors and measures in length, 6.2 cm.; width, 5.2 cm.; and thickness, 0.6 cm. The five fragments are midsections or tips of knives from the surface (2) and trash midden (3). These fragments are all bifacially pressure flaked and pressure retouched. Material utilized was chalcedony (1), jasper (1), and variegated chert (3).

A combination *scraper-graver* was found in the trash midden. The artifact (Fig. *31M*) is a nodular scraper, percussion flaked and with a projecting point. The point surface is ground smooth, somewhat polished, and extends 0.85 cm. from the tip of the tool indicating use for cutting or inscribing. One edge has been utilized for scraping. The implement is made of chert and measures 8.5 cm. long; 5.1 cm. wide; and 1.75 cm. thick.

Twenty-six *scrapers* were collected (Fig. *31N–R*): one from Structure 1, seven from the surface, and eighteen from the trash midden. The majority (21) are flake scrapers, the remainder being nodular. The flake scrapers are generally irregular in outline with a limited working area, usually part of one edge; however, several are either square or elongated and are flaked along most of one edge. Eight are bifacial and thirteen are unifacial; nineteen show evidence of pressure retouch or were marginally retouched to sharpen dull edges. Stone materials utilized include agate (1), chalcedony (4), quartzite (5) and variegated chert (11). The measurements range from: length, 3.3 to 5.8 cm.; width, 1.8 to 4 cm.; and thickness, 0.4 to 2.1 cm. The five nodular scrapers are discoidal, with steep edges. The working edge is unifacial. Two are of quartzite and three are of chert. The discoidal scrapers were excavated from the surface (1), from Structure 2 (1), and the trash midden (3). The measurements range from a diameter of 3.8 to 5.7 cm. and in thickness from 0.2 to 3 cm.

One chipped and ground stone artifact excavated from the trash deposits cannot be easily classified. The subrectangular object (Fig. *31D*) had been bifacially pressure flaked from a small piece of chalcedony. The object was then ground until the flaking scars were almost obliterated, creating a polished smooth surface. The artifact also possesses limited evidence of sandblasting. Although the intended function is unknown, the artifact may represent an unfinished *pendant*.

Choppers are represented by three artifacts (Fig. *31T–V*) collected from the surface (2) and the storage bin of Structure 2 (1). The tools were made from quartzitic water-worn cobbles, with one-third to one-half of the circumference having been unifacially spalled, forming a cutting and pounding edge. One of the choppers (Fig. *31V*) displays prolonged use. The lengths are from 8.8 to 10.8 cm.; widths, 7.8 to 9.9 cm.; and thicknesses, 2.5 to 4.5 cm.

Ten *cores* were found on the surface (3) and in the trash midden (7). The removal of numerous flakes on each artifact has resulted in irregular round shapes. The material utilized includes: quartzite (1) and variegated chert (9).

Utilized flakes were collected from thirty separate proveniences. A total of 268 were collected, mainly from the structures (35), broadsides (34), and the trash midden (199), some of which display use chipping, smoothed edges, or a combination of both. They range from thick to thin, from large to small, from convex to concave cutting edges, and possess from one to three working edges. A few retain remnants of the cortex, indicating that cobbles from the gravel terrace were utilized.

Stone chips or *waste flakes* showing no evidence of secondary use were numerous. Collected from thirty-three separate proveniences, these flakes represent the knapping debris—the flakes struck off and discarded during the manufacture of other implements. A total of 583 chips were collected, mainly from the broadsides (73), structures (242), and the trash midden (268).

Miscellaneous Stone Artifacts

Two unmodified river cobbles of quartzite were utilized as *hammerstones*. The artifacts evidence pounding scars on both ends, and are irregular in outline. The hammerstones were excavated from the floors of Structures 2 and 4.

Pigment was represented by *limonite* and *hematite*. Two small unworked pieces of limonite were excavated from the trash. Small amounts of ground limonite and hematite presumably once held in perishable containers were found on the floor of Structure 2, Room 2, together but not mixed.

Ceramic Artifacts

The study of the ceramic collection from Ariz. I:3:1 (Table 8) is greatly restricted and distorted by the condition of the sherds recovered. During the nine centuries since the sherds were discarded, a majority have been exposed to sand-carrying winds. The result has been the loss of painted designs, and even the loss of the applied slip in many cases. Of the 1,347 painted or decorated sherds, 59 percent, or 804, were badly weathered. Nevertheless, enough decorated sherds from buried proveniences escaped the effects of sandblasting to date the occupation between about A.D. 900 and 1050. The majority of the sherds are Kayenta Anasazi, with the temporal period represented by the sherds equivalent to the late Pueblo I and II periods, although some earlier and later sherds are also present. Final abandonment was probably at the eruption of Sunset Crater, between A.D. 1064 and 1067 (Smiley 1958:186–90; Breternitz 1967:72–76). The presence of only a few sherds of Moenkopi Corrugated and Sosi and Dogoszhi Black-on-white usually assigned beginning dates after the eruption (Breternitz 1966), confirms the date of abandonment.

The majority of pottery fragments collected from the surface and excavated units were found to be in accordance with the types described for Tusayan White and Gray Wares. Ceramic fragments classifiable under San Francisco Mountain Gray Ware, Tsegi Orange Ware, and San Juan Red Ware were present in fewer numbers. Ceramics made in adjoining culture areas, such as Deadmans Gray and Deadmans Fugitive Red, are considered Cohonina trade wares.

Nine *worked sherds,* not tabulated in Table 8, were shaped by chipping and grinding. Seven were fashioned from body sherds of Tusayan White Ware, of which only one can be classified as to type, Kana-a Black-on-white. The remaining two are Tsegi Orange Ware, one classifiable as Tusayan Black-on-red. Four of the worked sherds are subrectangular; the two complete examples are 3.6 and 3.7 cm. long; 3.4 and 3 cm. wide; and 0.5 cm. thick. One of the fragments has a biconical hole 5 mm. in diameter drilled near the center; the other fragment has a conical hole drilled halfway through the sherd from the exterior side. The remaining five worked sherds are irregular fragments, with one or more edges having been ground. The largest fragment is from a circular ground sherd, once 6.2 cm. in diameter. The other pieces are too small for accurate identification, and may have served as scraping and rubbing tools.

Two partially restorable Kana-a Gray *jars* were recovered. These range from a large restored rim and neck portion to a nearly complete vessel. The former example was assembled from fragments found scattered about the floor of the storage bin in Room 3, Structure 2. The neck band is 9.1 cm. wide and is composed of fifteen coils which have been emphasized by encircling horizontal tooling. The rim diameter is 29.4 cm. The other example of Kana-a Gray was partially restored from sherds on the floor in the northeast corner of Room 2, Structure 2. The neckband is 6.6 cm. wide, and is composed of nine flattened coils in typical Kana-a neckbanded fashion. The dimensions are: height, 34.6 cm.; rim diameter, 21.6 cm.; and body diameter, 28.7 cm.

Shell Artifacts

One olivella (*Olivella biplicata*) shell *bead* was excavated from Structure 1 fill. The bead is nearly complete, missing only a chip from the base. A single suspension hole, 2 mm. square, pierced one side of the shell. The length is 1.5 cm. and median width 8 mm.

A disc shell *bead* was excavated from Structure 4, Room 1 floor. The bead is circular with a central perforation 1.5 mm. in diameter. The species is unknown; however, the bead was constructed from a flat portion of shell and ground to a diameter of 4 mm. and thickness of 2 mm.

FLORAL MATERIALS

Eight small charred corncobs were represented by whole and fragmented specimens. Six of these were excavated outside of the northwest corner of Structure 2, and three from the fill of Hearth 1, Structure 4. This material has been submitted to Dr. Hugh Cutler of the Missouri Botanical Garden for analysis.

SUMMARY AND DISCUSSION

Ariz. I:3:1 was the sixth and final site excavated on the pipeline. Surface damage which resulted in the final decision to excavate enabled archaeologists to collect important new data on a Pueblo II Kayenta Anasazi occupation in a somewhat peripheral area. The ceramic record and the presence of windblown volcanic ash from the eruption of Sunset Crater indicate that the village was occupied from about A.D. 950 to 1064.

Evidence for population increase is evident in the architectural record as additional structures or contiguous rooms were added as needed. The absence of a kiva or ceremonial chamber is unusual. The kiva could not have been missed on excavation unless located an unusual distance from the main settlement. The lack of a kiva at a village of this period and size would seem to indicate that the inhabitants shared in the ceremonial activities of a nearby village where a kiva was maintained.

Although a paucity of ground stone artifacts was noted, the presence of many storage rooms and the sedentary nature which the architecture implies are adequate proof that the inhabitants possessed a basic agricultural economy supplemented by hunting and gathering. The chipped stone industry indicates

that hunting played an important role in the subsistence economy. The site's location would have been ideal for floodplain and mesa-top dry farming, riverside plant collecting, and hauling of water.

A number of Cohonina sherds were recovered at the site, but this is not particularly striking due to the geographical location of the site near a frontier between the Anasazi and Cohonina cultures.

It is likely that this site was occupied at the eruption of Sunset Crater, and that the final abandonment can be credited to this event at a period when the village was at its peak population. Since none of the structures caught fire from the accumulating ash, the inhabitants probably took the necessary time to collect their personal belongings, probably leaving as each family was ready. None of the structures was razed, and disintegration of the dwellings and storage rooms appears to be due to natural causes. The occurrence of ash on the collapsed roofing debris in Structure 1 clearly demonstrates that this unit had been abandoned prior to the eruption. However, the 5 to 10 cm. of clean windblown sand found between the ash and the roofing material of Structure 3 indicates that this room stood unused for some time before the roof fell. The roof of Structure 4 collapsed soon after abandonment as the volcanic ash was found between the floor and fallen roofing material. The lack of cinders in the storage rooms of Structure 2 suggests that the ash may not have fallen directly on the village, but was blown in after the eruption had begun. If this was the case, the winds carrying the cinders near the ground level could not deposit the cinders in these rooms through the roof entries. Caution should be exercised here; if the storage rooms were sealed, or the entries left covered for any reason, falling cinders could not have gained entrance.

This is the second site excavated in the Cameron region (Breternitz 1962) for which the abandonment can be related to the eruption of Sunset Crater. Breternitz (1967) pointed out that if we are ever to fully understand the aboriginal cultural consequences of and responses to the eruption of Sunset Crater, additional investigation is needed. The excavation of Ariz. I:3:1 has contributed toward this goal and clearly demonstrates that much remains to be accomplished. The Cameron region with numerous contemporary archaeological sites, seems worthy of primary consideration by future excavators.

Until such work can be accomplished and reported on, it remains open for speculation as to whether or not the inhabitants departing from Ariz. I:3:1 returned to the Kayenta homeland or journeyed to the Wupatki-Flagstaff region to join the hypothesized (Colton 1945b; 1946; 1960) prehistoric land rush created by this eruption.

Ariz. D:9:1

INTRODUCTION

The presence of a buried archaeological site at Station 1667 along the Black Mesa pipeline was detected through examination of the pipe trench; subsequent excavation revealed a small prehistoric settlement consisting of five structures and an associated trash midden. The site is of the Toreva phase of Kayenta Anasazi tradition, dating from about A.D. 1050 to 1150.

The site is located on Black Mesa, 3½ miles east of the western escarpment (Fig. 1). Ariz. D:9:2 is less than one mile to the east, while Ariz. D:13:1, located below the escarpment, is approximately 4 miles west. The elevation of the site is 5,900 feet. The soil mantle varies from a thin surface scattering of windblown sand to a large ridge dune upon which the structures were constructed. West of the site, wind has exposed the underlying Mesa Verde sandstone. This exposed bedrock probably supplied the inhabitants of Ariz. D:9:1 with water trapped in surface depressions for short periods of time after a rain. Otherwise, water was probably carried from a now undetectable seep spring located somewhere along the escarpment or the walls of Dot Klish Canyon.

Agriculture may have been practiced along the eastern edge of the large ridge dune and other plots were probably located along small arroyos north and east of the site which eventually enter a small open grassland valley half a mile to the east. The site is surrounded by growths of one-seed juniper (*Juniperus monosperma*) and Colorado piñon (*Pinus edulis*). The major undergrowth consists of the following species: big sage (*Artemesia tridentata*), cliff rose (*Cowania mexicana*), four-o-clock (*Mirabilis multiflora*), lupine (*Lupinus* sp.) larkspur (*Delphinum* sp.), Mormon tea (*Ephedra viridis*), narrow-leaf yucca (*Yucca angustissima*), needle grass (*Stipa* sp.), actinea (*Hymenoxys* sp.), a yellow variety of mariposa lily (*Calochortus* sp.), a variety of stickweed or wire lettuce (*Stephanomeria* sp.) with a long papus, prickly-pear cactus (*Opuntia* sp.), and cane cholla (*Opuntia* sp.).

Prior to the digging of the pipe trench the settlement was completely buried; only a few sherds were exposed by the trenching machine to indicate the site's presence. Exposed in the pipe trench were the cross sections of a bisected subterranean structure and trash midden. The site was excavated between June 4 and 19, 1969, requiring forty-eight man-days. Excavation began with the removal of the fill from the bisected structure; trenches were dug parallel to both sides of the pipe trench in search of others. As additional buried features were located strip areas were established to remove the overburden. Artifacts were collected from the disturbed soil in a provenience labeled "Construction Back

9. ARIZ. D:9:1. CERAMIC ANALYSIS

Ceramic Types	Surface	1 Fill	1 Floor	2 Fill	2 Floor	3 Fill	3 Floor	4 Fill	4 Floor	5 Fill	5 Floor	Extra-mural Storage Cist	Broadside 1	Broadside 2	Broadside 3	Test Trenches	Construction Back Dirt	Total
Tusayan White Ware																		
Kana-a B/W														1			2	3
Black Mesa B/W	4	12	8	4	5	26	1	3		9	6		35	12	4	12	44	185
Sosi B/W		2		4	6	10	1			10	8		34		5	15	27	122
Dogoszhi B/W	1	11	1	4	5	8	1			6	10		17	5	1	14	27	111
Unclassified B/W		41	13	7	6	86	3	3		32	40		85	52	10	55	79	512
Tusayan White Ware	3	50	14	23	12	101	9	4		36	47		128	19	22	73	139	680
Tusayan Gray Ware																		
Kana-a Gray											2		6					9
Coconino Gray		4				18	7			10			19	9		7	12	86
Honani Tooled						1											2	3
Tusayan Corr.	11	123	60	40	41	216	18	10		76	111	13	278	69	26	155	216	1,463
Moenkopi Corr.			1	13									9		1	6	1	31
Tusayan Gray Ware	20	171	44	35	37	348	19	30		87	86		356	115	11	147	247	1,753
Tsegi Orange Ware																		
Medicine B/R					1											1		2
Tusayan B/R		8	1	3	1	11				5	3	1	12	4	1	4	9	63
Tsegi Orange	1	5	1	3	2	15				8	3		23	9	1	7	12	90
Tusayan Poly.		1								2	1		1					5
Total	40	429	143	136	116	840	59	50		281	317	14	1,003	295	82	496	817	5,118

Dirt." In Table 9, Broadside 1 is associated with Structures 1, 3, and 5; Broadside 2 with Structure 4; Broadside 3 with Structure 2.

ARCHITECTURE

Structure 1 (Figure 32)

Type of Structure. Circular subsurface ceremonial room; kiva.

Dimensions. East-West, 4.8 m.; North-South, 4.75 m. Average depth of floor below present ground surface, 3.1 m.; from old occupation surface, 1.5 m.

Walls. Plastered vertical sides of original pit excavated into consolidated orange sand. Lower portion near floor burned. Vertical slabs placed at base of south wall; southwest portion of vertical slabs removed by trenching machine.

Bench. Constructed by leaving natural soil in place. Patches of plaster present. Constructed in at least two sections. Portion in north wall, 53 cm. above floor. Width varies from 40 to 46 cm.; length, 2.6 m. Single sandstone slab at west end of bench may have provided the footing for an additional roof support post. Most of bench in south wall destroyed by trenching machine. Height above floor, 52 cm.; width varies between 30 and 35 cm.

Ventilator. Opens into kiva through south wall, at floor level. Circular in cross section. Diameter of wall opening, 26 cm. Horizontal portion of shaft, 45 cm. long. Lined on each side with single vertical sandstone slab. Vertical portion of shaft, 1.9 m. Opening at old occupation surface rimmed with small unshaped sandstone pieces. Oval. East-West, 57 cm.; North-South, 69 cm. Unworked rectangular sandstone slab removed from shaft fill; probably utilized as opening cover. Length, 49 cm.; width, 33 cm.; thickness, 8 cm.

Damper. Subrectangular sandstone slab covered interior ventillator opening. Slab shaped by unifacial chipping. Length, 36 cm.; width, 26 cm.; thickness, 6 cm.

Entrance. Through opening in roof also serving as smoke hole. Evidenced by position of ladder holes between ventilator and ashpit.

Floor. Plastered and burned bottom of original pit. Wall-floor juncture at right angles. Two sandstone slabs plastered in floor; location suggests use as base for roof support posts.

Hearth. Irregular circle; slab-lined with seven unshaped pieces of sandstone. Bottom of baked sand; basin-shaped. White wood ash in fill. Diameter, 55 cm.; depth, 15 cm.

Ashpit. Rectangular. North end contiguous to south side of hearth. East and west walls formed by vertical sandstone slabs; south end open. Length, 40 cm.; width, 18 cm.; and depth, 31 cm.

Storage Pit. Circular; located along vertical slabs at base of south wall. Diameter, 32 cm.; depth, 28 cm. Walls vertical and unplastered. Floor concave.

Postholes. Six postholes were located on the floor. Two represent primary roof supports, while three along west wall represent secondary roof supports. The remaining two are ladder holes. The roof support posts were placed between 6 and 16 cm. below the floor; diameter, 6 to 13 cm. The ladder posts were 18 cm. apart; depth below floor level, 8 cm.; diameter, 12 cm.

Roof. Rectangular arrangement of roof support posts (two postholes and two slabs plastered in floor) suggests a rectangular plate on which horizontal timbers were placed. Covered with daub. Ten randomly placed postholes on old occupation surface north of structure may represent additional attempts to brace the roof. Depth below old occupation surface, 4 to 31 cm.; diameter, 9 to 20 cm.

Fill. Wind- and water-deposited fine orange sand containing charcoal flecks, which increase in size and number with depth. On floor burned roofing material consisted mainly of charcoal and burned daub. Few sherds and artifacts intermixed.

Material Culture. Slab metate fragment, one-hand mano fragment, two worked sherds, one utilized flake, and seven waste flakes in

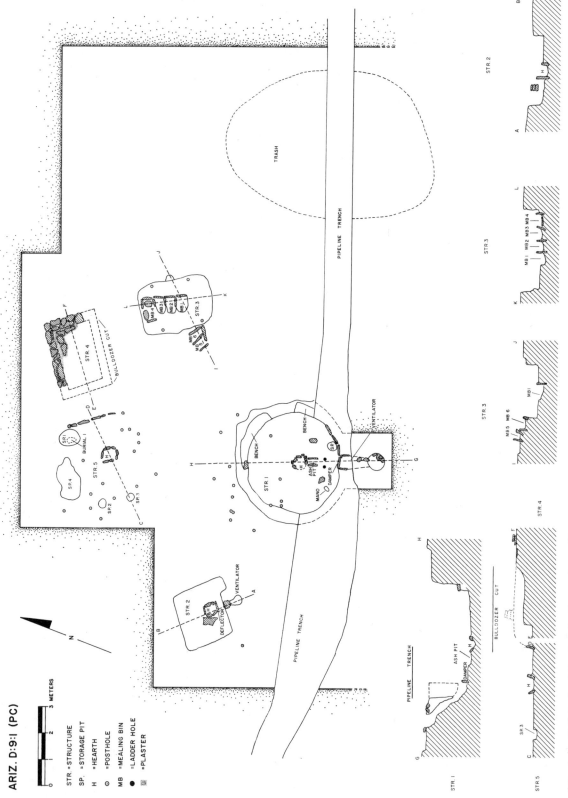

ARIZ. D:9:1 (PC)

STR. = STRUCTURE
SP. = STORAGE PIT
H = HEARTH
⊙ = POSTHOLE
MB = MEALING BIN
● = LADDER HOLE
▦ = PLASTER

N

0 1 2 3 METERS

32. *Ariz. D:9:1. Architectural plan and profiles*

fill. One-hand mano fragment, pebble pounder, scraper, three worked sherds, three utilized flakes, and seven waste flakes on floor.

Structure 2 (Figures 32, 33, 34)

Type of Structure. Square pithouse.

Dimensions. East-West, 2.2 m; North-south, 2 m. Average depth of floor below present ground surface, 58 cm.; from old occupation surface, 40 cm.

Walls. Lower portion formed by vertical sides of pit dug into consolidated orange sand. No evidence of plaster. Structure set into side of dune. North wall, 40 cm. high; south, 58 cm. East and west walls range between these two heights. Upper portion con-

structed of perishable material with the base resting on the old ground surface. Covered with daub.

Ventilator. Opens into the pithouse through the south wall, at floor level. Shaft constructed by digging open trench. Wall opening formed by two vertical sandstone slabs, which support lintel and three slabs plastered above. Five Tusayan corrugated sherds used as chinking along slab on east side of opening. Wall opening square; height, 28 cm.; width, 27 cm. Horizontal portion of shaft, 70 cm. Vertical portion, 55 cm. Opening at old ground surface elongated oval; length, 50 cm.; width, 32 cm. A sandstone slab, from the fill shaped by bifacial chipping along one end. The slab was D-shaped and probably was

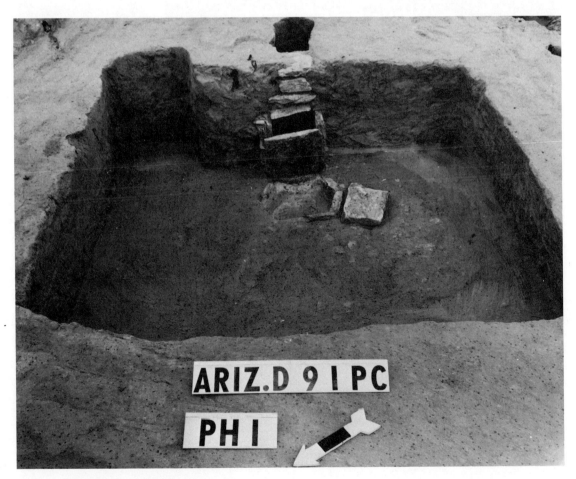

33. *Ariz. D:9:1. Pithouse; Structure 2*

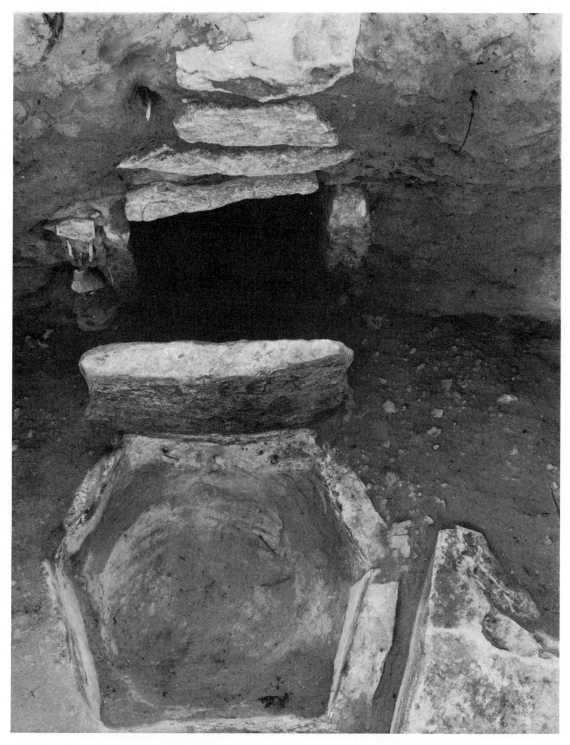

34. *Ariz. D:9:1. Detail of ventilator shaft, deflector, and hearth complex; Structure 2. Note sherd chinking on left side of ventilator opening*

utilized to cover the ventilator's surface opening. Length, 43 cm.; width, 36 cm.; thickness, 1.5 cm.

Entrance. Probably through south wall. Indicated by recess in south wall at juncture with east wall. Recess may have provided footing for ladder; it extends to the floor and is cut back into wall 40 cm.; width, 57 cm.

Floor. Plastered; well-preserved bottom of original excavation. Flat, but curves up to meet walls. Unshaped sandstone slab plastered in floor contiguous to west side of hearth. Function unknown. Length, 42 cm.; width, 22 cm.; height above floor, 10 cm.

Hearth. Subrectangular; lined by six unshaped vertical sandstone slabs. Bottom of baked sand; basin-shaped. Contained white wood ash. Length, 43 cm.; width, 40 cm.; depth, 17 cm.

Deflector. Unworked rectangular sandstone slab plastered vertically into the floor on southeast side of hearth. Located 16 cm. in front of ventilator opening. Extends 26 cm. above the floor with a width of 35 cm.

Roof. No evidence. Single posthole located out from southwest corner may be associated. Depth below old occupation surface, 20 cm.; diameter, 17 cm. Probably of perishable material.

Fill. Wind- and water-deposited orange sand containing charcoal flecks, sherds, and a few artifacts.

Material Culture. Two hammerstones, worked sherd, unworked piece of limonite, and waste flake from fill. One-hand mano in ventilator fill.

Structure 3 (Figures 32, 35, 36)

Type of Structure. Subrectangular pithouse utilized as mealing room.

Dimensions. East-West, 2 m.; North-South, 3 m. Average depth of floor below the present ground surface, 1.67 m.; from old occupation surface, 0.61 m.

Walls. Lower portion formed by unplastered sides of original pit excavated into consolidated orange sand. Vertical. Upper portion constructed of daubed perishable material resting on old ground surface, with the top leaning against the roof. Niche in east wall at old ground surface; width, 35 cm.; height, 19 cm.; cut back into wall 20 cm.

Entrance. Probably through roof.

Floor. Packed sterile orange sand.

Mealing Bins. Six. Four are contiguous, occupying the center of the room along its long axis. Metates removed prior to abandonment of structure, however, outlines were visible on floor (Fig. 36). The metates rested on the floor so that they slanted down toward the open sides of the catching bins. The catching basins were faced on three sides by thin sandstone slabs; floors were plastered, curving up to meet the bin sides. Only Bin 4 possessed evidence of framing slabs for the metate; length, 78 cm.; width, 46 cm.; depth of catching basin, 25 cm. Two mealing bins were connected to the exterior west wall at the old occupation level. Due to their exterior position only the vertical slabs remained, delineating the catch basins. Lengths, 48 and 60 cm.; widths, 30 and 27 cm.; depths, 31 and 20 cm.

Postholes. Four primary roof supports located along walls. Depth below floor level, 20 to 43 cm.; diameter, 14 to 20 cm. Rotted juniper fragments in southwest posthole.

Roof. Rectangular arrangement of roof support posts suggests a rectangular plate on which horizontal timbers were placed. Covered with daub.

Fill. Wind- and water-deposited orange sand containing charcoal flecks, charcoal, sherds, and artifacts. Small lenses of charcoal and ash 16 cm. above floor indicate small amounts of trash deposited after final abandonment of structure.

Material Culture. Restorable Tusayan corrugated jar, partial Tusayan Black-on-red bowl, six worked sherds, two one-hand mano fragments, two-hand mano fragment, gypsum pendant fragment, hammerstone, two pieces of worked gypsum, and one piece of worked

35. *Ariz. D:9:1. Mealing room; Structure 3*

silt stone from the fill. Two pebble pounders, one worked sherd, two utilized flakes, and five waste flakes on floor.

Structure 4 (Figure 32)

Type of Structure. Rectangular masonry storage room, partially destroyed by construction equipment.

Dimensions. Estimated dimensions, East-West, 3 m.; North-South, 2 m. Average depth of floor below present ground surface, 90 cm.; constructed on surface of ridge dune.

Walls. Masonry. Constructed of unshaped sandstone blocks; laid in large amounts of brown mortar. Originally much higher; rem-

nants are three courses high and average one to two stones in width. Maximum wall height above floor, 30 cm.; above old occupation surface, 40 cm.

Entrance. Probably through opening in roof.

Floor. Masonry-lined with unshaped sandstone slabs; plastered on leveled occupation surface in large amounts of brown mortar. Floor-wall juncture at right angles.

Roof. Daubed perishable material; poles laid north-south horizontally across upper course of wall.

Fill. Wind-deposited orange sand containing charcoal flecks. Sherds were collected in combined fill and floor provenience because

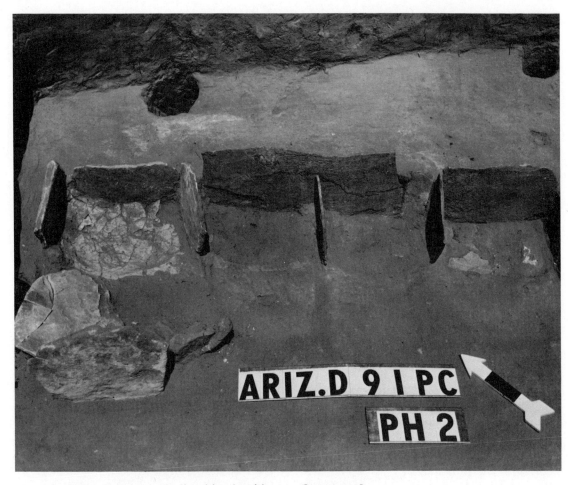

36. *Ariz. D:9:1. Detail of mealing bins in pithouse; Structure 3*

of disturbance. Some daub fragments intermixed.

Material Culture. Nothing but sherds in fill.

Structure 5 (Figure 32)

Type of Structure. Jacal dwelling.

Dimensions. East-West, 3.9 m.; North-South, 4 m. Structure originally built into side of sand dune so that the western portion of the floor rested on the old ground surface; the eastern portion 77 cm. below it. The eastern portion was 1.13 m. from the present ground surface; the western, 27 cm.

Walls. Jacal. Complete wall pattern not preserved. Posthole pattern indicates single-room structure, either square or subrectangular in outline, with additional roof support posts. Base of east wall excavated into dune, reinforced with low masonry wall of unshaped vertical sandstone slabs. Length of masonry, 1.89 m. Highest standing portion 31 cm. above floor, lowest, 27 cm. Width one stone, varying between 8 and 15 cm.

Entrance. No evidence. Probably through roof.

Floor. Native orange sand packed by use. Poorly preserved.

Hearth. Circular, 53 cm. in diameter; 24 cm. deep. Lined with seven vertical unshaped sandstone slabs. Bottom baked sand; basin-shaped. White wood ash constituted half of fill; remainder gray ash. The gray ash may be derived from coal, as eleven unburned coal pieces were removed from the hearth fill.

Storage Pits. 1. Located at north end of masonry retaining wall. Oval; length, 84 cm.; width, 67 cm.; depth, 50 cm. Walls vertical. Floor flat; curves up to meet walls. Fill of orange sand contained remains of human burial, artifacts, sherds, and charcoal flecks. 2. Located 1.45 m. west of hearth. Circular, 29 cm. in diameter; 13 cm. deep. Basin-shaped. Plastered walls. Fill consisted of orange sand intermixed with a few sherds and charcoal flecks. 3. Located 1.42 m. southwest of hearth. Circular, 25 cm. in diameter; 20 cm. deep. Walls vertical. Floor flat. Fill of orange sand intermixed with charcoal flecks. Few sherds. 4. Located on north side of room. Irregular outline. Maximum length, 1.6 m.; maximum width, 0.95 m.; average depth, 0.5 m. Walls vertical to irregular along east side. Floor flat. Fill deposited in two layers. Bottom, 38 cm., consisted of burned roofing debris and orange sand. Upper 22 cm. consisted of trash with large number of artifacts and ceramic fragments.

Postholes. Fifteen postholes. Depth below floor, 5 to 30 cm.; diameter, 10 to 20 cm. Many of these represent primary roof supports, and additional supports probably placed after the roof began weakening. The remaining posts were in the walls, which also supported the superstructure.

Roof. Perishable materials resting on walls and ridge poles supported on primary posts. Daubed. Probably gabled.

Fill. Resting on floor, 7 to 15 cm. layer of burned roofing material and intermixed artifacts. Above that, 15 to 18 cm. of trash containing numerous artifacts. Capping the above material was approximately 80 cm. of wind-deposited sand and charcoal flecks. Small amount of construction back dirt and masonry rubble from Structure 4 completed the fill.

Material Culture. From the fill: burned through metate, slab metate fragment, two-hand mano fragment, three hammerstones, coal pendant fragment, scraper, five worked sherds, two utilized flakes, seven waste flakes, piece of unworked gypsum, and a lump of potter's clay. Two worked sherds on floor. Miniature Tusayan Gray Ware jar with burial in Storage Pit 1. From the fill of Storage Pit 1: bone awl, rectangular ground piece of shell, shale disc, utilized flake, four waste flakes, lump of potter's clay and forty-seven pieces of worked or molded potter's clay. Storage Pit 3 fill: one gypsum pendant fragment. From partially trash filled Storage Pit 4: two trough metates, two slab metate fragments, one-hand mano, two indeterminate mano fragments, two hammerstones, pebble pounder, four unworked river pebbles, ground sandstone disc, five worked sherds, unworked piece of limonite, sixteen pieces of worked or molded potter's clay, eighteen unworked gypsum flakes, one utilized flake, and five waste flakes. In addition to the above items, ninety-three pieces of ground stone disc beads in various stages of manufacture were found scattered throughout the proveniences (thirty-three pieces of unworked raw material, forty-three pieces of ground raw material, six bead blanks, four bead blanks with drilled centers, five disc beads, and two bead fragments) .

Extramural Storage Pit

Located 70 m. southeast of site. Pentagonal; formed by five slanting unshaped sandstone slabs. East-West, 40 cm.; North-South, 40 cm. Average depth of floor below present ground surface, 20 cm. Walls slant outward at the top. Floor flat; packed sand. No evidence of roofing. Wind-deposited orange sand and sherds constituted fill.

ARCHITECTURAL SUMMARY

The position of the architectural units in relation to each other and the trash midden at Ariz. D:9:1 corresponds to a front-oriented village plan: 1. surface rooms, 2. pithouses and kiva, and 3. refuse (Reed 1956:11). Although no clear indication of different construction periods could be recognized, the mealing room and jacal dwelling had evidently fallen into disuse before the rest of the group. Structure 3 served as a workroom where corn was ground. The mealing room possessed a total of six metate bins. The metates had been placed so that the meal ground on them fell into the appropriate catch basin. The catch basins were plastered, curving up to the bin sides to facilitate retrieval of the ground meal. This construction trait was best preserved in Bin 4 (Fig. *36*). Then, for some unknown reason, the metates were removed, leaving only the catch basins. The structure stood unmolested for some time, accumulating 16 cm. of wind and water deposited fill on the floor. For a limited time the structure was then utilized as a trash dumping pit. Before the subsurface room was completely filled, two ceramic vessels were placed in an upright position along the north wall.

Prior to the final abandonment of the mealing room, Structure 5 burned and was utilized as a trash dump. Two trough metates, presumably from the mealing bins, were found above the burned roofing debris filling Storage Pit 4 of the jacal dwelling.

Structure 4 was the settlement's granary. This storage room was constructed with a slab-lined masonry floor, which would have deterred rodents from entering the structure.

Structure 2 was the only domicile occupied after fire forced the abandonment of the jacal dwelling. The pithouse was small and could not have been occupied by many people.

Structure 1 was a circular kiva serving the ceremonial needs of the settlement. Part of the kiva was destroyed by the pipeline trench.

REFUSE

A formalized refuse midden was located at the southeastern limits of the settlement. The trash consisted mainly of organically stained soil-bearing sherds, stone artifacts, charcoal fragments and flecks. There were no interments in the midden. The trash was shallow, measuring only 29 cm. at its deepest point. On a north-south axis the trash extended 8 m.; its east-west extent was 5.8 m. Since the trash was shallow and represented a homogenous short occupation, it was not excavated by stratigraphic levels. Rather, it was excavated by a series of parallel test trenches 1 m. wide.

Additional trash had been deposited in the abandoned and partially filled mealing room, and on the burned jacal dwelling. The composition of the deposits was similar to that described for the midden; the exception being that the refuse associated with the jacal remains contained more discarded artifacts. The cultural deposits above the burned roofing debris were screened to increase artifact recovery.

OTHER EXCAVATIONS

Ten test trenches were placed to test the regions adjacent to the excavated features, and to completely excavate the refuse midden. The trenches were 1 m. wide and totaled 79.4 m. in length. Depths ranged from 25 to 75 cm. below the disturbed surface; each was dug slightly below the old occupation surface into sterile soil.

ARTIFACTS

Ground Stone Artifacts

Ground stone artifacts from Ariz. D:9:1 are of two basic types: those utilized for food processing, and those made for personal adornment. Eight *one-hand manos* of sandstone are represented in the collection; three are complete. Two of the complete specimens are subrectangular. One possesses two convex grinding faces; the other, one. Length, 10.2 and 12.5 cm.; width, 6.8 and 9.5 cm.; thickness, 3.4 and 4.6 cm., respectively. The complete specimen is square and possesses two flat grinding surfaces; limonite stains are present on both faces. Length, 10.7 cm.; width, 8.9 cm.; thickness, 4 cm. The five mano fragments represent subrectangular manos, three of which possess a single convex grinding surface; two are faceted. Width, 6.4 to 10.7 cm.; thickness, 1.8 to 3.8 cm.

Two-hand manos are represented by two rectangular sandstone fragments. One is burned and possesses traces of hematite on both flat working surfaces. Width, 11 cm.; thickness, 3.3 cm. The other fragment represents a *mano blank* which had been pecked to shape. The implement probably broke during shaping and was discarded. Width, 11.5 cm.; thickness, 2.5 cm.

Two *indeterminate mano fragments* are constructed of sandstone and represent subrectangular manos. Both possess a single convex grinding surface, although one is slightly faceted. Width, 8.2 and 9.4 cm.; thickness, 3.4 and 4.7 cm., respectively.

Three complete *trough metates* were associated with Structure 5—the burned jacal dwelling. One metate, on the roof when the structure burned was broken into seven fragments. A slab of Mesa Verde sandstone had been pecked and chipped to shape a subrectangular block 43 cm. long, 31 cm. wide, and 4.2 cm. thick. The grinding surface is a shallow trough, open at one end; 32 cm. long, 23 cm. wide, with a maximum depth of 2 cm. The other two metates were found unburned in the upper fill of Storage Pit 4, where they had presumably been thrown after removal from the mealing bins of Structure 3. Both were shaped by pecking and chipping slabs of Mesa Verde sandstone. The smaller example measures: length, 39 cm.; width, 30.5 cm.; thickness, 15 cm. The trough is open at both ends and measures: length, 35 cm.; width, 25 cm.; maximum depth, 4 cm. The larger metate measures: length, 45 cm.; width, 33 cm.; thickness, 13 cm. The shallow trough is open at one end and measures: length, 29 cm.; width, 25 cm.; maximum depth, 2.5 cm.

The three metates were constructed of fine-grained sandstone, which has resulted in similar grinding surfaces.

Five *slab metate fragments* were also of fine-grained sandstone; supporting the hypothesis that graded metates were not present at Ariz. D:9:1. The fragments represent five separate metates. Each was shaped by pecking, and used slightly on one surface. Thickness varies from 1.4 to 9 cm.

Four ground *pendants* were excavated; two are complete. One whole specimen is subrectangular, the other is square. Both were constructed from pieces of opaque gypsum, and possess edges that are ground flat; the faces are smooth and polished as are all edges. The subrectangular pendant measures: length, 2.2 cm.; width, 1.2 cm.; thickness, 0.4 cm.; the square specimen: length, 1.4 cm.; width, 1.25 cm.; thickness, 0.3 cm. Both fragments are the lower or bottom portion of ground subrectangular pendants. The larger fragment is constructed of red shale, the other of gypsum. Both fragments possess rounded edges and smooth faces. Width, 3 and 2.1 cm.; thickness, 0.7 and 0.2 cm.; respectively.

Two ground *stone discs* were recovered. The artifacts were formed by edge grinding thin pieces of brown sandstone and shale; the faces are flat and smooth. The shale specimen is slightly subrectangular; a conical hole is drilled halfway through near the center. Length, 3 cm.; width, 2.5 cm.; thickness, 0.3 cm. The sandstone specimen is circular, with a chip missing from one edge. Diameter, 2.7 cm.; thickness, 0.7 cm. A flat piece of gypsum was hexagonally chipped. Slight grinding on six sides resulted from preliminary rounding of the object. The piece of gypsum is not translucent, and probably represents a disc in the process of manufacture. Length, 5.5 cm.; width, 4.5 cm.; thickness, 0.4 cm.

A total of ninety-three items, illustrating the steps required for the ground stone manufacture of *disc beads* (Fig. *37*), were excavated from four proveniences within Structure 5. The majority had been discarded in the fill above Burial 1, Storage Pit 1, after

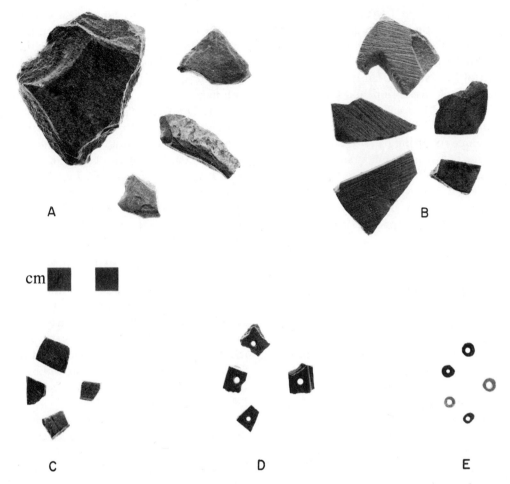

37. *Five successive stages for creating stone disc beads:* A, *raw material;* B, *ground raw material;* C, *bead blanks;* D, *center drilled blanks;* E, *finished ground beads*

the dwelling burned and are not directly associated with the interment.

Individual objects include: thirty-three pieces of raw material, forty-three pieces of ground raw material, six bead blanks, four bead blanks with drilled centers, two bead fragments, and five complete beads. The raw materials consist of irregular fragments struck from larger pieces of gray (28) and yellowish or buff (5) shale. Although irregular in outline, the fragments are nearly all thin pieces. Size of the fragments varies considerably: length, 1.1 to 6.4 cm.; width, 0.7 to 3.4 cm.; thickness, 0.5 to 1.6 cm. Forty-three pieces of yellowish or buff shale were ground on oppos-

ing faces, creating smooth thin slabs from which the bead blanks were to be made. The slabs were then edge ground creating square, rectangular, and triangular bead blanks. Length, 3.5 to 5 cm.; width, 1.9 to 4.7 cm.; thickness, 0.45 to 1 cm. Six bead blanks are irregular square or rectangular forms; gray (2) and buff (4) shale. The edges and faces are ground flat. Length, 0.9 to 1.4 cm.; width, 0.9 to 1.1 cm.; thickness, 0.35 to 0.5 cm. Four additional bead blanks are center drilled; the suspension holes are cylindrical—diameter, 0.2 to 0.25 cm. These particular blanks are not edge ground, but were chipped from ground slabs; only the faces were ground. Length, 0.8

to 1.3 cm.; width, 0.9 to 1.1 cm.; thickness, 0.3 to 0.4 cm. Two fragments represent similar bead blanks broken during the drilling. Five finished disc beads were found; three of dark gray, two of buff shale. Diameter, 0.5 to 0.6 cm.; diameter of suspension holes, 0.1 to 0.2 cm.; thickness, 0.15 to 0.25 cm.

To summarize, the disc beads were created by a technique requiring five stages (Fig. *37*) : 1. fragments or flakes were first struck from a selected piece of shale; 2. these flakes were ground flat on two opposing faces creating thin slabs; 3. square or rectangular bead blanks were either chipped or ground from the slabs; 4. suspension holes were drilled; then 5. ground to the desired size and shape. Similarity was achieved by stringing the roughly shaped blanks and working them down simultaneously on an abrasive surface. The precise method used to drill the minute and exactly cylindrical holes remains unknown; however, one of the two forms of the bow drill was probably utilized.

A *cylindrical* or *tubular bead* of pink shale was the only example of this variety of bead. The artifact was ground to shape and polished. A suspension hole, 0.25 cm. in diameter passes through the long axis of the bead. Length, 1.2 cm.; maximum body diameter, 0.95 cm. One piece of similar pink shale, which has been ground into an elongated object, represents tubular beads in the process of manufacture. Length, 3.8 cm.; width, 1.2 cm.; thickness, 0.8 cm.

Chipped Stone Artifacts

Chipped stone artifacts were sparse at Ariz. D:9:1. A *projectile point* from the surface is triangular; both the tip and base portions are missing. The artifact was pressure flaked from a primary percussion flake of gray chert. Two diagonal side notches are present to aid hafting. Estimated length, 3.2 cm.; width, 1.5 cm.; thickness, 0.3 cm.

Five *scrapers* of variegated chert (4) and quartzite (1) were excavated from separate proveniences. One rectangular scraper is well-made, possessing a bifacial working edge around the entire tool. The other irregular scrapers possess single unifacial or intermittent cutting edges. The entire collection was made by pressure retouching primary percussion flakes. Length, 2.6 to 5 cm.; width, 1.9 to 3.8 cm.; thickness, 0.9 to 1.2 cm.

Eleven *utilized flakes* were identified by minute use scars along one or more edges. Material: variegated chert (8) and quartzite (3). Forty-five *waste flakes,* representing the knapping debris from tool manufacture, were collected. Material: gypsum (21), variegated chert (19), and quartzite (5).

Miscellaneous Stone Artifacts

The twelve *hammerstones* found can be divided into two types: spherical (4) and unmodified cobbles (8). Outlines are circular to subrectangular. Circular to oval specimens measure: length, 6.3 to 8.1 cm.; width, 4 to 6.6 cm.; thickness, 2.2 to 6.3 cm. Subrectangular: length, 5.5 to 9.6 cm.; width, 3.6 to 5 cm.; thickness, 2.9 to 4 cm.

Four oval *pebble pounders* evidence little use; two are unmodified quartz river cobbles, the remainder chert cobbles. One of the quartz artifacts possesses hematite stains on one slightly battered end. Length, 4 to 6.4 cm.; width, 3.4 to 5.6 cm.; thickness, 1.75 to 3.5 cm. Four unmodified water worn *river pebbles* of various colored quartzite were similar in size and shape to the pebble pounders, but lacked evidence of use.

Two pieces of *limonite* were excavated; one had several ground faces. Length, 3.9 and 4 cm.; width, 3.3 and 2 cm.; thickness, 2.7 and 1.5 cm., respectively.

Ceramic Artifacts

The ceramics at Ariz. D:9:1 were of the Kayenta Anasazi tradition; the 5,118 sherds recovered have been assigned to types listed in Table 9. Among the pottery types present, the best indicators of temporal placement are Black Mesa, Sosi, and Dogoszhi Black-on-white. These three types, in conjunction with the utility wares, would seem to indicate that the settlement was occupied during the middle to late portion of the twelfth century. The remaining utility and decorated ceramic types found, agree with a temporal placement between A.D. 1050 and 1100.

The only departure or deviation from the ceramic types described by Colton and Hargrave (1937) and Colton (1955) were twenty-five sherds of Tusayan White Ware and seven

of Tusayan Gray Ware. These thirty-two sherds were excavated from nine separate proveniences and include the following types: Black Mesa Black-on-white (14), Dogoszhi Black-on-white (5), unclassified Tusayan White Ware (6), Tusayan Corrugated (6), and Coconino Gray (1). These sherds possess a yellowish cast; normally black design elements were yellowish orange in appearance. It has been hypothesized that this discoloration resulted from an overfiring due to the

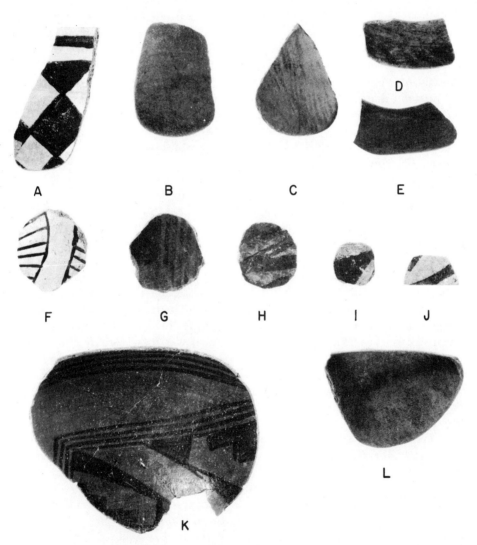

38. *Ariz. D:9:1. Worked sherds: A, B, C, K, L, scoops; D, E, scrapers; F, G, H, I, discs; J, unfinished pendant*

use of coal as fuel. Since coal was found in the hearth of the jacal domicile the inhabitants must have understood the potential of coal as a source of fuel.

Five sherds exhibiting the characteristic of Shato Black-on-white (Colton 1955) were recovered. Corrugated exteriors were present on Black Mesa (1), Dogoszhi (1), and unclassified black-on-white (3) sherds.

Not included in the pottery tabulations are thirty-eight *worked sherds* of various sizes, shapes, and pottery types (Fig. *38*), all of which show modification by chipping, scraping, and grinding. Only painted sherds were utilized: twenty-two of Tusayan White Ware; fifteen of Tsegi Orange Ware; one of San Juan Red Ware. Nine of the sherds were circular, or nearly so. Four are complete (Fig. *38F–I*) and range in diameter from 2.9 to 6.1 cm.; thickness, 0.4 to 0.7 cm. These artifacts were made from body sherds of Black Mesa (2), Sosi (1), and Dogoszhi Black-on-white (1), Medicine (1), and Tusayan Black-on-red (2), Tsegi Orange (1), and Deadmans Black-on-red (1). None of the whole sherd discs possessed a drilled hole; however, one fragment did. The piece probably represents an oval *pendant* ground from a body sherd of Tsegi Orange Ware. A biconical hole is located 4 mm. from the edge, and is 3 mm. in diameter.

Another form of worked sherd is the *scoop*. Shapes range from oval to subrectangular. The two oval scoops (Fig. *38K–L*) are made from body sherds of Medicine and Tusayan Black-on-red. The larger specimen (*K*) may have served as a small receptacle, being a shallow dishlike vessel. Length, 13.9 and 8.1 cm.; width, 10.9 and 6.4 cm.; thickness, 0.4 and 0.5 cm., respectively. Additional scoops (Fig. *38A–C*) are subrectangular. Two with pointed fragments at one end are ground only on the opposite end, while the other subrectangular specimens are ground along all edges. One Black Mesa Black-on-white rim sherd and three body sherds of Tusayan and Medicine Black-on-red and Tsegi Orange pro-

vided the necessary raw materials. Length, 5.5 to 8.8 cm.; width, 2.7 to 5.15 cm.; thickness, 0.4 cm. Twenty-two sherds of various shapes generally are considered to be *ceramic scrapers*. The specimens are oval to rectangular, and include fragments too small to determine the original shape. Ten were rectangular (Fig. *38D–E*), four oval to circular. Raw materials selected include the following ceramic types: Black Mesa (3), Dogoszhi Black-on-white (2), unclassified Tusayan White Ware (11), Tusayan (4) and Medicine Black-on-red (1), and Tsegi Orange (1). Three were made from rim sherds, the remainder from body fragments. A general characteristic of these sherds is steeply beveled working edges, often with an acute angle along the sherd interior, although seven possess rounded or flat working edges at right angles to the sherd surface. Measurements for the two ceramic fragments (Fig. *38D–E*) are: length, 5.5 and 6.5 cm.; width, 3 cm.; thickness, 4 cm., respectively.

One unclassified Tusayan White Ware body sherd has four straight edges and resembles a *pendant,* but lacks the hole for a suspension cord (Fig. *38J*). Length, 3.5 cm.; width, 1.8 cm.; thickness, 0.3 cm.

In addition to the ceramic artifacts described above, three vessels were recovered. A restorable Tusayan Corrugated jar was found in the fill of the northwest corner of the mealing room. When first discovered, the vessel was intact but fractured, placed vertically with the rim 5 cm. below the old occupation surface, the bottom 37 cm. The exterior is corrugated and is heavily coated with carbon. Rim diameter, 15 cm.; maximum body diameter, 28.5 cm.; height, 30 cm.; volume 10,000 ml. Two small sandstone slabs were found in place as *vessel covers*. The slabs were unworked and measure: length, 17 and 11 cm.; width, 11 and 9 cm., respectively; thickness, 1 cm. Immediately east of the Tusayan Corrugated jar was found a partial Tusayan Black-on-red bowl. The vessel was vertical, with the rim at the old occupation surface. A portion of one side was missing. The black design is located on the bowl interior extending completely around the rim. The design is Dogoszhi Black-on-white. Rim diameter, 11.3 cm.; height, 6 cm.; volume, 300 ml.

The third vessel recovered was a miniature Tusayan Gray Ware water jar or canteen. The vessel had been placed with Burial 1; interment was in Storage Pit 1, Structure 5. The miniature vessel was found resting on its side, where it had slumped since placement in the vicinity of the skull. The vessel is an elongated sphere with a flat bottom and small neck. Two opposing lug handles are present; each pierced with a suspension hole 3 mm. in diameter. Rim diameter, 2.4 cm.; maximum body diameter, 6.3 cm.; height, 8 cm.; volume, 50 ml.

Bone Artifact

A single bone implement was excavated from Storage Pit 4 of the jacal domicile, where it had been discarded with the refuse. The tool is a bone *awl* of the split bone variety. The bone had been split at an angle so that the entire articular end formed the proximal end or handle. The distal end or tip was ground to a tapering point. Weathering removed all traces of any body grinding or polishing. The awl is complete and measures: length, 14 cm.; width, 1.7 cm.; thickness, 1.2 cm.

Clay Artifacts

Sixty-seven unfired artifacts of clay were recovered from the trash deposited on the jacal dwelling. Twenty-one objects are *sand tempered sherds* representing at least two unfired vessels. Two rim sherds represent a medium-size bowl; a third, a miniature bowl. Both surfaces of the sherd representing the miniature vessel were smoothed and probably polished. However, the exterior sherd surfaces of the larger bowl are rough, due to decom-

position. The interiors are smooth with traces of a white slip—indicating that a Tusayan White Ware vessel was in the process of manufacture.

Twelve objects are *clay coils,* demonstrating that the vessels were constructed by the coiling technique. Both Tusayan White and Gray Wares, the decorated and utility wares of the Kayenta Anasazi culture, were made by the coiling technique (Colton 1955).

The remaining pieces are balls and lumps of *potter's clay*. Both sand tempered and untempered clay is represented. The balls are all small, less than 1.7 cm. in diameter. The lumps of clay are generally amorphous and defy formal description. The largest lump is 5.1 cm. long; 3 cm. wide; and 2.1 cm. thick.

Coal Artifacts

One piece of worked low-grade bituminous coal was excavated from the trash deposited on the jacal domicile. The artifact is broken and represents the lower portion of a sub-rectangular *pendant*. Both faces were ground flat, the edges are rounded. The entire pendant had been highly polished. Width, 2.1 cm.; thickness, 0.3 cm.

In addition to the coal pendant fragment, eleven unworked pieces of bituminous coal were recovered from the hearth fill of the jacal dwelling.

Shell Artifacts

A small rectangular piece of ground shell was found among the stone bead items in the jacal dwelling. The object may be a disc bead in process of manufacture, or intended for inlay. Length, 1 cm.; width, 0.7 cm.; thickness, 0.2 cm.

FLORAL MATERIALS

Three small charred corncobs were represented by specimens excavated, one each from Storage Pits 1 and 4 of the jacal domicile and the mealing room. A fragmented seed shell was also recovered from the jacal structure, Storage Pit 1.

NONARTIFACTUAL MATERIALS

Seventy-seven white eggshell fragments, probably representing more than one egg, were excavated from the trash deposited on the burned jacal structure. These are not turkey eggs, but are from some tree-nesting bird as the shell is quite thin (Lyndon L. Hargrave, personal communication).

HUMAN BURIAL

Before the jacal structure burned, a human burial had been placed in the lower portion of Storage Pit 1. The upper 22 cm. of fill consisted of burned roofing debris and trash deposited sometime after the interment, indicating that the pit had not been completely filled at the time of burial. The burial was definitely not placed in the pit after the fire, as the burned debris formed a continuous layer over the floor and into the storage pit.

The bones were almost completely disintegrated, with only fragmented splinters and brown stain present. The burial was of an infant, and it had apparently been a primary inhumation in a flexed position. The head had faced toward the west, with the body placed on its left side on a slight southeast-northwest axis.

The only grave offering was a miniature Tusayan Gray Ware water jar, placed at the head of the skeleton.

SUMMARY AND DISCUSSION

Ariz. D:9:1 was the first site excavated on the Black Mesa pipeline project. The village layout is reminiscent of the front-oriented ground plan of most late Pueblo II-early Pueblo III settlements of the Colorado Plateau. The small size would seem to indicate an occupation consisting of a few families. The inhabitants were of the Toreva phase, oc-cupying the site between A.D. 1050 and 1150.

Labor specialization occurred at the site; corn grinding activities were centered around Structure 3—a subterranean mealing room. Limited rooftop grinding may have been performed on the jacal dwelling. Other sites exhibiting a similar pattern for specialization of corn grinding have been reported for Black Mesa (Gumerman 1970). The common or repeated occurrence of specialized mealing rooms, both subterranean and surface structures, on Black Mesa would appear to have developed as an adjunct to the kiva.

Analysis of the archaeological data has suggested a hypothesis regarding the settlement's final abandonment. The small settlement originally consisted of two domiciles, a specialized mealing room, kiva and granary or storage room, occupied by an extended family group. When the jacal dwelling caught fire and burned, forcing its final abandonment, the inhabitants of that domicile were left with four possible alternatives for future action: to move into the other domicile if the individuals there were willing; to occupy the kiva as a domicile; to construct another dwelling; or to move away from the site. Several of these alternatives can be eliminated on the basis of the archaeological evidence. The other domicile or pithouse is small, rendering it very doubtful that this structure housed the entire village after the fire. The possibility that the kiva was occupied as a domicile is practical, although evidence for this could not be found or recognized. Had a new structure been built the excavation surely would have located it. Thus, it would seem most likely that the people involved chose the fourth alternative and left the village. If this were the case, then we can explain the sudden abandonment of the mealing room during the site's occupation. It appears that the family whose home burned possessed a number of females who had previously been active in the operation of the mealing room. When it came time for them to leave, they removed their metates from the mealing bins for transportation to the new village or home site. For some unknown reason, two of these metates were discarded on the burned home. Meanwhile, the inhabitants of the pithouse remained in residence for an unknown period of time, utilizing Structures 3 and 5, which were then both abandoned, as trash-dumping pits. Later, when the kiva required major construction repairs, and perhaps also because the kiva society could no longer conduct ceremonials due to the population decrease, the kiva was intentionally fired and the settlement was totally abandoned.

SUMMARY OF EXCAVATIONS

The second major section of this report presents the results of archaeological investigations at six Kayenta Anasazi settlements.

The earliest component discovered and subsequently excavated was Ariz. D:13:4, a multiroomed jacal structure provisionally assigned to the Basketmaker II tradition (approximately A.D. 1 to 500). The settlement represents a semipermanent or temporary campsite of a small band or group of hunters-and-gatherers, who probably wandered from one seasonally occupied camp to another in their quest for food. Evidence from Ariz. D:13:1, an early Dot Klish occupation, suggests that individuals of the former tradition remained in regional residence until the acquisition of new traits brought about the transition into the latter period (approximately A.D. 450 to 700). Basketmaker III settlements of the region generally tend to be located near plots of arable farmland adjacent to large sandy dunes, as at Ariz. D:9:2, or along aggrading floodplains, as at Ariz. D:10:1. Excavation of a Forestdale Smudged container from Ariz. D:9:2 suggests that the farming and ceramic techniques may have diffused from the Mogollon region to the southeast.

Architecture of the excavated Dot Klish phase sites was diversified and varied within each site, reflecting a period of transition and culture change. Multiroomed jacal domiciles and a ramada were constructed early. An intermediate Basketmaker III settlement, Ariz.

D:9:2, possessed the best examples of pithouse construction. The three circular subterranean domiciles are similar to others of comparable age, including examples from the Basketmaker III type site—Schabik'eshchee Village (Roberts 1929). However, there are two major architectural differences between the latter structures and those of Ariz. D:9:2. The major difference is the complete lack of antechambers at Ariz. D:9:2. Abandonment of the side entrance or antechamber, and its conversion into a ventilator shaft, was a well-established construction trait. The other major difference was an absence of the low ridge or partition wall found at Jeddito 264 (Daifuku 1961:43) and elsewhere; this ridge served to separate the southern or eastern portion of the floor area from the rest of the room. At Ariz. D:9:2, one domicile possessed faint traces of once having had this feature, but the structure had been abandoned before the rest of the group. Architectural features at Dot Klish Village, Ariz. D:10:1, consisted of a jacal domicile and surrounding surface and subterranean storage rooms. The contiguous masonry storage rooms, one of which served as living quarters for some part of the year, records the transition of these storage rooms to surface dwelling units. Even at this early stage of house-building, there is evidence that horizontally laid slabs forming true masonry walls were beginning to develop. Yet, it was some time before it progressed to the point where multiroomed pueblos were constructed. By most standards the quality of masonry found in the three contiguous surface rooms must be considered crude although it remains superior to that of others reported for this period (Gladwin 1945:11–19; Daifuku 1961:30–34; Carlson 1963:22–26).

Ceramics from the Dot Klish phase can be classified under Tusayan Gray Ware. The most abundant pottery type from sites of this age was a plain gray ware fitting the type description (Colton 1955) for Lino Gray. Second in abundance are sherds classified as Lino Smudged. It is interesting to note here that the sherds classified as Lino Smudged, although containing smudged interiors, are not highly polished and smudged in the characteristic Forestdale Smudged fashion (Haury 1940:85). Thus, the complete blending of the two ceramic techniques had not yet occurred. Third in abundance are sherds of Lino Fugitive Red; Lino Gray sherds altered by the application of an exterior red wash (iron oxide). Fourth in abundance are sherds and vessels which exhibit painted decorations on a gray to white surface and are classified as Lino Black-on-gray. The presence of Tallahogan Red, proportionately a very minor element of the ceramics collected, demonstrates that the potters of this period knew the properties of red and white firing clays and also knew how to apply a slip. Such evidence would tend to suggest that the decorated slipped white wares of the following period, such as Kana-a Black-on-white, resulted from a combination of known techniques.

The occupants of these settlements were certainly heavily dependent upon agriculture in their subsistence pattern, a pattern reflected by a large number of food processing tools rather than those generally associated with hunting and related activities. Just how much the harvesting of wild plant and animal resources supplemented the fruits of agriculture is unknown. The small size of the Dot Klish settlements suggests group organization was probably one of autonomous households occupying dwellings adjacent to cultivated fields. An exception to this is Ariz. D:9:2, which perhaps represented a limited-activity agricultural settlement. A definite community pattern had not yet developed, unless the arrangement of structures at Dot Klish Village, Ariz. D:10:1, represented an early attempt at village planning. The excavated portion of that settlement suggested a single family unit consisting of a surface domicile surrounded by surface rooms and subterranean cists for the storage of food.

In addition to the four Dot Klish sites, two front-oriented villages representing the late Pueblo II period (approximately A.D. 1000 to 1100) were excavated. Although the settlement pattern differed at the two sites, both were probably inhabited by extended family groups.

Ariz. D:9:1, a Toreva phase site, was constructed as a segmented village with subterranean and surface domiciles associated with an above-ground storage room. The presence of a specialized mealing room suggests that centralized corn grinding took place. It was hypothesized that the communal grinding of corn may have developed as an adjunct to the kiva.

A late Pueblo II, frontier or peripheral Anasazi occupation, Ariz. I:3:1, located near Cameron, Arizona, was abandoned at the eruption of Sunset Crater. The exodus was not in haste; personal belongings were collected and little of value was left behind. The settlement pattern consisted mainly of multi-roomed domiciles and storage units. The architectural features also recorded population increase at the village, as additional structures or contiguous rooms were added as needed. It would appear that the population increase resulted from a successful economic adaptation to a relatively stable riverine environment.

Ceramics and artifacts for the two late Pueblo II settlements were typical of that period. Ariz. D:9:1 possessed an abundance of ground stone or food processing tools, while the Ariz. I:3:1 assemblage consisted mainly of chipped stone implements, probably is due to the sites location on a gravel terrace, rather than to a predominance of hunting activities.

Evidence suggesting coal fired ceramics (Gumerman 1970:24) was found at Ariz. D:9:2, Ariz. D:10:1, and Ariz. D:9:1. Although these sites were located on Black Mesa, they do demonstrate a larger or regional distribution of this trait. The paucity of these altered sherds, when compared to the total ceramic collection, precludes their being of statistical value. The discontinuous distribution of these sherds tends to imply that they were not fired at each settlement. Although somewhat tenuous, analysis of the individual sherds reinforce this hypothesis. Sherds from Ariz. D:10:1 are from the same container, while those from the remaining two sites represent only one or two sherds from separate vessels.

The sites excavated on Black Mesa were located along canyon walls or near the mesa's edge close to outcropping coal beds. That the inhabitants of Ariz. D:9:1, a Toreva manifestation relatively dated at A.D. 1050 to 1150, utilized these coal resources was demonstrated by the presence of unburned coal and coal ash in a domicile hearth. It is my hypothesis that the discolored sherds reflect early experiments at firing ceramics with coal; a technique that was not to be fully achieved until the beginning of the Pueblo IV period (beginning about A.D. 1300) with the ceramic types classified under Awatobi Yellow Ware.

2 Carbonized Corn Remains From the Excavations

HUGH C. CUTLER AND
LEONARD W. BLAKE

Carbonized corn remains were recovered from five Anasazi sites excavated along the Black Mesa coal slurry pipeline right-of-way (Table 10). A combined total of twenty-seven cob fragments were collected from the floors of two Dot Klish phase pithouses at Ariz. D:9:2. This collection was large enough to provide us with a reliable picture of the nature of the corn being grown during the Basketmaker III period on Black Mesa; the actual occupation having been ceramically dated between A.D. 620 and 775. The few remaining cobs—recovered from each of the other sites—conform very well with the pattern revealed at Ariz. D:9:2 (Figs. *39, 40*).

Most of the cobs are medium-sized, usually with little thickening of the cob and lower glumes. The cupules, in which the paired grains were borne, are open, that is, they are relatively long in the direction of the length of the cob, as compared to width of the cupule. Nearly all of the cobs were fully developed. This does not prove that growing conditions, seed stock selection, and techniques were good, because softer and poorly developed ears are more likely to have burned than firm and good ones which would be carbonized.

The corn investigated here was a small to medium-sized form of Onaveño, and the grains probably flint as were others found in many other sites in northern Arizona (Cutler

10. PERCENT OF COBS OF EACH ROW NUMBER FOUND IN SITES ALONG THE COAL SLURRY PIPELINE

| Site | Phase | Number of Cobs | Percent of Row Number | | | | Mean Number |
			8	10	12	14	
Ariz. D:13:1	Dot Klish	3		67	33		10.7
Ariz. D:9:2	Dot Klish	27	4	18	63	15	11.8
Ariz. D:10:1	Dot Klish	6		50	50		11.0
Ariz. I:3:1	Pueblo I-II	5		60	20	20	11.2
Ariz. D:9:1	Toreva	3	34		33	33	11.3
Total		44					

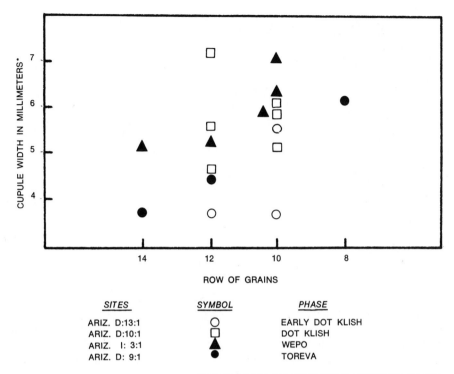

39. *Diagram showing rows of grains and cupule width of corncobs recovered from sites excavated along the coal slurry line*

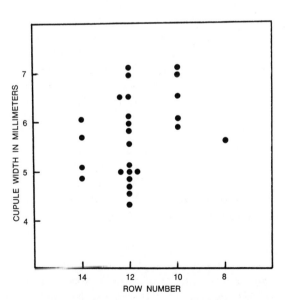

40. *Diagram showing rows of grains and cupule width of corncobs from Ariz. D:9:2*

1966:14). There were very few eight-rowed cobs. Between 35 to 73 percent of the cobs from Mogollon sites to the south had eight rows of grains during the periods represented by these pipeline sites. The corn is similar to that recovered from Basketmaker III level of Mummy Cave in Canyon del Muerto, Step House in Mesa Verde, and from NA 7523, a site northeast of Navajo Mountain (Cutler and Meyer 1965:149; Cutler 1969:372–75). The larger proportion of the twelve-rowed cobs from Ariz. D:9:2 (635) as compared to the 47 percent in the above sites may suggest a greater conservatism, a greater emphasis on the older twelve-rowed types, than was exhibited in the three sites mentioned above. However, the sample is small and more material should be examined.

Similar kinds of corn are still grown by the Hopi and Papago and are considered by native informants to be the older varieties.

3 Faunal Remains From the Excavated Sites

CHARLES L. DOUGLAS

Bones uncovered during excavation of the archaeological sites discussed in this report are identified and analyzed in this report. Six of the sites yielded 143 bones representing 69 individuals of various species. Table 11 lists the percentages of unworked and worked bones in each taxon from each of the sites containing faunal materials.

Bones and fragments were identified to element and taxon by comparing them with bones in a comparative osteological collection housed at Prescott College. In addition to the identification, other data such as charring or butchering marks, and relative age of the individual as determined by tooth-wear or epiphyseal closure, were reported as the situation warranted.

One of the persistent problems in faunal analysis is the interpretation of fragmentary bones. Diagnostic characteristics often are obscured on broken bones, especially small ones. In order to analyze the significance of fragmentary bones, they are listed under one of two headings: Rodentia-Lagomorpha for fragments that cannot be separated into either order with precision, and Artiodactyla for fragments of large bones that obviously are from one of the large artiodactyls. There were only a few broken bones that could be identi-fied to element, but not to taxon. These are listed under Mammalia.

The data in Table 11 show that the percentage of small fragments (Rodentia-Lagomorpha) in each site is inversely related to the numbers of bones from rodents and rabbits that were identifiable. One could not expect such a relationship to exist in other archaeological sites. Ariz. D:10:1 had the largest faunal assemblage and also had the largest number of bones that were identifiable to species. This site had relatively few fragmentary bones that could not be identified to a taxon lower than Order.

It is interesting to note that the faunal assemblages contained no remains of carnivores. This is somewhat unexpected, but probably is due to the small size of the samples. The species listings are judged to be incomplete, owing to the small sample sizes. Nevertheless, the species of mammals represented in the faunal assemblages are the same as those one would expect to find in the areas today.

Table 12 shows the distribution of percentages of individuals of various species represented in each of the sites. It is somewhat difficult to evaluate these data because of the small samples. The data are too limited to

11. VERTEBRATES IDENTIFIED FROM FAUNAL REMAINS FOUND IN SIX ARCHAEOLOGICAL SITES ON BLACK MESA *

Vertebrates	BM II	Early Dot Klish	Dot Klish	Tallahogan	Dinnebito	Toreva
Mammalia (frags)				4		5
Lagomorpha (rabbits and hares)						
Sylvilagus sp. (cottontails)			8	41		11
Sylvilagus audubonii (Audubon's cottontail)				3		
Lepus sp. (jackrabbit)		16	6	4		11
Lepus californicus (black-tailed jackrabbit)				12		
Rodentia-Lagomorpha (fragments)		75	37	4		55
Rodentia (rodents)				3		
Cynomys sp. (prairie dog)				1	14	
Eutamias sp. (chipmunks)				6		
Thomomys sp. (pocket gopher)			3	3		
Dipodomys ordii (Ord's kangaroo rat)				4		
Neotoma sp. (woodrat)			3	1		
Neotoma albigula (white-throated woodrat)				3		5
Artiodactyla (fragments)	100	8	16	6	86	5
Odocoileus sp. (deer)				1		5
Antilocapra americana (proghorn)				3		
Total Number of Individual Animals	5	12	32	69	7	18

Note: Bm II = Ariz. D:13:4; Early Dot Klish = Ariz. D:13:1; Dot Klish = Ariz. D:9:2; Tallahogan = Ariz. D:10:1; Dinnebito = Ariz. D:13:3; Toreva = Ariz. D:9:1.

* Fragments that were identifiable to class, but not to order or lower taxon are so indicated.

12. PERCENT OF INDIVIDUAL ANIMALS REPRESENTED IN EACH TAXON OF VERTEBRATES FOUND IN SIX ARCHAEOLOGICAL SITES ON BLACK MESA

Vertebrates	BM II	Early Dot Klish	Dot Klish	Tallahogan	Dinnebito	Toreva
Mammalia				9		9
Lagomorpha (rabbits & hares)				1		
Sylvilagus sp. (cottontails)			33	18		8
Sylvilagus audubonii (Audubon's cottontail)				6		
Lepus sp. (jackrabbit)		20	13	9		17
Lepus californicus (black-tailed jackrabbit)				6		
Rodentia-Lagomorpha		60	27	6		42
Rodentia (rodents)				6		
Cynomys sp. (prairie dog)				3	50	
Eutamias sp. (chipmunks)				3		
Thomomys sp. (pocket gopher)			7	6		
Dipodomys ordii (Ord's kangaroo rat)				3		
Neotoma sp. (woodrats)			7	3		
Neotoma albigula (white-throated woodrat)			3			8
Artiodactyla	100	20	13	12	50	8
Odocoileus sp. (deer)				3		8
Antilocapra americana (proghorn)				3		
Total	1	5	15	34	2	12

allow evaluation of possible faunal changes through time, and any fluctuations in percentages from one time period to another are probably of little importance, here.

Charred Bone

Only five pieces of charred bone were found, and these were in Ariz. D:9:2. Two of these were fragments assigned to Rodentia-Lagomorpha. Two fragments of long bones from cottontail rabbits (*Sylvilagus* sp.), and one distal end of a tibia from a jackrabbit (*Lepus* sp.) represented the other supposed food items. It was surprising that such a small percentage of the rabbit and hare bones were charred.

Bone Artifacts

Six bone artifacts were recovered. These artifacts are identified below by site. Table 13 lists the distributions of animals among the artifact types, and summarizes the ways in which bones were modified to construct the various implements.

Ariz. D:9:1–9, *Odocoileus* sp. One awl on the distal half of the cannon bone (metatarsal) of a deer. The entire bone was used and it was not split. The distal articulating end has been eroded away.

Ariz. D:10:1–2, *Odocoileus* sp. One awl on a split cannon bone (metacarpal?) from the proximal one-third of one side of the bone. The proximal end and the sides and tip are worked.

Site D:10:1–6, Mammalia. One awl from a fragment of heavy, split and worked bone, probably from the leg bone of a large mammal (carnivore or artiodactyl). Tip of the awl tapers from one side, as a knife does.

Ariz. D:10:1–7, *Antilocapra americana.* A short awl (58.7 mm) on a split, distal half of a cannon bone. The awl is badly eroded; the distal end is intact.

Site D:10:1–15, cf. Artiodactyla. Broken tip of awl from heavy bone.

Ariz. D:13:1–5, cf. Artiodactyla. Badly eroded awl constructed on one side of a long bone.

None of the above artifacts is unusual in the method of construction, nor in the species of mammal represented. Nevertheless, compilation of data on such implements eventually will permit a more complete interpretation of how aboriginal peoples in various cultures utilized the available raw materials in their habitats. Future publications concerning the ethnobiology of cultures that have occupied the Black Mesa region will attempt to clarify the relationship of aboriginal peoples to their biotic and abiotic environment.

13. SUMMARY OF BONE IMPLEMENTS FROM SIX ARCHAEOLOGICAL SITES ON BLACK MESA *

Implements	Unidentifiable Mammals	Artiodactyls	Odocoileus sp. (Deer)	Antilocapra Americana (Pronghorn)	Total
Bone not split, head intact			1		1
Bone split, head unmodified				1	1
Bone split, head partly modified			1		1
Awl on fragment of bone	1				1
Other worked bone		2			2
Total	1	2	2	1	6

* The number of implements in each taxonomic group is given, as is the kind of modification of the parent bone that was carried out to create the implement.

Part 2

**New Directions
in the Archaeology
of Black Mesa**

4 Aspects of Prehistoric Social Organization on Black Mesa

ROBERT T. CLEMEN

INTRODUCTION

Gumerman, Westfall, and Weed (1972: 196–97) have documented that three major demographic changes occurred during or directly prior to the Toreva phase (A.D. 1075–1150) on northeastern Black Mesa. First, the inhabitants had moved from the floodplains of the washes to the upland areas of the Mesa, and secondly, the significant rise in the number of sites points to an almost certain population increase. Both of these changes seem to have been triggered by environmental stimuli Thirdly, the settlement pattern on Black Mesa took on a very definite form, having previously been vaguely defined at best. During the Toreva phase, we find two kinds of sites: larger, formalized villages and smaller settlements with no special pattern. Phillips (1972) has termed these two kinds of sites "Primary" and "Secondary" sites respectively. The main point of distinction is the kiva; present in the primary site, absent in the secondary site. Phillips has suggested that this new settlement pattern reflects the population's response, within cultural restraints, to their new location and their increase in numbers. As the larger population moved to the uplands, the people chose either to live in small dispersed settlements close to their fields, or to reside in larger villages, which encompassed the increasing number of inhabitants and allowed for close social contact. Phillips suggests that by having the "family center" at the primary site and moving small household groups to peripheral secondary sites, the inhabitants arrived at a compromise solution to the problems presented by the new situation.

In addition to the task of demonstrating the validity of Phillips's hypothesis, we are left with a number of unanswered questions. What exactly was the nature of the relationship between primary and secondary sites? What sort of social organization would lead to such a settlement pattern? What integrating factors formed a society of the groups of people? Beginning with Phillips's ideas and the problems posed by these questions, this paper will build specific, testable hypotheses of intra- and inter site social organization on Black Mesa, looking particularly at the number of residence groups present in a primary site, and at the possible relationships among these groups and other groups represented by surrounding secondary sites.

113

DETERMINING THE NATURE AND NUMBER OF RESIDENCE GROUPS

Developing the Hypotheses

Our first problem is to determine the number and nature of residence groups occupying a primary site and to suggest how these groups were drawn together by common use of the kiva, mealing room, and storage rooms. As a starting point we must show that a primary site is a multipurpose habitation site. Such sites have structural evidence for food storage in the masonry rooms; food preparation in the hearths and the mealing room; ritual activity in the kiva; and other living-working activities in the *jacal* wings. We can test the hypothesis that the various rooms and areas were used in different ways by determining the ratio of plain and decorated ware in these areas (Hill 1968).

Hill (1968) has developed the proposition that plain utility ware shows up in greater proportion in living areas than in storage areas. Table 14 shows the distribution of plain and decorated ware through a Toreva phase primary site. The masonry rooms, hypothesized to be storage areas, show a lower incidence of plain ware, while the jacal areas show a higher incidence of plain ware. The hypothesis that this is a multipurpose site seems to be substantiated.

For reasons of simplification, we will operate on the assumption that we are dealing with a closed system; we will not consider the possibility of groups migrating onto the Mesa. This we do for three reasons: 1. The apparently marginal living conditions of Toreva phase Black Mesa make it seem highly unlikely that anyone would be moving into this area; 2. It is unlikely that an incoming group would build a primary-type site or be able to inhabit an abandoned one, due to the poor construction quality; 3. During the Toreva phase we find evidence of site abandonment (burned kivas, smashed metates), painting a picture of migration away from (or within) the Mesa rather than onto it.

Looking at the structure of a primary site, we would hypothesize one or two residence groups: one occupying the entire village, or one in each jacal wing. From ethnographic analogy and from other archaeological study we can hypothesize that these were matrilocal residence groups. Titiev (1944), Eggan (1950), and Dozier (1970) have documented that the Hopi, presumably the descendants of prehistoric Black Mesans (Euler and Dobyns 1971), use a matrilocal residence pattern. Longacre (1964; 1968; 1970a) and Hill (1970b) appear to have demonstrated, using the same technique we propose to use here, that a matrilocal pattern of residence was in use prehistorically at the Carter Ranch and Broken K Pueblos in east-central Arizona. There are problems with this. As Stanislawski

14. NUMBER OF SHERDS AND PERCENTAGES OF DECORATED AND UTILITY WARES IN TEST AREAS OF ARIZ. D:11:93

Area	Decorated Ware		Utility Ware		Total
Room 1	200	57	150	43	350
Room 2	251	47	278	53	529
Room 3	80	43	107	57	187
Kiva	269	38	432	62	701
Mealing Room	307	29	764	71	1,071
Jacal Wing 1	1,432	32	3,087	68	4,519
Jacal Wing 2	3,992	28	10,420	72	14,412
Total	6,531	30	15,238	70	21,769

Note: $x^2 = 285.7$ with 6 degrees of freedom. Significance = .999. This does not appear to be a nonrandom distribution.

(1973) has reported for the Hopi, and as Goodenough (1956) has also noted concerning the Trukese, one rarely finds a situation where the "residence rules" are followed strictly. Under certain circumstances it becomes impossible for a society to adhere to the ideal norm. For example, a matrilocal or patrilocal system with a growing population must eventually send offspring away from the group when conditions become too crowded.

Allen and Richardson (1971) have pointed out the difficulties involved in showing that a given norm applies to a particular society. If a society does appear to conform to an idealized pattern, it is almost never a matter of total adherence to the rules, but a case of the majority of the people conforming to the pattern. Stanislawski (1973) has criticized Longacre for talking in terms of "ideal explanatory models as matrilineal and matrilocal descent and residence rules," and for stating that "the archaeological remains of cultural behavior are so precisely patterned in the ground that they closely reflect the 'ideal' behavior of prehistoric social groups, and thus allow archaeologists to reconstruct the *normative* patterns of such groups." More generally, archaeologists have argued that the patterns of archaeologically retrieved material reflect the *actual* social behavior of the prehistoric society, and that the only way to talk intelligently about that behavior is to show that it

approaches a given generally understood norm. The application of statistics, the science of probabilities, allows the archaeologist to confirm, as does the ethnologist, that the behavior of a society does approach that norm. Anomalies in the indirect archaeological data parallel ethnological anomalies as evidence of less than 100 percent conformation to the norm.

Hill (1970a) has compiled a table which shows the distributions of male and female stylistic elements in various types of ideal residence patterns (Table 15). The reasoning behind these results is that parents teach children both technology and style; hence a son will use more or less the same style that his father used, and a daughter will use her mother's style. If a society practices a matrilocal pattern of postmarital residence, for example, then daughters living with or near their mothers will perpetuate the family's female stylistic characteristics in that area. The sons, on the other hand, will move away from the family, and thus spread the family's male stylistic characteristics randomly through the community. In the archaeological record of this case, we would expect to find female-linked stylistic elements clustered nonrandomly through the community, and male-linked stylistic elements scattered randomly about the area.

We will use ceramic design elements as an

15. RESIDENCE PATTERNS AND THEIR HYPOTHETICAL DISTRIBUTION CORRELATES (AFTER HILL 1970a)

		Stylistic Distributions	
Pattern	Description	Female Elements	Male Elements
Uxorilocal (including matrilocal)	Couple lives near wife's relatives	Nonrandom	Random
Virilocal (including patrilocal and avunculocal)	Couple lives near husband's relatives	Random	Nonrandom
Neolocal	Couple lives away from either mate's relatives	Random	Random
Bilocal	Couple lives near either mate's relatives	Random	Random
Duolocal	Couple separates, each living with own relatives	Nonrandom	Nonrandom

index of female-linked stylistic characteristics, a technique developed by Deetz (1960; 1965) and Longacre (1964; 1968; 1970a). It is questionable whether or not ceramic design elements actually are transmitted from mother to daughter in the way our model suggests. Stanislawski (1973:121) has pointed out that at present among the Hopi there are "a minimum of four ceramic teaching models in use, three of which involve cross-clan teaching of ceramic techniques, designs, and styles." Furthermore, Stanislawski found that Hopi potters agreed that they can use any designs and styles they wish, and that a potter's style changes through time as she learns new ideas from outside sources. What Stanislawski has not specifically pointed out is that Hopi ceramic design elements do not cluster according to the matrilocal residence groups, or that mother-daughter ceramic instruction is not the most important and influential instruction in a potter's career. Essentially, he has said that there are many exceptions to the so-called rules; he has not demonstrated that these deviations make the entire system unrecognizable or even significantly different from our idealized model. Furthermore, Stanislawski's extensive ceramic teaching models could be due to a revival of pottery-making, and to the fact that in the course of the twentieth century, Hopi pottery has become almost completely a tourist souvenir item and now is hardly used in its previous utilitarian mode.

The most important problem with the use of ceramic design elements stems from the fact that no one has defined the term "design element" to the general satisfaction of archaeologists, nor has anyone shown where design elements end and artistic style begins. Longacre (1964:162–63) has said regarding this technique: "we hoped to define elements that would not be consciously selected from an artistic point of view. Rather, we hoped to isolate the smallest meaningful elements of design that would be nonconsciously selected based on learning patterns within the social frame." We *hope* to have done the same in

this study. We have used design elements similar to those used by Longacre and Hill, and will certainly encounter similar criticisms. This author recognizes the problems involved in basing a scientific study on a concept whose meaning is imprecisely determined, "More work is needed in this overlooked area."

Due to the poverty of the archaeological record on Black Mesa, we shall not be able to check the distribution of male-linked stylistic elements in the primary site. Hence the number of multiple hypotheses is drastically reduced. With the ceramic design elements, we can hope to find two clusters of design elements to satisfy the hypothesis that the site was occupied by two matrilocal groups. Without the use of male stylistic elements, all the alternate possibilities for residence groups (for example, one matrilocal group, one or more groups of any other type) are indistinguishable. Also, we cannot really distinguish between duolocal and matrilocal groups in this test. On the basis of overwhelming ethnographic evidence it seems highly unlikely that duolocality would apply to Black Mesa.

Provided that we do find two definite areas ascribed to two residence groups, we can proceed to test the second aspect of the hypothesis, that which deals with forces of social integration within the site. For example, the kiva and the mealing room might act as vital focal points of social interaction serving to bind the two groups together. The storage rooms also could have a strong integrative effect if they were used in common by the entire community. The existence of common storage areas would not of itself indicate that food was pooled for general redistribution, although this is a possibility. Nevertheless, any common utility area would indicate at least a minimum degree of integration of the community. For test implication, we should see stylistic similarities among a group's living area and its special-purpose areas.

We can now state the test implications for our hypothesis succinctly and specifically: 1. If there are two matrilocal residence groups, then there will be two clusters of design elements, one centered on each jacal wing in the primary site. If part one is substantiated, then: 2. If any of the special-purpose areas (kiva, mealing room, storage rooms) are used by only one group, then design element assemblage from that area will show an association with only one of the two residence groups. 3. If any area is a common area, then its design element assemblage will show association with both residence groups.

Testing the Hypotheses

We decided to test the hypotheses against the actual design element distribution of site Ariz. D:11:93, a multicomponent site excavated by the Black Mesa Archaeological Project in the summer of 1971. On the basis of pottery type distributions and the accepted orientation of a primary site, we extracted the Toreva component from earlier Wepo phase substructures. As shown in Figure *41*, we delineated the site into seven areas for test purposes: the two jacal wings, the kiva, the mealing room and the three masonry rooms. For each area, we analyzed the decorated potsherds according to their design elements. In all, we analyzed about 2,600 sherds. For the analysis, we used a chart of 105 design elements previously determined by Black Mesa Project students for Toreva phase ceramics. Of those 105, we found 82 to be represented in the site. The design elements and their distributions through the site are shown in Appendixes 1 and 2.

A number of minor problems arose. First, we accidentally included in the distribution of jacal wing 1, the sherds from an earlier pithouse. This we did not realize until the study had been completed. Second, we had originally intended to use only "floor" and "floor-filled" sherds as these are the best indicators of primary cultural activity. It becomes immediately apparent, however, that the number of such sherds was so small as to make the test meaningless. We decided, therefore, to use all the sherds found in the fill of the areas in question. Thirdly, we discovered

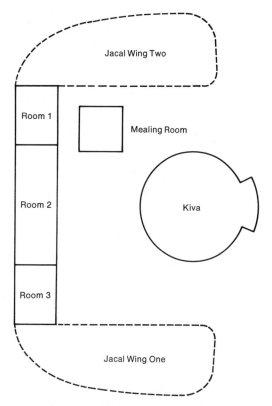

41. *Test areas used in design element analysis of Ariz. D:11:93*

that when the site was excavated a mechanical blade was employed to strip the sandy overburden off of jacal wing 1. This could have had an effect on the ceramic distribution of that area. Finally, we found less than 20 classifiable design elements in room 3, and decided to exclude it from the statistical tests since its sample was so small. With these problems in mind, we elected to continue, deciding that even though the reliability of the test was somewhat lessened, the results would be worthwhile, if only for stimulating future ideas.

Statistical Analysis

There were two parts to the statistical analysis of the design element data. First, we did a cluster analysis to determine whether or not the design elements formed two distinct clusters. Secondly, we executed a chi-square analysis, comparing each jacal area with each of the special-purpose areas, finding which areas possibly were associated in having similar design element distributions, and hoping to show that these special-purpose areas do provide some social integration in the community.

Cluster Analysis

The idea behind a cluster analysis is to find groups of objects or variables which "behave" in the same way. Here we want to find out which design elements pattern similarly. Our hypothesis implies that we should find a cluster of design elements located primarily in each jacal wing.

Before the cluster analysis is meaningful at all, we should determine that the overall distribution of design elements is nonrandom. This we can do with the chi-square statistic presented in Appendix 3. The result is that the observed distribution has less than .00001 chance of being random. Thus we see that a cluster analysis probably will be helpful.

We calculated a measure of similarity comparing every design element's distribution with every other element's distribution across the site. This statistic was:

$$S = 2.00 - \frac{\Sigma}{X}\left|F_x{}^{(i)} - F_x{}^{(j)}\right| 2 \leq S \leq O$$

where $F_x{}^{(i)}$ is the fraction of the total number of occurrences of the ith design element that occurs in area X ($F_1{}^{(i)} + F_2{}^{(i)} + \ldots + F_7{}^{(i)} = 1.00$). At this point, we had an 82 x 82 matrix of similarity values. This matrix then was used as input for the cluster analysis. The particular clustering technique we used is a hierarchical clustering method developed by Stephen C. Johnson (1968). In this technique, individual objects are formed into clusters, and these clusters are then grouped into higher-order clusters. The results of our analysis are given in Figure *42*, showing how the first-order clusters actually formed into super-clusters.

In this method of clustering, the final evaluation is based on visual inspection of the hierarchical structure of the clusters. In Figure *42* we can see that there is a basic dichotomy; the two super-clusters are circled. It seems that design elements in super-cluster 1 appear mostly in jacal wing 1 and that super-cluster 2 represents jacal wing 2. We can check this statistically by comparing the observed distributions of each design element in the jacal wings with the expected values (that is, what we would expect if the distribution were independent among the areas). For example, if a cluster really represents jacal wing 2, then those design elements will show up more in jacal wing 2 than we would expect, and less in jacal wing 1 than we would expect. Table 16 shows the results of comparing observed and expected values for all design elements; "+" indicates that the observed < expected, and "−" indicates that observed > expected. We see that the first three clusters, which make up super-cluster 2, do show a positive association with jacal wing 2; for the most part, these design elements appear more than expected in jacal wing 2, and less than expected in jacal wing 1. For super-cluster 1, we see that clusters 4 and 5 are positively associated with jacal area 1, but that cluster 6 shows up more than expected in both jacal areas. As far as the two remaining clusters go, we see that cluster 7 is positively associated with jacal wing 1. Cluster 8 seems to be more or less associated with jacal wing 1 also, but shows an even stronger association with the special-purpose areas. The remaining four design elements generally appear more in special purpose areas than in the jacal areas.

Summarizing the results of the cluster analysis, we found jacal wing 2 to be represented by super-cluster 2, and jacal wing 1 to be represented by super-cluster 1 as well as cluster 7. The remaining design elements tend to be associated with the special-purpose areas. We conclude that there are two basic super-clusters of design elements, one representing each

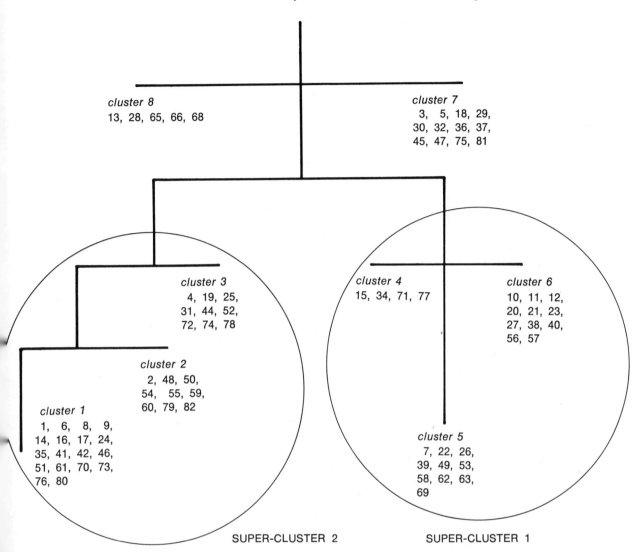

cluster 8
13, 28, 65, 66, 68

cluster 7
3, 5, 18, 29,
30, 32, 36, 37,
45, 47, 75, 81

cluster 3
4, 19, 25,
31, 44, 52,
72, 74, 78

cluster 4
15, 34, 71, 77

cluster 6
10, 11, 12,
20, 21, 23,
27, 38, 40,
56, 57

cluster 2
2, 48, 50,
54, 55, 59,
60, 79, 82

cluster 1
1, 6, 8, 9,
14, 16, 17, 24,
35, 41, 42, 46,
51, 61, 70, 73,
76, 80

cluster 5
7, 22, 26,
39, 49, 53,
58, 62, 63,
69

SUPER-CLUSTER 2   SUPER-CLUSTER 1

. Hierarchical structure of design element clusters. Each number represents one of eighty-two design ele-
ents. (See Appendix 1.) Higher position in the hierarchy indicates less similarity with the other clusters. Thus
sters 1 and 2 are more similar than clusters 2 and 3. This structure is from the results of Johnson's (1968)
iameter Method"

jacal wing, substantiating the hypothesis of two matrilocal residence groups.

Chi-Square Analysis

We used a chi-square statistic to determine the relationships between jacal areas and special-purpose areas (Fig. *43*). By comparing two distributions (for example the kiva and jacal wing 1) the chi-square statistic shows how likely it is that the two distributions are random samples from one overall distribution. For our purposes, the lower the chi-square for two areas, the greater the *probability* that those two areas are stylistically-socially related. Table 17 shows the results.

We can see that both jacal areas are asso-

16. OBSERVED DESIGN ELEMENTS COMPARED TO EXPECTED VALUES

Elements	Jacal Area 1	Jacal Area 2	Elements	Jacal Area 1	Jacal Area 2	Room 2	Kiva
Cluster 1			Cluster 5				
1	−	+	7	+	−		
6	−	+	22	+	−		
8	−	+	26	+	−		
9	−	+	39	+	−		
14	−	+	49	+	−		
16	−	+	53	+	−		
17	−	+	58	+	−		
24	−	+	62	+	−		
35	−	+	63	+	−		
41	−	+	69	+	−		
42	−	+	Cluster 6				
46	−	+	10	−	+		
51	−	+	11	−	−		
61	−	+	12	−	+		
70	−	+	20	+	−		
73	−	+	21	+	+		
76	−	+	23	+	−		
80	−	+	27	+	+		
Cluster 2			38	+	+		
2	−	+	40	+	+		
48	−	+	56	+	+		
50	−	+	57	+	+		
54	−	+	Cluster 7				
55	−	+	3	+	−		
59	+	+	5	+	−		
60	−	+	18	+	−		
79	+	+	29	+	−		
82	+	+	30	+	−		
Cluster 3			32	+	−		
4	−	+	36	+	−		
19	−	−	37	+	−		
25	−	+	45	+	−		
31	−	+	47	+	−		
44	−	+	75	+	−		
52	−	+	81	+	−		
72	−	+	Cluster 8				
74	−	+	13	−	+	+	+
78	−	+	28	−	−	+	+
Cluster 4			65	+	−	+	−
15	+	−	66	+	−	−	+
34	−	−	68	+	−	+	+
71	+	−	Remaining Elements				
77	+	−	33	−	−	+	−
			43	+	−	−	+
			64	−	−	−	+
			67	−	−	+	−

Note: "+" indicates observed > expected, and "−" indicates observed < expected.

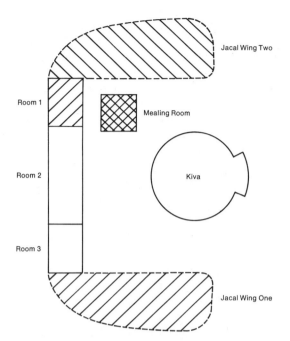

43. *Graphic representation of inter-area stylistic relationships, as determined by chi-square analysis*

ciated with the mealing room, and that jacal area 1 is strongly associated with room 1. Not surprisingly, room 1 and the mealing room also are closely associated, according to the chi-square comparing their distributions. (They have a 49 percent chance of being related.) Thus we see that more than likely both groups used the mealing room and that the group in jacal wing 1 probably used room 1 more than did the second group. Thus the mealing room can be proposed as a central point of social interaction and community integration.

What happened in room 2 and in the kiva?

In the chi-square analysis, neither of these areas showed any particular affinity with any other area. One possibility is that these functionally-specific areas are correlated with special design elements (such as those in cluster 8 and the four leftover design elements) in such a way that normally their design element assemblages are very different from the assemblages of other areas. Whether such a phenomenon occurs with design elements is unknown. Freeman and Brown (1964) found that traditional ceramic types in the Carter Ranch site were distributed about the site according to the various functional types of areas (storage, ceremonial, and so on). It is not completely inconceivable, then, that such could be the case for design elements as well; here is a potentially testable hypothesis.

FURTHER HYPOTHESES OF TOREVA PHASE SOCIAL ORGANIZATION

Growing and Branching Clans and Matrilocal Communities

Dean (1970) and Eggan (1950) have suggested that at one time or another the traditional Hopi clans grew out of localized lineages. Considering the population increase on Black Mesa, it is completely possible that this transformation was taking place there before and during the Toreva phase. If both matriliny and matrilocality were the case in early Black Mesa prehistory, then localized lineages could begin to grow in size, branching into a number of extended families centered at a certain site, presumably under rule of the eldest member. As population continued to

17. CHI-SQUARE RESULTS. PERCENTAGE SHOWS THE PROBABILITY THAT THE TWO AREAS ARE STYLISTICALLY-SOCIALLY RELATED

Special-Purpose Area	Jacal Wing 1	Jacal Wing 2
Room 1	82.0	1.8
Room 2	0.00001	0.000001
Mealing Room	82.0	99.9
Kiva	0.00001	0.0000001

increase and as older members passed away, the result would be a collection of related lineages. This is what Fox (1967:97) has called a "clan."

A clan could certainly encompass more extended families than the two groups occupying the primary site. It is suggested that secondary sites represent groups or branches of clans centered at specific primary sites. The kiva at the primary site would provide the clan's ceremonial focus, and hence provide intrasite integration. If Black Mesa clans operated as do Hopi clans in terms of exogamy and ritual function, then the kiva society would include men who had married and moved away from the clan to live with their wives' relatives in a separate site cluster. Such an interfacing of a number of clans would provide social interaction across the entire multiclan demographic structure on the Mesa.

How does this hypothesis of growing clans coincide with the regional prehistory of northeastern Arizona? Consider the Tsegi phase, A.D. 1250–1300 in the Tsegi Canyon complex just north of Black Mesa (Dean 1969). The cliff dwellings found there presumably were at least partially settled by refugees from abandoned Black Mesa. A striking difference between Tsegi and Black Mesa sites, in addition to the village structure, lies in the ratio of kivas to population, cliff dwellings such as Betatakin or Kiet Siel have very few kivas whereas every small primary site on Black Mesa has at least one kiva. We can explain this discrepancy simply by the idea that one or two clans collectively migrated north to settle in a cave. The ratio of kivas to people for a cluster of primary and secondary sites (provided such clusters exist) should be roughly equivalent to the kivas to pe̶o̶p̶l̶e̶ ̶f̶o̶r̶ ̶a̶ large Tsegi phase site.

̶T̶h̶e̶ ̶h̶y̶p̶o̶t̶h̶e̶s̶i̶s̶ of growing clans also fits ̶w̶h̶a̶t̶ ̶w̶e̶ know ethnographically ̶a̶b̶o̶u̶t̶ ̶t̶h̶e̶ Hopi have used a matri-̶l̶i̶n̶e̶a̶l̶ ̶o̶r̶g̶a̶nization for as long as we ̶k̶n̶o̶w̶ ̶h̶i̶s̶t̶ory (Titiev 1944; Eggan

1950). It is not unlikely that a matrilineal organization developed on prehistoric Black Mesa. Eggan (1950:80) has suggested "that the groups moving into the Hopi country may well have been organized around matri-local households and matrilineages as a base and that the more elaborate clan and phratry organization was developed to integrate the larger population." Here we would modify Eggan's statement to suggest that those groups already had some familiarity with clan organization as well as with lineages.

This author does not pretend that matri-locality and matrilineality are equivalent, nor that one implies the other. What we have tentatively shown on Black Mesa is the possible existence of matrilocal residence groups. The relationships among matrilineages, matrilocal residence groups, collections of matrilocal residence groups, and full-fledged clans are apparent, as shown ideally in Figure 44. Nevertheless, it is important to distinguish between residence rules and descent rules, and in the balance of this paper, it will be necessary to maintain that distinction. Definitions are in order. By "matrilineage" we mean a group of people all of whom recognize their membership in the group by virtue of descent, through female lines, from a common living ancestor. For "matrilineal clan" the same definition holds with the exception that the common ancestor is usually deceased. A "matrilocal residence group" is a group of people who share a residence as a result of the postmarital residence practice of husband and wife residing with or near the wife's mother. A "matrilocal community" will be a collection of matrilocal groups related through female lines. These related groups, which need not recognize their relationship, must reside in close proximity to each other as the result of the continued general use of matrilocal residence rules. We must stress, as we did earlier, that these are normative definitions, and we assume that the actual behavior of the people only approaches the ideal patterns here defined.

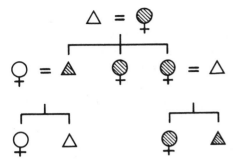

a) Simple Matrilineage

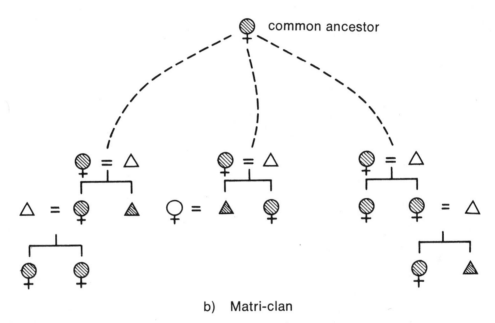

b) Matri-clan

44. *Genealogical diagram showing the relationship among matrilocal residence groups, matrilineages, and matrilineal clans. Shading indicates membership in the lineage or clan; matrilocal residence groups are circled*

The first assumption this model of growing clans and matrilocal communities makes is that both matrilocality and matriliny were well established on Black Mesa by Toreva times. There is debate as to the processes which generate matrilineal systems and residence rules (Fox 1967; Schneider and Gough 1962; Steward 1955) and, specifically, question about the development of pueblo matriliny. Steward (1955) has proposed that matrilineal clans developed in the Southwest as a result of women controlling land during the rise of agriculture. According to Steward, men were absent most of the time engaged mostly in hunting. This left the women to tend the fields as agriculture gained importance; the women maintained their control over the land, leading eventually to the Pueblo land-oriented, *matrilineal* clan system of organization. Arguing along the same lines, Helms (1970) has suggested that *matrilocality* develops as a result of men being absent, leaving women with the bulk of the responsibility for maintaining the household and socializing the children. These two notions complement each other well, as Steward's emphasizes the development of matriliny and Helm's stresses the development of matrilocality. Presumably processes similar to these helped to establish matriliny and matrilocality as characteristics of Black Mesa society.

The next problem is to determine whether or not a matrilocal residence group can actually grow into a matrilocal community simply as a result of population increase. Ecological and demographic stimuli, such as the move from the floodplains to the uplands, could have triggered the population increase; however, this is a different problem. Our hypothesis here is that lineages and clans are so similar structurally that no outside stimulus other than population increase is necessary to transform a simple residence group into a collection of groups.

To test this hypothesis of population growth, a computer simulation of a growing matrilocal residence group was executed. The object of the simulation was to determine whether or not a single matrilocal group can expand into a matrilocal community, and how this expansion occurs. We began with a "founding mother" and her children. The following simplifying assumptions were made: 1. People live an average of thirty-five years; the distribution is normal with mean = thirty-five years, standard deviation = ten years, and maximum = seventy-two years; 2. No couple has more than four children; 3. People can have children anytime after they are fifteen years old and before 70 percent of their married life (that part after fifteen years) has passed. Along with these simplifications, we also ass-- sal adherence to matrilocal th the simplifications, the m to deviate significantly e.

ed to family size assured population. The simu- he "founding mother" ocal group for seven-

teen generations. Then, within two generations, several branches formed, as shown in Figure 45 which represents the entire genealogical structure as it was created by the computer.

The fact that the computerized matrilocal residence group did grow into a matrilocal community is not absolute proof of the hypothesis by any means. It could, however, provide some insight into the dynamics of growth of such social groups. For example, Figure 46 demonstrates clearly the idea that population must reach a "critical value" before it will increase indefinitely. The true power in this simulation would lie in repeating the simulation perhaps a hundred times, using a different progression of random numbers on each occasion. This would produce a statistically valuable sample from which parameters could be accurately determined and hypotheses concerning the dynamics of growth could be generated.

For example, such a sample would show that a certain percentage of the matrilocal residence groups would die out, a certain percentage of the matrilocal groups would evolve into matrilocal communities, and a certain percentage of the matrilocal communities would devolve into a single matrilocal residence group. Also, using different growth rates in the model would change the percentages of extinction, evolution, and devolution (Martin Wobst, personal communication). As it stands, this project represents only an initial attempt to develop the techniques which could yield truly valuable results.

What about test implications for the hypothesis of growing matrilocal communities and matrilineal clans? It is very difficult to prove that at a given time in prehistory a particular extinct society used a specific method of social organization. Probably the best way to do this is to study in great detail the material culture of a number of societies with a certain type of social organization to find out what, if any, archaeologically retrievable patterns are unique to and universal within societies of that type. Finding this unique pat-

45. Computer-simulated genealogy showing growth of a single matrilocal residence group into a matrilocal community (M = Male, F = Female)

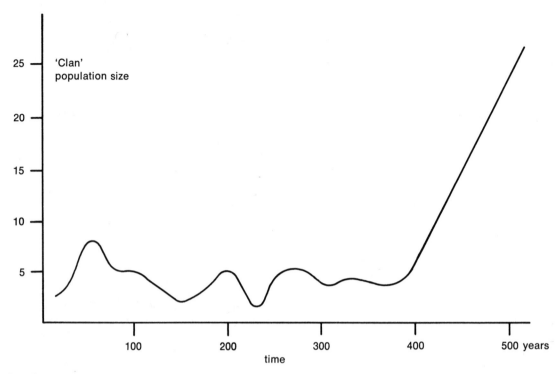

46. *Population of simulated clan through time*

tern in the archaeological record would indicate that the ancient inhabitants used the correlated system of organization.

This paper has not studied matrilineal and matrilocal societies in detail, but has and will continue to confine itself to archaeological tests. First, we can test early Black Mesa sites for matrilocality using a method similar to the one used in this study. Perhaps we could find a set of male-derived stylistic traits to make the test more complete. Another possible test for matrilocality involves measuring the living floor area; matrilocal households seem to have living areas generally greater than 600 square feet (Ember 1973).

Showing that the people of Black Mesa were organized into matrilineal clans is a more delicate task. We have already shown that a Toreva phase primary site probably was occupied by two matrilocal households; extending the interpretation to say that these households were part of a clan is not neces-

sarily warranted. The existence of matrilineal clans could mean that females would rank at least as important as the men; this status might be indicated in burials by the amount and quality of grave goods associated with the deceased.

If the growing clan-community hypothesis is correct, we would expect that the secondary sites would cluster about the primary sites, both stylistically and spatially. In determining the existence of spatial clusters, locational analysis will be useful (Haggett 1965). We can consider the primary site as a central place (Christaller 1933; Lösch 1938; 1954) and expect that the secondary sites will cluster nonrandomly in the vicinity of the primary sites. Distortions will occur as a result of topographic distortion, residence group population variation, associations among clans, and communities, and resource distribution. Hopefully some spatial clustering would be apparent, although it is conceivable that sites' spatial distribution depends primarily on other factors and does not reflect social organization.

Another possible test is the ceramic analysis, again in terms of design elements. We might expect that a clan's members would show a relatively high degree of stylistic homogeneity, and that each clan would have its own stylistic characteristics. We can represent the difference between two distributions of design elements as a Euclidean distance in n-dimensional space. We should find that sites belonging to the same matrilocal community would cluster about a particular point in this n-dimensional space, and that there are as many clusters of sites as there are matrilocal communities. Also, the stylistic clusters should correlate with spatial site clusters.

Finally, we need to demonstrate that the primary site is the group's central place in terms of social and ritual activity. The kiva would provide much of this focus, and we would expect to find ceramic artifacts, stone artifacts, pollen specimens, food remains, and other refuse which would indicate that this area was used by all or most of the clan members for ceremonial purposes. The ceramic design elements from the kiva might show consistent affiliation with all the sites in the clan's cluster.

Dual Organization

The use of a system of dual organization is another possible method of social organization on Black Mesa during the Toreva phase. This possibility was discovered by comparing the Black Mesa primary site with village plans from societies ethnographically known to use a dual system of organization (Levi-Strauss 1967). Figure 47 shows examples of such villages. In this system the social functions centered at the kiva would show a pattern of using members of separate moieties for various rituals or parts of rituals. There is still the possibility that descent is traced through the female line, but this would no longer have much effect on the gross social organization within the community.

Unfortunately, this hypothesis does not fit at all with the archaeological and ethnographic evidence from northeastern Arizona. The Hopi have never been known to use a system of dual organization. The Tsegi phase cliff dwellings and open sites in the area do not show the sort of village structure one would associate with dual organization. On the other hand, we can look eastward to Chaco Canyon ruins such as Pueblo Bonito or Chetro Ketl. The orientation and structure of these sites have led Vivian (1970) to hypothesize that the inhabitants were organized around a dual pattern. Also we can look to the eastern Pueblos which are ethnographically known to use a dual system of social organization (Dozier 1970; Ortiz 1969). Dozier has suggested that this dual organization resulted as a social adaptation to a situation which required a well integrated and efficient system for accomplishing tasks. If the organization on Black Mesa was of a dual nature, then this opens a new range of questions. What was Black Mesa's relation if any to the Chaco and to the eastern Pueblos? Did the Hopi ever have dual organization? What was there about Black Mesa life that required such organization, and why do we find no evidence for such organization at nearby sites?

The test implications for the hypothesis of dual organization are somewhat simpler than those for the previous hypothesis of growing clans and communities. We would expect there to be two moieties, one represented by each jacal wing. Moieties need not be defined as either matrilocal or patrilocal. The two residence groups already defined in Ariz. D:11:93 could easily represent moieties. To check on this, we would determine the distribution of the secondary sites around the primary site. If the population is great enough to have members of the system occupying nearby secondary sites, then each related secondary site should show close affiliation with one or the other of the jacal wings. This af-

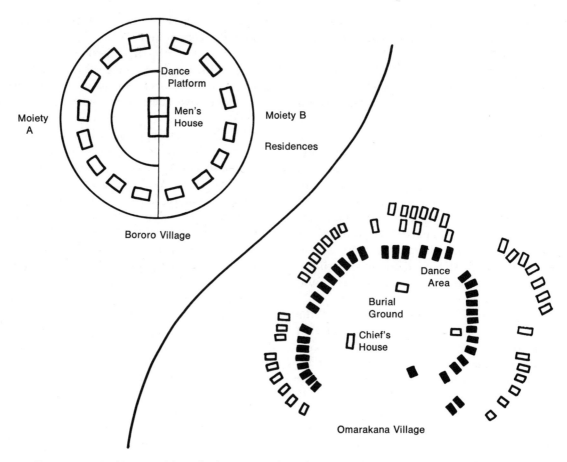

47. *Examples of villages with a dual pattern of social organization (after Levi-Strauss (1967)*

filiation could be manifest spatially, stylistically, or both, and we could test this using the same locational and statistical techniques suggested for the previous hypothesis. A rather difficult aspect of the test would be to show that the kiva represents the ceremonial-ritual focus for the two groups, and that these rituals were patterned around moieties.

Research Possibilities

In order to adequately test these hypotheses, a number of things must be done. First, and most important, the term "design element" must be carefully defined, and the conceptual area surrounding the idea of design elements must be thoroughly and rigorously developed. Answers to certain questions must be sought. Are there levels of design elements and design variability? What information can be gained from the various levels, individually and in combination? Is the mother-teaching-daughter model for ceramic-style perpetuation really a valid model in pueblo society? How could that model be tested in a prehistoric context? How rapidly does an array of design elements change within the framework of the model, and does it change slowly enough to generate the nonrandom distributions we find? What else could affect the randomness of a design element distribution? The answers to such questions as these would provide the much-needed strong theoretical base for residence-group studies.

With the theoretical groundwork laid, the hypotheses and test implications must, of course, be elaborated upon, made specific and operational. A good deal of data must be collected. An intensive site survey across a large section of the Mesa would be in order. The survey data would include accurate spatial coordinates as well as excavation samples taken randomly from both midden and living areas. Carefully controlled excavations of Toreva phase primary and secondary sites would be necessary. Kiva excavation must be especially well controlled. Virtually all the ceramic material must be analyzed with respect to design elements as well as to traditional pottery type classification. Much pertinent data has already been collected in the five summers of excavation; these data should be analyzed in light of the hypotheses presented here. Undoubtedly, data we already have would be enough to execute the major portion of these tests and help clarify some problems in this relatively poorly known area of Southwestern archaeology.

NOTE

This paper was prepared as a senior Honors Thesis in the Stanford University Honors Program in Anthropology in 1973. Essentially a yearlong project, research for this paper began the summer field session at Black Mesa in June and July 1972, where George J. Gumerman provided the initial information and opportunity to develop some of my ideas. Gumerman's enthusiasm and encouragement continued throughout the project. Ezra Zubrow provided valuable insights and arguments which led me to consider some of the more subtle aspects of the "new archaeology." Renato Rosaldo, George Collier, Bert Gerow, Alan Swedlund, James N. Hill, H. Martin Wobst, and Robert Euler, as well as Gumerman and Zubrow, all made valuable comments on drafts of this paper, although their advice was not always followed. Dr. Collier was particularly helpful with the statistical part of the study, and Claudia Chang helped with the ceramic analysis.

APPENDIX 1   Eighty-two Design Elements found in
Ariz. D:11:93

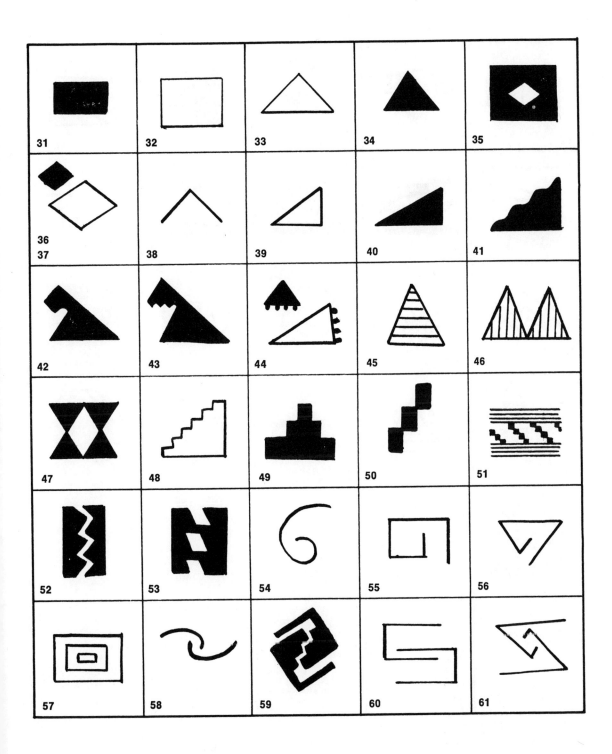

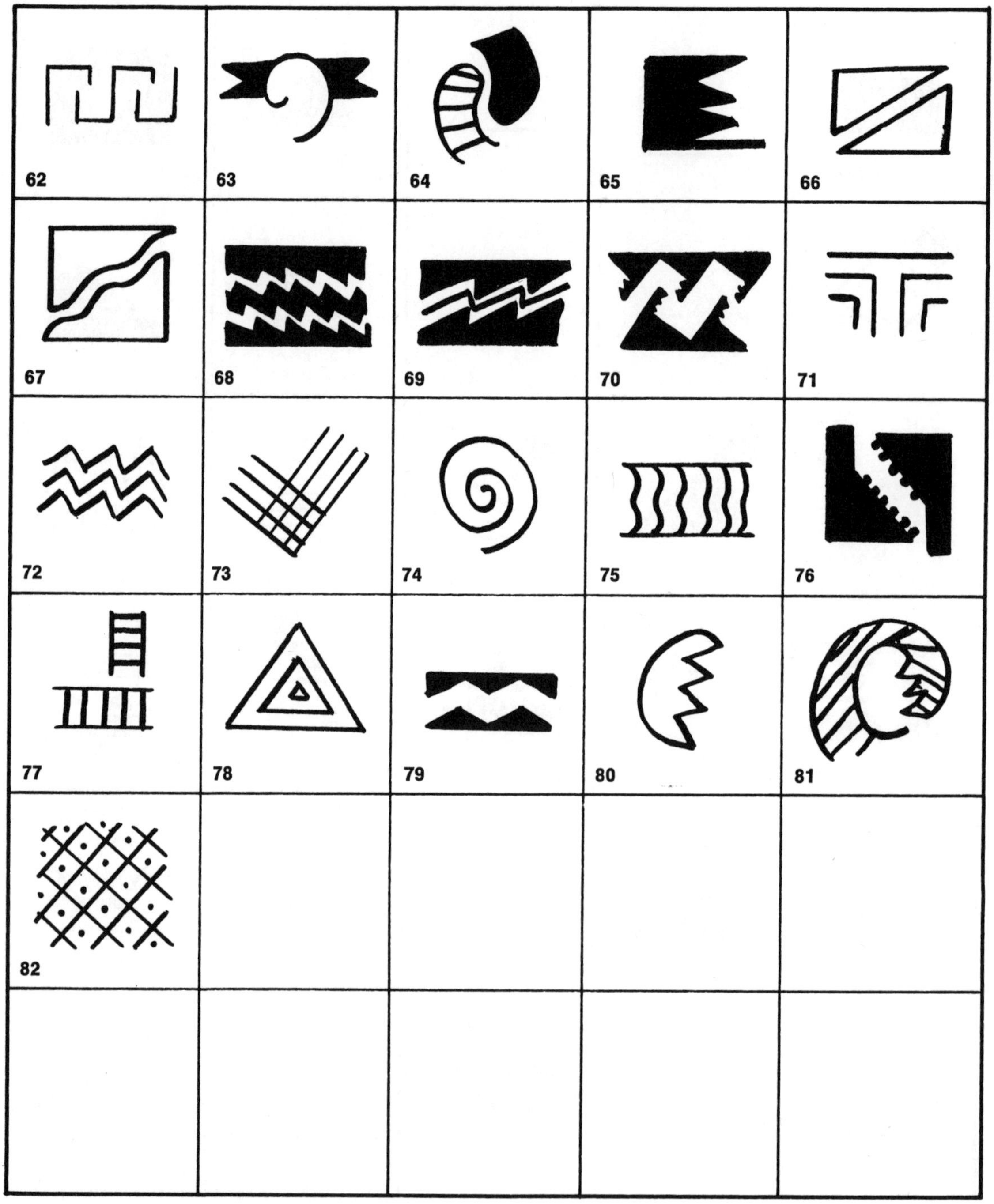
62
63
64
65
66
67
68
69
70
71
72
73
74
75
76
77
78
79
80
81
82

APPENDIX 2   Design Element Distributions in Ariz. D:11:93

DESIGN ELEMENT	ROOM 1	ROOM 2	KIVA	MEALING ROOM	JACAL WING 1	JACAL WING 2
1	—	—	—	—	—	1
2	—	—	—	—	2	14
3	2	—	—	—	14	15
4	—	2	2	1	5	21
5	—	—	—	—	5	—
6	—	—	—	—	—	1
7	—	—	—	—	1	1
8	—	—	—	—	—	1
9	—	1	1	2	2	67
10	5	5	5	11	18	61
11	17	74	41	26	118	403
12	32	27	30	33	107	369
13	—	2	2	—	—	2
14	—	—	—	—	—	1
15	2	2	2	2	13	20
16	—	—	—	—	—	1
17	—	—	—	—	—	1
18	—	—	—	—	3	1
19	1	—	2	—	1	6
20	1	2	4	3	15	35
21	6	2	9	5	25	77
22	—	—	—	—	2	2
23	16	11	10	12	61	152
24	—	—	—	—	—	3
25	—	—	1	—	—	4
26	—	—	—	—	2	2
27	—	1	—	—	4	8
28	—	3	14	1	1	10
29	1	—	—	—	1	—
30	—	—	1	—	4	3
31	—	—	1	—	—	2
32	1	—	—	—	2	1
33	—	4	—	—	—	—
34	—	4	3	1	3	10
35	—	—	—	—	—	3
36	—	—	—	—	3	2
37	—	—	—	—	1	—
38	2	—	—	3	5	16
39	—	—	—	—	1	1
40	1	—	1	—	3	9
41	—	—	—	—	—	2
42	—	—	—	—	—	1
43	—	—	2	—	1	—
44	2	1	11	1	5	37
45	—	—	1	—	4	2
46	1	—	—	—	—	7
47	—	—	—	—	8	5
48	1	—	1	—	4	32
49	—	—	—	—	2	2
50	1	—	—	—	1	6
51	—	—	—	—	—	1
52	1	—	9	4	6	40

APPENDIX 2 (Continued)

DESIGN ELEMENT	ROOM 1	ROOM 2	KIVA	MEALING ROOM	JACAL WING 1	JACAL WING 2
53	—	—	—	—	1	1
54	—	—	—	—	1	7
55	—	1	—	—	1	7
56	—	—	1	—	3	10
57	2	—	1	1	4	9
58	—	—	—	—	2	2
59	—	—	—	—	1	4
60	1	2	—	—	—	5
61	—	—	—	—	—	1
62	—	—	—	—	1	1
63	—	—	—	—	2	2
64	—	—	1	—	—	—
65	1	1	—	—	2	2
66	—	—	1	—	1	1
67	—	2	—	—	—	—
68	1	1	2	—	3	1
69	—	—	—	—	3	4
70	—	—	—	—	—	2
71	1	1	3	—	5	10
72	—	3	2	—	1	11
73	—	—	—	—	—	1
74	—	—	1	—	—	3
75	1	—	—	—	2	1
76	—	1	—	—	—	5
77	—	2	2	—	8	12
78	—	3	1	1	3	22
79	—	—	—	—	2	7
80	—	—	—	—	—	1
81	1	—	—	—	1	—
82	—	—	—	—	1	3
Totals	101	158	168	107	501	1595
Grand Total	2630					

Note: Chi-square = 650,601.4, with 405 degrees of freedom.

APPENDIX 3   Chi-square Analysis

	Room 1	Room 2	Kiva	Mealing Room	Jacal Wing 1	Jacal Wing 2
Room 1	—					
Room 2	76.12	—				
	37					
Kiva	64.74	68.68				
			—			
	41	35				
Mealing Room	29.33	53.03	47.20			
				—		
	29	27	32			
Jacal Wing 1	46.79	119.07	126.28	45.83		
					—	
	58	61	61	56		
Jacal Wing 2	100.50	154.21	173.80	35.41	173.13	—
	75	75	75	73	78	

Note: These results come from comparing the two indicated areas' design element distributions against the expected distribution (that is, design elements distributed independently in those two areas). Top number is the x^2 statistic, and the bottom number is the degrees of freedom. The overall chi-square, comparing the entire site distribution against a distribution with independence among the areas, is 650,601.4, with 405 degrees of freedom.

EDITORS' NOTE: The results derived from the chi-square analysis may not be valid because of the low frequency in each cell.

5

A Developmental Model of Prehistoric Population Growth on Black Mesa Northeastern Arizona

ALAN C. SWEDLUND and STEVEN E. SESSIONS

INTRODUCTION

Before the reader undertakes the main body of this paper, we would like to very briefly amplify the editors' comments in the Foreword of this volume. This paper presents a hypothetical, speculative approach to a problem. We make no apologies for this, but we hope that it will be viewed in the same light in which it is written. Its inclusion in the Black Mesa series is an attempt to let other anthropologists know about the kinds of thinking that are evolving concerning the culture history of the region. Furthermore, by formulating these hypotheses and attempting to test them we hope we are able to contribute to the theoretical literature on the archaeology of the Southwest. Stanislawski (1973) has recently criticized Longacre (1970) for his honest questioning of his own conclusions. We question our own conclusions and join Longacre in the hope that the open exchange of ideas will contribute to a sound theoretical base for southwestern archaeology.

The writing of this paper was stimulated by the original observation by Gumerman (1970) that the frequency of sites increased very significantly from earlier to later phases

on Black Mesa, but that the site frequencies dropped rapidly towards the end of the Toreva phase. The growth of habitation sites raises the question of the nature of the actual population growth in a region and we wanted to determine if we could devise some estimates of population growth, based on site size and frequency through time, that would make sense in terms of known demographic models.

We were also interested in investigating the kinds of demographic analyses that might be open to the archaeologist who has mostly survey data. It must be emphasized at the outset that our study is based primarily on the archaeological survey of Black Mesa, with some excavated sites for an information base. It was our thinking that if the archaeologist had some means for better making demographic and/or settlement hypotheses prior to large-scale excavation, then better testing could be done once excavation was actually undertaken. One question that immediately came to mind was whether or not the growth observed was likely to have been the result of immigration, or rather, that the amount of growth observed could easily be explained by normal, internal population growth. We should state at this time that our *initial* research of the problem was done without specific knowledge about the kinds of hypotheses and inferences that were being made by the archaeologists working on Black Mesa (for example, Gumerman, Westfall, and Weed 1972; Phillips 1972; Clemen, this volume). After some initial research we were able to arrive at some specific hypotheses of our own that can now be stated formally. Our working hypotheses came to include: 1. The growth represented by the remains on Black Mesa can be explained as internal population increase. Although some immigration was probably inevitable, this was probably not the major source of growth observed. 2. The population growth on Black Mesa bears directly on abandonment, although the actual causal factor(s) may be multiple and complex. This hypothesis, in turn, stimulated a number of secondary hypotheses concerning abandonment of Black Mesa and the larger issue of Anasazi migration and abandonment in the twelfth and thirteenth centuries. These secondary hypotheses will be discussed below.

The purpose of this paper is, then: 1. to relate our methods for estimating population growth from archaeological evidence; 2. to explain our findings in terms of some existing ecological and cultural theories; 3. to relate the immediate situation on Black Mesa to similar situations in the greater Southwest. We see this paper, because of its speculative nature, as a generator for further hypotheses and for critical examination of findings in the future.

The reader should be advised that there exists a long history of concern about the population growth, settlement, and abandonment of the northern Arizona region by the prehistoric occupants (for example, Colton 1936, 1949; Reed 1954; Hester 1962; Jett 1964; Woodbury 1961; Longacre 1970, Zubrow 1970). A recent summary of much of this work has been provided by Kunitz and Euler (1972) and it should not be necessary to repeat it here. Insofar as specific studies are

deemed relevant to our discussion they will be included in the text below.

MATERIALS AND METHOD

Our first need in this research was to obtain an index of population growth from the available data. Our best primary evidence was the growth curve of actual sites that was constructed by Gumerman (1970). An expanded version of this curve, based on more sites, is presented in Figure *48*. From these sites we attempted to ascertain the *relative rate* of population growth and not the absolute population numbers. We deductively inferred that the settlement sizes and their temporal variation should be reflective of rates of population growth. Although our data are not the product of a complete survey of the whole Black Mesa region, the areas which were surveyed were done so intensively. The areas include all the predominant ecological settings in this Upper Sonoran zone and all the recognized chronological stages of the Anasazi on

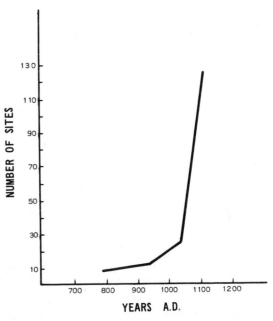

48. *Frequency of sites over 300 years on Black Mesa*

Black Mesa. Therefore, the data are thought to be representative of population patterns in this section of the Mesa (Gumerman, Westfall, and Weed 1972). The assumption made here is that the survey approaches a representative sample of all sites in all phases of the Anasazi occupation of northeastern Black Mesa.

A total of 169 sites was catalogued in the survey. The curve in Figure *48* is constructed by plotting the sites at the midpoint of their particular phase in an attempt to adjust for those sites occupied in the same phase but over different time intervals. The number of sites from each phase are, from early to late; 8, 12, 25, and 124, respectively. The sites surveyed and excavated on Black Mesa are characteristically single component sites of relatively short duration. This makes the clustering of sites into discrete phases somewhat more reasonable than would be the case in many archaeological samples. By plotting the sites in this fashion we believe we are approximating the relative growth trends between those phases.

One of our first objectives in the actual analysis of the sample was to assess the demographic nature of the few surveyed sites that had also been excavated. There are several methods of estimating a site's population that are available to the archaeologist (see Cook 1972). The number of burials, food residue, artifacts, houses, rooms, and sites are all valuable when the evidence exists. On Black Mesa the number of burials is insignificant, food residue is lost to decay, and the types of artifacts and their reflection of population is difficult to determine, therefore the identification of rooms and sites proved the most accurate means of population estimate for this area.

The smallest population unit the archaeologist might identify through the analysis of sites and rooms is probably the house and its equivalent set of occupants—the household. The smallest type of household is the family, but these two terms are not necessarily synonymous. A family may consist of only the nuclear or biological family made up of the procreative couple and offspring. This unit may include from two to several members. The addition of any relative such as grandparents, siblings and sons or daughters-in-law, is common and in such a case becomes an extended family.

As Cook (1972) points out, "family size must conform to certain biological and demographic principles. If a population is to maintain itself, each reproductive pair must produce two offspring who survive to maturity. Hence, the absolute minimum family size if the group is not to head for extinction is four. Under usual circumstances, in order to allow for death in early years, each pair must produce at least three children. Hence, the family size will approach five. If additional members are to be allowed, and these average one per family, the household reaches close to six."

From these data we can assume that under normal conditions the number of people in a biologically viable household will range from 4.5 to 6.0 (with a mean of 5.25). This range includes the addition of a limited number of secondary relatives. If a more permissive addition of secondary relatives is practiced, the value may reach 6.5 or 7.0 (Cook 1972).

A primary tool in archaeological research is, of course, the use of ethnographic sources. For this study, ethnographic data from the Hopi were believed to be the most reliable source for household estimates. Turner and Lofgren (1966) compared seven ethnographic estimates for the Hopi and gave an average of 5.55 for a Hopi household. This estimate falls well within the range predicted for a normal household with a limited addition of secondary relatives, and is very close to the mean 5.25.

Turner and Lofgren (1966) define the archaeological household as "the number of persons usually dependent on food preparation around a single fire hearth. This would include the biological family plus any married, unmarried, or widowed relative who habitually ate meals with the biological family." For the purpose of this study this will serve as an adequate definition, and the household number of 5.55 as an adequate measurement of the number of persons in this unit.

With this figure as a base, the excavated sites of the various time periods were then examined and estimates of the number of households occupying those sites were made. There are several forms of habitation structures on Black Mesa, including pithouses, masonry rooms, jacal rooms, and rooms constructed of masonry and jacal. The identification of a household unit was dependent on the location of a well-defined and used hearth located in an identifiable jacal, or masonry room, or pithouse.

The site samples were analyzed in terms of temporal units surveyed and excavated to determine the average number of households per excavated site and to extrapolate that data to our nonexcavated sites. Table 18 gives us a clearer picture of the site population patterns at different periods on Black Mesa.

The Tallahogan phase has eight sites with one excavated (Ariz. D:11:113). The excavated site has one pithouse and was discovered after work on a pipeline had been begun and uncovered it. It is located in the largest wash on Black Mesa, the Moenkopi. Because of the heavy alluvial overburden, no cultural material was seen on survey. One pithouse was all that was found although "it must be stressed that further test excavation was impossible due to the great amount of overburden and it seems extremely likely that there are additional features in the immediate area" (Gumerman, Westfall, and Weed 1972). It was therefore thought that this site only provided fragmentary evidence concerning the typical number of households in this

18. ESTIMATED HOUSEHOLD NUMBERS BY PHASE

Phase	No. Sites	No. Excavated	Household No.	Ave. Household No. per Site
Tallahogan BM III-PI				
700–875 A.D.	8	1	2	2.0
Dinnebito P I				
875–1000 A.D.	12	2	2	4.5
			7	
Wepo-Lamoki P I-P II				
1000–1075 A.D.	25	2	4	7.5
			11	
Toreva P II-P III				
1075–1150 A.D.	124			
Primary		5	2	
			2	
			3	
			4	
			7	3.6 *
Secondary		11	0	
			0	
			0	
			1	
			1	
			1	
			2	
			2	
			2	
			3	
			5	1.54 *

* Combined average for Toreva = 2.19.

particular phase, so surveyed sites were examined. All of the sites of this phase on the Mesa appear quite small. The mean area of the surveyed sites of this phase is 445 square meters. The largest surveyed site is 600 square meters, and the typical survey remark is: "no masonry, depression probably containing a couple of pithouses." For this reason the average household size was arbitrarily placed at two. The Tallahogan phase is the one we know the least about. The fact that the majority (60 percent) of these sites lie in the lowlands along the major washes and not on secondary washes and in the uplands like later phase sites, may have caused more sites to be lost due to alluviation. This would affect the original assumption that the survey represents a random sample of all the sites. However, the significant part of the growth curve is not seriously affected by errors in this phase, and also, the curves visually appear very reasonable in terms of population growth models.

There are twelve Dinnebito phase sites. Two have been excavated and there appear to be two variants of habitation site in this phase. One, Ariz. D:11:57, contains only two pithouses, while the other, Arix. D:7:98, contains five pithouses, one masonry room, and one jacal structure. The surveyed sites also tend to cluster into these two types with four sites representing the larger variety, and seven the smaller variety. One site in this phase appears to be a limited use or special activity site at which no permanent habitation took place.

The Wepo and Lamoki phase sites were combined due to the short time duration of the latter phase (twenty-five years). By combining these two phases a more comparable time period of seventy-five years was established. Ceramically, these sites represent a stage with late Pueblo I, transitional, and Pueblo II pottery. Two sites have been excavated in this time range, again, apparently representing two different habitation sizes. The smaller one, Ariz. D:7:11 has one pithouse and three masonry dwelling rooms; the

larger, Ariz. D:11:18, contains four pithouses, one masonry dwelling room and two jacal structures, which probably represent six households. A total of eight hearths were found in these two jacal structures but only six show extended use and can be identified with particular rooms. The surveyed sites again also appear to fall into these two size ranges of large and small.

The Toreva phase represents a unique settlement pattern. Phillips (1972) has identified two distinct types of habitation site in the Toreva of Black Mesa, the primary and the secondary or "daughter" site. The primary site is defined "as having those facilities required by the Anasazi for complete maintenance of their cultural system, including facilities for habitation, storage, and socioreligious activities." The critical feature in the primary site is the presence of a kiva. The secondary sites are defined "as capable of satisfying the immediate biological needs of the inhabitants, but lacking at least the important dimension of socioreligious facilities, i.e., a kiva." The largest sample of excavated sites comes from the Toreva phase. Both primary and secondary sites have been excavated and the expected variation in the two noted. Five primary sites that have been excavated were used in this analysis. One additional primary site was excavated, but due to erosional damage an estimate of household number was impossible to make. The number of household units per site drops considerably from the previous phase. The range is from 2 to 7, with a mean of 3.6. A total of eleven excavated secondary sites make up the sample from which the average of 1.54 was gained. Three of the sites appeared to have had no habitation and served only as storage facilities in proximity to agricultural land. One or 2 households is the common number with one site containing 3 households and another with 5.

An important demographic question arises in respect to these secondary habitation sites: do they represent unique population units or are they the product of summer habitation by a population unit from a primary site utilizing them for their proximity to crops? One example of this kind of habitation may be represented in Ariz. D:11:109, a single pithouse with associated extramural cists and hearths. The excavation report describes the hearth in the pithouse as "an irregular shaped hearth which showed little use." It goes on to explain that, "the external hearth had been utilized extensively suggesting that the domicile was occupied during the summer or growing season" (Euler and Ward 1971). Careful examination was made of the other secondary habitation sites to determine if they might also represent only summer residences, but the presence of adequate storage facilities and well-used interior hearths points to their year-round use. The overall (both primary and secondary) excavated site average was 2.19 household units, considerably lower than all but the Tallahogan phase sites.

The criterion for the identification of household units in a particular site was, as stated before, the location of a permanent hearth associated with a room large enough to have supported such a household unit. The smallest structure designated as representing a household unit was a pithouse with a 3.96 square meter floor area. The largest was a pithouse with 23.1 square meters. Although this represents a large range of sizes for a fixed designation of 5.55 individuals, the application of this figure is intended as an arithmetic mean with the assumption that range and variance may be great. Also, the 23.1

square meter pithouse is an isolated event in the sample and is considerably larger than the next largest pithouse (about 10 square meters). Table 19 shows the mean size distribution of dwellings through time. The average size dwelling unit designated as containing a household is 10.89 square meters with one standard deviation of 4.43. The change in square meters of dwelling area per structure through time would indicate a variability of structure size possibly corresponding to slight increases or decreases in the household unit, but for the purposes of this study the change was believed to be too small to warrant adjusting the standard household number.

Population Ratio Estimates by Phase

This section should be prefaced with a statement regarding the survey information and the reliability of site size estimates. As has been stated previously, the architecture on Black Mesa varies temporally and spatially. Pithouses, jacal structures, and masonry rooms commonly can be found in a single site. When initially surveying a site the estimated perimeter was recorded. In the case of pithouse sites, or sites with jacal structures, this estimate was often found to be inaccurate when the site was excavated. What was found, however, was that the size of the masonry structures was a relatively good indicator of the size of the jacal portion of the site. That is, there is a predictable ratio between masonry architecture and total site size. The

19. MEAN SIZE DISTRIBUTION OF DWELLING UNITS BY PHASE (FIGURES IN SQUARE METERS)

Phase	Ave. Pithouse	Ave. Masonry Dwelling	Ave. Jacal Dwelling	Ave. Dwelling
Tallahogan	9.92	0.0	0.0	9.92
Dinnebito	11.63	7.50	10.90	10.93
Wepo-Lamoki	9.83	9.20	15.14	12.40
Toreva				
Primary	8.44	7.01	10.87	9.31
Secondary	6.92	0.00	12.05	10.76
Total Average	10.30	7.90	11.93	10.89 ± 1SD4.43

sample of excavated sites for any particular phase is a problem we readily acknowledge. However, our attempts to use the available information in various estimates (as discussed below) has indicated to us that the excavated data are, indeed, applicable.

To extrapolate the data found from the examination of the excavated sites to non-excavated sites, three methods were employed. The first was a direct application of the average number of household units per excavated site to all other sites in that time period. The second was an attempt to look at the surveyed sites in terms of their size and architectural remains and to apply the household number of a similar excavated site. This basically involved separating the surveyed sites into three categories: large, small, and special activity. The large and small categories refer to the excavated sites of a particular phase. Surveyed sites were placed in the large or small category according to their similarity with the excavated site. The identification of special activity sites where it was not likely habitation took place, was a factor in this second method. Small sherd areas with no architectural features and little trash were designated special activity sites. As stated before, in the case of Wepo-Lamoki phases, two sizes of excavated sites were manifest. We assessed the data on the surveyed sites and divided them into special activity, small and large categories and applied the relative household numbers accordingly. In the case of the Tallahogan sites, they were divided into two categories: 1. special activity, and 2. those appearing to have two dwelling units (pithouses). In the case of Dinnebito phase surveyed sites, they were divided into three categories: 1. special activity, 2. those appearing similar in size and architectural remains to the site with two household units, and 3. those appearing similar in size and architectural remains to the site with seven household units. The Wepo-Lamoki sites were divided similarly into three categories: 1. special activity, 2. those similar to the excavated site with four household units, and 3. those similar to the exca-

vated site with eleven household units. The Toreva phase sites were the easiest to manipulate in that the two variants of primary and secondary sites were used. The designation of primary site was given to a surveyed site if it possessed a kiva depression, and evidence of the associated surface structures (masonry room block), characteristic of the excavated primary sites. The designation of secondary site was given to sites without kiva depressions with or without other attributes. Since excavated secondary sites with no habitation were included in the figures to obtain the mean of secondary sites, no effort was made to designate special activity sites. A direct application of the mean household units per both primary and secondary sites (2.19) was the first method employed. Applying the two distinct means for primary (3.60) and secondary (1.54) sites to the respective classified surveyed sites was the second method employed.

The third population estimate involved a critical examination of surveyed sites wherein we made estimates based on the excavated sites and their household number for that particular phase, expanding the values used to include values from all the excavated sites in that phase and their mean. This method like the second, takes into account those sites which probably represent special activity areas rather than habitation and consequently would contain no households. It also takes into account the variability in surveyed sites. Although many sites conveniently fit into the relative large and small categories, some sites as would be expected, appeared to fall in varying degrees into these two categories. Special activity sites were always given a 0 household figure. The other figures were from the household figures obtained from the excavated sites, the mean of those excavated sites and, in two cases, midpoints between those figures.

For the Tallahogan phase, three figures were used; 0 for special activity sites, 1 for surveyed sites that were small and appeared to have only 1 pithouse depression, and 2 for those appearing to have 2 pithouse depressions. The figures used for Dinnebito phase were 0, 2, 4.5, and 7. These figures represent special activity, small, medium and large sites respectively. The 2 and 7 figures are from excavated sites with 4.5 being their mean. Wepo-Lamoki phase surveyed sites were divided between household figures of 0, 2, 4, 7.5, and 11 representing the various use and size sites. The 4 and 11 figures are from excavated sites with 7.5 being their mean and 2 representing a surveyed site smaller than the excavated site with 4 households but not appearing to be a special activity site. There are 124 surveyed Toreva phase sites and the range in size varies greatly. Once they were divided into primary and secondary sites,

they were compared with the excavated sites of the specific type and were given household figures like the comparable excavated site. The figures obtained from excavated primary sites were 2, 3, 4, and 7 households, The figures obtained from the excavated secondary sites were 0, 1, 2, 3, and 5 households. In this case a mean was not used, only figures obtained from excavated sites.

Results

Using the ethnographic figure of 5.55 persons per household, the three population estimates were made. Table 20 shows these three estimates and the average estimate, with the average annual increase from the same previous phase estimate. The total average

20. THREE POPULATION ESTIMATES AND AVERAGE ESTIMATE BY PHASE, INCLUDING AVERAGE ANNUAL INCREASE FROM PREVIOUS PHASE AND AVERAGE NUMBER OF PERSONS FOR SITE

Phase	Estimate No.	Ave. No. Pers. per Site	Pop. Est.	Percent Ave. Annual Increase from Previous Phase Estimate*
Tallahogan (BM III-P I)	I	11.10	88.80	
700–875 A.D.	II	9.71	77.70	
	III	8.33	66.60	
	IV ($\overline{X}$)	9.71	77.70	
Dinnebito (P I)	I	24.98	299.76	.81
875–1000 A.D.	II	25.40	305.76	.93
	III	17.80	213.68	.79
	IV ($\overline{X}$)	22.70	272.90	.83
Wepo-Lamoki (P I-P II)	I	28.30	708.70	.86
100–1075 A.D.	II	24.40	610.00	.69
	III	23.50	587.00	1.00
	IV ($\overline{X}$)	25.40	635.20	.86
Toreva (P II-P III)	I	12.15	1507.00	1.00
1075–1150 A.D.	II	12.60	1560.00	1.30
	III	8.60	1070.00	.81
	IV ($\overline{X}$)	11.12	1379.00	1.00

Note: Estimate I. All sites multiplied by average household figure.

        II. Sites designated into three categories: special activity, small, and large, and multiplied accordingly.†

        III. Sites designated into various categories reflective of their use, size, and architectural attributes and multiplied accordingly.

        IV. Average of the three estimates.

* Average annual increase from BM III-P I (est. IV) to P II-P III (est. IV): .86%.

† For Tallahogan only two categories, special activity and average (2.0). For Toreva only two categories, primary and secondary.

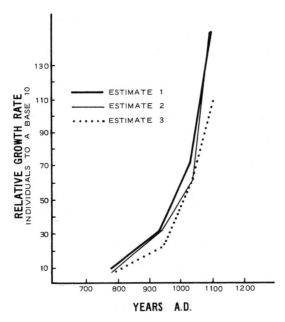

49. *Comparison of three population growth estimates on Black Mesa*

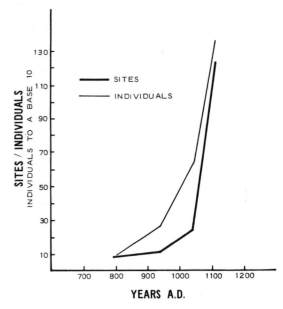

50. *Comparison of population growth with site frequency over time on Black Mesa*

annual increase of the population figures from early to late phases is 0.86 percent per year. Figure *49* shows the three curves representing the three estimates. It will be seen that all three curves are similar in their expression of growth rates. Figure *50* presents the average of the three growth estimates and compares that curve to the site frequency curve given in Figure *48*.

The population figures obtained for each phase were placed at the temporal midpoint of that particular phase in an attempt to adjust for those sites that were occupied over different time spans within a phase. If growth is constant during any particular phase, then this method may approximate the actual population size of the subject sites during the middle period of the phase. This is not an object of the estimate, however. The main objective is only to have some indicator of *relative* growth from one phase to the other, and not to intimate that we are dealing with absolute values. The calculation for average annual increase was also made from the midpoint of each phase using a compound in-

terest formula for biological population growth.

The curves we derived were then tested for fit and compared to known growth models. All of these curves fit the general family of exponential curves ($y = ae^{bx}$). Two commonly observed population growth curves are called the **J** curve and the **S** (sigmoid) curve (Odum 1971). Although actual field data may not exactly fit the classic types, a pattern related to one or the other is common. Our curves for Black Mesa resemble the **J** type quite closely.

With the relative population estimates developed from excavated and surveyed sites in the study area, we have a point of departure before proceeding to further analysis. First, the question arises whether or not the 0.86 percent growth rate is a reliable figure. Improving the method for obtaining that figure would certainly increase its reliability, and its reflection of true population fluctuation. We can make one simple check by comparing this rate with that of other populations living under similar conditions. The problem is that census data for nonindustrial, "primitive" subsistence agriculture populations are lacking. From Bogue (1969) we find a somewhat comparable figure of 0.91 percent annual growth rate for Latin America between 1800 and 1850, but Latin America in this time period probably had more varied factors affecting its population than does the area under study here. The doubling time for a population with a 0.86 percent annual growth rate is approximately eighty-seven years. Bogue classifies this as a moderate population growth rate. From Trewartha (1970) a comparable annual increase of 0.8 percent is found for Middle and South America between 1750 and 1800 but again the many variables accounting for that population growth were probably quite different from those affecting our study population. Cook and Borah (1971) have found a rate of 1.00 percent for the Indians of Mexico in the eighteenth century. Perhaps our best indirect sample comparison comes from the work of Sanders (1972). Sanders has developed population growth curves for several prehistoric populations in Mesoamerica and, although rates are not given, the shape and grade of selected curves in the Aztec and Mayan regions appear quite similar. Recent studies (Hassan 1973; Cook and Borah 1971; Sherburne Cook, personal communication) all suggest that the moderate rate of 0.86 percent is quite reasonable.

Basically, we believe that the 0.86 percent annual population increase falls within an expected range for a nonindustrial, subsistence agricultural population. The real value could certainly vary on either side of this value (see Table 20) and yet still be within reasonable limits of known rates for such populations. Although we cannot state unequivocally that the differences observed between the various phases are not the result of immigration, we can easily account for those differences by the rate of natural growth estimated.

In other cases where this type of study is undertaken it may be possible to estimate other demographic parameters if large skeletal samples are available. Weiss (1973a; 1973b) describes methods for fitting model life tables and estimating fertility rates where such large samples exist. However, the skeletal remains recovered from Black Mesa to date (Swedlund and Hanson 1972) only represent nineteen individuals.

Population Growth and Cultural Ecological Considerations

Assuming that the 0.86 percent rate is reflective of real events occurring on Black Mesa, it remains for us to relate our findings to cultural and ecological causes and effects. We can start by explicitly stating two assumptions: 1. We assume that the increase in sites over time is a real phenomenon and that the survey reflects the prehistoric reality about settlement. 2. We also assume, at this point, that the curves expressing rates of population growth are reflective of trends that actually occurred prehistorically. One might ask at this point, "If the curve of sites is accurate then why is it necessary to speculate further and more tenuously about actual population size?" We would answer that an increase in site frequency does not necessarily mean an increase in population. The increase could be due to a different settlement pattern but a stationary population (that is, more but smaller sites). Furthermore, the population rates give us an estimate of growth that can be analyzed in light of known biological characteristics of human populations.

In addition to these two assumptions, we have things (artifacts) and events (for example, occupation, abandonment) that are known about the subject population on Black Mesa. For example, we know that there were not significant advances in cultural sophistication through time as demonstrated in the artifacts and architecture. There was, however, technological innovation in agriculture, as evidenced by exploitation of different environmental zones. We know that, as time passed, the prehistoric occupants of Black

Mesa moved from lowlands and major drainages to the uplands where water was more scarce. We know that the settlement pattern changed through time so as to include primary, larger sites surrounded by secondary sites of smaller size (Gumerman 1970; Gumerman, Westfall, and Weed 1972; Phillips 1972). These and other observations are available for correlation with the predicted population growth.

Now we turn to the "unknown." There are two major unknowns that are of concern to us: 1. We know there was a change in settlement pattern through time, and that this occurred primarily during the Toreva phase, but we do not know specifically why. 2. We have good evidence for population growth through time, but we do not know what the effects of this growth might have been.

Our construction of the pertinent events on Black Mesa is as follows:

Basketmaker populations have moved to a relatively new resource base (intensive agriculture) and are succesfully settling in the areas most conducive for the purposes of growing crops while at the same time making widespread use of hunting for a protein supplement to their diet. As time passes the Basketmakers emerge into bona fide Puebloan cultural patterns and are successfully adapting to a more settled way of life. At this time resources and life styles are conducive to accelerated population growth and by about A.D. 1050 the effects of this growth are beginning to be felt. However, improvements in food production and gathering enable the population to continue to grow very rapidly and also to inhabit new areas and subenvironments as old areas become too densely populated or too depleted in resources. Eventually, by about A.D. 1125, the effects of this growth are very strongly felt and the inhabitants of the Mesa are having to settle in increasingly less desirable areas and are going farther and farther for game. By about A.D. 1150 the internal growth, with its consequent depletion of resources and a variety of external factors, has brought about emigration from the area and, very shortly, large-scale abandonment.

What are the relevant variables in this sequence and how do they relate? The major hypotheses concerning abandonment of many areas in the greater Southwest have been drought, competition from "other" peoples, and disease. Many accept an explanation using all three. Kunitz and Euler (1972) have recently reviewed the literature pertaining to these various arguments and the criticisms of each. They note that, although there is good evidence that the Southwest did sustain drought beginning about A.D. 1100, there were earlier droughts that the indigenous groups sustained. Also, Jennings (1966) has commented that the Anasazi were very skillful in quickly adapting to climatic fluctuations. So, although paleoclimatic conditions were certainly influential, they may well not have been the major factor. In regard to the hypothesis about enemy peoples, there does not seem to be adequate evidence for this; however, when any populations are in stress conditions, some competition can probably be expected, and we certainly do have evidence for "defensive" sites in some areas. Disease was most likely a significant factor, although we do not find the high frequency of burials and ancillary evidence that might be expected with large-scale epidemics. Thus, it does not seem to be a question of these factors not being significant so much as it is a question of *why* these factors come about and are so significant at this particular time. We might ask why, although agricultural technology was probably increasing, the Anasazi would be abandoning several areas within a relatively short time? It is our contention that the major factor could have been population growth and available resources, and that the three above hypotheses are concommitant to this major factor.

Longacre (1970), Zubrow (1970) and several others have observed similar trends in site frequencies over time as we have observed for Black Mesa. In the Hay Hollow area Zubrow (1970) has contrasted the site frequency growth to various indicators of food resources and concludes that the carrying capacity of the land was exceeded and abandonment quickly followed. Carrying capacity refers to the ratio of resources to biomass (of a species) in a given environment or locality (Odum 1971). When the carrying capacity of a region is exceeded by a species then decline of the vitality of that species in the region is virtually assured. When the carrying capacity is met, but not exceeded, then a leveling off of population can be expected, but a subsequent drop in numbers is normally the case. These two conditions show the characteristic population curves referred to above as the J curve and the S (sigmoid) curve types (Odum 1971). In the cases of the Black Mesa (Gumerman 1970; this paper) and the Little Colorado River valley (Longacre 1970; Zubrow 1970), the curves of site frequencies tend toward the J type, while Schwartz (1956) has observed the S type for prehistoric populations of the Coconino Plateau in northern Arizona.

It would certainly be unwarranted for us to assume that the existence of these curves is absolute proof of critical carrying capacity relationships in these or other areas of the greater Southwest, or, that population decline in these and other areas is always the result of resource limitations. However, we believe that the carrying capacity argument does seem very reasonable for Black Mesa and the Little Colorado River valley and that this may have been a precipitating factor in increasing the incidence of disease as well as making the effects of drought more severely felt. If one views the Black Mesa region as a case where a highly adaptive species (*Homo sapiens*) has recently occupied a new ecological niche (agriculture), then the growth we hypothesize makes sense. Occupation of the new niche allows for rapid expansion of the population. Eventually the population has cultivated all the available arable land

and exhausted the growing capacity of some of it. Finally, the available resources can no longer sustain the existing population and rapid decline occurs.

Turning now to other cultural manifestations of settlement pattern, we will attempt to explain the consistency of the population data with observations that are not directly related to abandonment. Gumerman, Westfall, and Weed (1972), and Phillips (1972) have observed that the settlement pattern on Black Mesa shifts from a lowland pattern to a use of the upland areas as well when sites are geographically plotted through time. As they have also noted, this would seem to demonstrate exploitation of slightly different environmental areas and, perhaps, the development or acquisition of new varieties of maize as well as improved technology (George Gumerman, personal communication). Phillips has observed that the sites of the Toreva phase can often be found in a pattern where a major site is surrounded by "daughter" sites. The major sites, as noted above, are distinctive from the daughter sites in having a kiva present and by being larger than their surrounding sites. Phillips suggests that the smaller sites are related to the larger ones, are dependent on the larger ones for certain socioreligious activities, and that they may be functionally explained as habitations that are more closely located to the agricultural fields. Clemen (this volume) would support at least the first two of these observations.

If we place these hypotheses in the context of the population growth model, we find additional support. Population growth can readily be seen as a stimulus for occupation of the upland areas, where additional land for crops and settlement was available. This does not mean that the lowlands would necessarily be abandoned in favor of the uplands, only that the uplands were also important to the continued success of the local population. As fields became more scattered the cultural response may have been, as Phillips (1972) suggests, to also scatter the habitation pattern.

Eventually, however, the population growth and diminishing resources were too far out of equilibrium with each other, and emigration followed.

CONCLUSIONS

Our major conclusions are as follows:

1. With the adoption of agriculture the prehistoric occupants of Black Mesa were in a position similar to that of a species that has just recently occupied a very favorable environmental region. The conditions were very conducive to rapid population growth. The presence of agriculture and a more settled way of life were the most significant of these conditions.

2. As time passed and technology evolved, the exploitation of the new ecological niche increased in intensity. Population growth occurred exponentially, and the amount of available resources diminished rapidly as the population increased. By approximately A.D. 1100 the population was too large for the available resource base, and resembled the ecological model of a species that has exceeded the carrying capacity of its habitat. Paleoclimatic factors and other external stimuli were unfavorable and abandonment of the area by large numbers followed. This process is probably most appropriate to a dynamic view of carrying capacity. That is, as the population changes, the carrying capacity can also be subject to change. The more the grow-

ing population exploits the environment, the greater the carrying capacity may be diminished. This view would predict that some biodegradation occurred on Black Mesa as a result of the human occupancy.

In an analysis of faunal remains in sites on Black Mesa, Douglas (1972) found that the ratio of small mammals to large mammals increases as more recent sites are sampled. He suggests that there would have been an increasing dependence on small mammals as a food resource in the later phases. This certainly seems feasible as an effect of man's presence. As hunting and area of cultivation increases, the density and proximity of large animals probably decreases. Small mammals (rodents, lagomorphs) would not necessarily be as limited by these human activities. If extreme biodegradation were the ultimate result, large-scale abandonment (J curve) seems more likely than population equilibrium and a leveling off of population growth (sigmoid model).

3. Although these conclusions are very hypothetical, we believe there is support for them, and we would apply this argument to other areas in the prehistoric Southwest as well.

NOTE

We would like to thank the late Sherburne Cook, George Armelagos, and Steven Clarke for their useful comments and criticisms.

6 Paleoenvironmental and Cultural Correlates in the Black Mesa Region

THOR N. V. KARLSTROM

GEORGE J. GUMERMAN

and

ROBERT C. EULER

INTRODUCTION

Geologic investigations of the late Quaternary alluvial and colluvial deposits in the Black Mesa region over the past four years have been closely coordinated with archaeological, dendroclimatic, and palynological research of the Black Mesa Archaeological Project (Fig. *51*). This project has been directed toward deriving detailed reconstructions of both prehistoric cultural history and the accompanying changes in the physical environment so that cultural processes can be better understood.

The geologic research has focused on the stratigraphic evidence of past environmental changes that may have directly or indirectly affected the activity of prehistoric man in the region. Sufficient time-stratigraphic data are now available to reconstruct the general pattern of hydrologic and, by inference, climatic changes during the critical last two thousand years of the cultural record extending from the beginning of Lolomai phase, through the Toreva phase to the present.

The contributions that paleoenvironmental studies can make toward understanding prehistoric culture change have long been recog-

nized. The reverse of that situation, the potential contributions that archaeology can make to aid understanding of past environmental reconstructions have not been utilized to their fullest extent. In this paper we first discuss the appropriate archaeological data and then the geologically and biologically derived environmental data. These combined data are then jointly assessed in terms of cultural-environmental relations; finally, some broader regional implications are suggested relating to cultural history, process dynamics, and paleoclimate.

ARCHAEOLOGICAL DATA AND CONCEPTS

Regional résumé and conceptual problems

Numerous archaeologists (c.f. Martin and Plog 1973) have commented on the seemingly important events that took place about A.D. 200–300 among the early Basketmaker II Anasazi, the spread of these Anasazi and the development of certain traditions of the Hakataya about A.D. 700, the population increase and spread to the uplands about A.D. 900, the widespread movement of both Anasazi and Hakataya around A.D. 1150, and the pro-

149

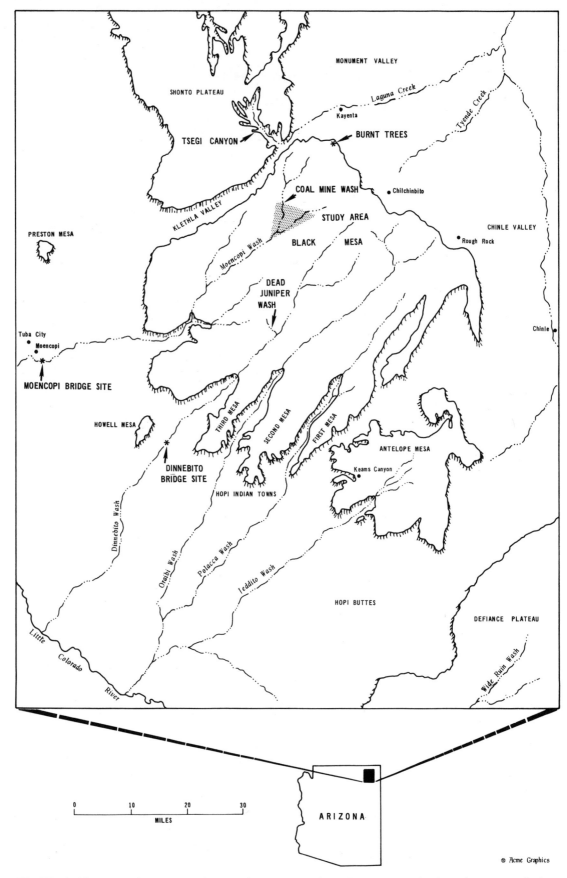

51. *Black Mesa, northeastern Arizona, showing location of archaeological study area and sites with C-14 dated stratigraphy*

nounced abandonment of certain regions after A.D. 1300.

The movements of populations in the prehistoric Southwest have long been of interest to archaeologists, and summaries of several causative hypotheses have been presented by Reed (1954), Jett (1964), and Kunitz and Euler (1972). In the latter study, emphasis was placed upon paleoenvironmental factors and their relationship to epidemiology. The conclusions reached were that more attention should be given to the role that disease may have played in these populations shifts, and that while ecological changes are very likely to have led to an increase in morbidity and mortality, one "does not need to invoke large-scale, dramatic epidemics" as the explanation. Rather, "prosaic entities like malnutrition and infectious diarrhea are more than sufficient" (Kunitz and Euler 1972:40). In this paper we shall simply review the recent concerns that archaeologists and biologists have had with paleoclimatological explanations for cultural dynamics and processes.

Since we also attempt to apply archaeological concepts of the phase system to our work on Black Mesa, we shall briefly comment upon our philosophy of classificatory systems so that our position is clear. Following that, we shall discuss cultural development for the particular area of northeastern Black Mesa in which we have been working and, most importantly, present new data relative to paleoclimatology there.

General Environmental Considerations

Recent studies of past environments in the northern Southwest have seemed to indicate that changing climatic conditions played a more complex role in cultural and demographic change than had earlier been realized. For example, archaeologists no longer refer glibly to the so-called "great drought" of the last quarter of the thirteenth century as a primary factor in the depopulation of the Mesa Verde and Tsegi Canyon. Fritts and his associates (Fritts, Smith, and Stokes 1965: 120) have shown through tree-ring indices that the Mesa Verde people survived periods of drought at A.D. 1276–89. Dendroclimatic studies by Robinson and Dean (1969:7) further indicate that the period from A.D. 1140–89 was "an interval of extremely dry conditions prevailing in the Four Corners regions." Palynological research by Schoenwetter (1970: 45) suggests evidence for drought conditions in the northern Southwest between A.D. 800–815 and A.D. 1112–30. Archaeological excavations and associated climatic studies in the Navajo Reservoir district of northwestern New Mexico, east of Mesa Verde, and north of Chaco Canyon, suggest that inadequate precipitation beginning about A.D. 1100 on the Colorado Plateau caused the agricultural Anasazi to begin an exodus (Dittert 1968:14). Detailing the paleoenvironmental aspects of those Navajo Reservoir studies, Schoenwetter and Dittert (1968:41–66) have postulated a summer-dominant rainfall pattern between A.D. 1100 and 1300 coupled with a drought between A.D. 1275 and 1300 and continuing erosion of valley agricultural fields utilized by the Anasazi. They believe that alluvial degradation is common in periods of summer-dominant storm patterns. In summary, they have suggested that the widespread erosion of farmlands plus drought were factors instrumental in the Pueblo abandonment of much of their heartland. It has been noted, in this connection, that during those centuries the Anasazi built more extensive water and soil conservation systems on Mesa Verde and in Chaco Canyon (Rohn 1963:441–45; Vivian 1970:69–78). Although Martin and Plog (1973:331) assume that "environmental stresses were present at the time of abandonments," they also suggest "that it is probably unnecessary to search for major environmental disruptions." We believe, however, that the high correlation of environmental changes with demographic changes on the Colorado Plateau makes it highly desirable to explore these correlations in more detail.

Paleoclimatology and the Archaeological Record

Climatic regimes can be interpreted from the archaeological record because nonindustrial societies articulate directly with their environment. As a result, change in the environment of a certain order of magnitude demands changes in a culture's subsistence-adaptive strategy. For example, if annual or seasonal precipitation falls below that necessary for successfully raising crops until no surplus remains, a primarily agricultural people must take adaptive action, such as reversion to a hunting and gathering subsistence base or migration to wetter zones. This is an obvious example and one which would be readily detectable in the archaeological record.

However, a number of factors complicate the interpretation of past climatic shifts based on phase changes in the archaeological record. Archaeological phases, as described below, are abstractions which may involve stylistic change within the cultural sequence and not any major change in adaptive strategy. Furthermore, even if change in the archaeological record reflects major cultural change in the adaptive strategy, it does not necessarily follow that the cultural change reflects climatic change. For example, the adoption of agriculture by a hunting and gathering society will have far-reaching implications for changes which may not be associated with climatic fluctuations. The introduction of the horse on the western United States plains resulted in vast changes in the cultural systems of the Plains Indians with no recognizable change in the climatic regime. In short, changes in the archaeological record do not necessarily reflect environmental change.

Care must also be exercised in comparing absolute dates of cultural sequences when seeking change over large areas which might be due to environmental variation. Similarities in dates between different cultural sequences may be due in some cases, not to an accuracy of dating or change at a particular time, but to a cross-dating of one cultural sequence by another. One sequence may be established by well-dated intrusive sherds from another sequence and consequently, the phase boundaries in both sequences will appear to be of similar age but may in reality not be contemporaneous.

In spite of the difficulties described in using archaeology as a device for understanding past climatic change, when used with caution and with other independent lines of evidence such as geology, tree-ring analysis and palynology, archaeology can be most helpful in reconstructing paleoenvironments.

Phase Concept

The phase concept has been of incalculable value in archaeological research; the history of the phase concept in the Southwest has been well documented (Olson 1962). Its critics have been many (among others, Brew 1946). While we would agree with Lister (1966:75) that it presents many problems both locally and regionally, we would also concur in his acceptance of Kluckhohn's statement (Kluckhohn and Reiter 1939:162) that: "Surely, all classifications can but, at best, express modal tendencies and must be used purely heuristically, with constant awareness that they are most crude categorizations of the human acts we are trying to reconstruct."

The tentative phase system developed for Black Mesa is based primarily upon temporally sensitive ceramic types. It is a system based on observations to date and is certainly subject to refinement and extension (Gumerman, Westfall, and Weed 1972:26). We would, of course, hope ultimately to arrive at phase distinctions based upon more "quantitative, qualitative, and other relational data" (Taylor 1948:138) so that they will be more culturally relevant (Taylor 1948:122).

Furthermore, while we are aware of recent attempts to utilize computer-assisted statistical procedures such as factor analysis and cluster analysis in defining archaeological units (Michaels 1972:114), we have not had the opportunity to apply these techniques to our Black Mesa data.

The Black Mesa Phase Sequence

The Black Mesa phase sequence, as we have described it elsewhere (Gumerman, Westfall, and Weed 1972:30–35; Euler 1973:77–81) and in this volume, in many ways reflects what happened in the entire Kayenta area tradition. This phase sequence has been developed through seven years of archaeological survey and excavation in the northeastern part of Black Mesa. Hundreds of ruins in and near the upper Moenkopi Wash drainage are located on lowland terraces and in piñon pine, juniper, and sage covered uplands at an elevation of about 6,500 feet.

The earliest manifestation is Lolomai, which is equivalent to Basketmaker II in the Pecos Classification (Fig. 52). The one excavated site on Black Mesa, investigated as recently as 1973–74, consists of several shallow pithouses or storage structures, outdoor cooking areas and a large slab cist. Basketmaker II projectile points, stone and shell beads, ground stone and carbonized corn were recovered. Preliminary radiocarbon results range from 65 B.C. to 630 B.C. Population was low throughout the entire Kayenta area, and sites appear to have been located to take advantage of agricultural land near streams and

major washes as well as good hunting and gathering locations. In the Dot Klish phase there was increasing sedentism and increasing population, probably due to a greater dependence on cultivated foods. Sites were situated on low knolls on the floodplains of the major washes, or else in heavily duned areas which were preferred for agriculture because of their water-holding characteristics (Hack 1942).

There does not seem to have been much change in the adaptive system from the Dot Klish to the Tallahogan phase, except for a tendency to occupy the first terrace along the major drainages, perhaps as a result of increasing population (Fig. 52) or drier conditions. Tallahogan sites are marked by upright sandstone slab cists and buried pithouses. Again, there is little change during the Dinnebito phase, except that occasional sites are found in the uplands. Large and small pithouses and crude surface masonry and jacal structures for both storage and living were constructed during this phase. These sites are commonly buried in present washes under layers of coarse sand and gravel.

The Wepo phase is truly transitional; its termination signals major changes in the entire cultural system. There was an increase in the use of the uplands for habitation, a large population increase, a transition from subsurface to surface masonry rooms, and the beginning of a more formalized village plan. These changes began to accelerate about A.D. 1000 and may have had multiple causes, one of which was almost certainly a climatic shift that permitted dry farming in the uplands.

The Lamoki phase was short-lived, and little is known about it except that change was still rampant and the trend to upland habitation continued. Sites consisted of single components with five or six masonry rooms and an associated pithouse or kiva. One fifty-three-room cliff dwelling also has been recorded. The culmination of northeastern Black Mesa cultural development was in the Toreva phase, with an increase in population which successfully adapted to dry farming in

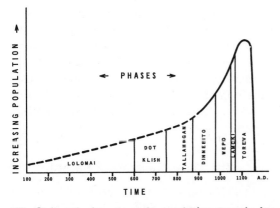

52. *Cultural phases and population trends for northeastern Black Mesa*

the uplands. The end of the phase was marked by an abandonment of the northeastern part of the mesa about A.D. 1150. Sites of this period commonly consisted of storerooms, jacal domiciles, and an associated masonry kiva.

The period from about A.D. 1000 to 1150 involved a rapid population increase; a movement to drier, previously sparsely occupied areas; an increase in farming and a corresponding decrease in the hunting of large game animals; and a distinctive uniformity in village pattern. The cause for the abandonment of northeastern Black Mesa was seemingly another change in the climatic regime that made dry farming impossible. Change during this period is reflected in prehistoric societies throughout most of the Colorado Plateau.

Little is known about the Klethla phase from A.D. 1150 to 1250, but it was apparently a period of great instability and the beginning of larger villages, only a few of which have been recorded in the marginal environment of northeastern Black Mesa. The Tsegi phase represents an agglomerating population into large cliff dwellings, such as those in the Tsegi Canyon area like Betatakin and Kiet Siel (Dean 1969). There are some Tsegi phase sites in the central part of Black Mesa in more favorable environmental locations; two are on or near Dead Juniper Wash. The greatest Tsegi-phase population, however, was in the Tsegi Canyon system and around nearby Navajo Mountain.

Earlier, Tsegi Canyon had been sparsely populated, owing to somewhat limited amounts of arable land. The presence of perennial water, however, made it a desirable habitat during the early part of the Tsegi phase. At about A.D. 1300 the Kayenta people were again forced to move, this time in part by headward extension of arroyos which depressed water supplies below their field systems. The movement was apparently to the south edge of Black Mesa, where the Hopi villages are today and where there are more dependable sources of water and available agricultural land.

GEOLOGIC DATA AND METHODS

Objectives and Methods

The ongoing geologic investigations of the Black Mesa Project are designed to place the surface and buried archaeologic sites in their geologic context, and to derive from the late Cenozoic depositional record a detailed C-14 dated chronology of the past hydrologic and inferred climatic changes in the region.

Our stratigraphic observations build on the pioneer work in northeastern Arizona by Hack (1942), and on extensive published and unpublished observations by Cooley (1958; 1962; written communication, 1973).

The stratigraphy of two main groups of sediments is locally being analyzed in detail: 1. the fluvial sequences exposed in the walls of deep arroyos cut in alluvial floors of the washes throughout the region; 2. the slope and upland deposits including extensive landslide complexes associated with the outer scarp of the Mesa.

Variations in the number and heights of terraces within and between washes, and rapid lateral variations in depositional units resulting from typical cut-and-fill structures pose problems in the reconstruction of a valid regional fluvial chronology. As a consequence, numerous sections in widely spaced areas must be analyzed and dated to distinguish depositional units of regional significance from those representing local facies changes. Sections have been selected for detailed study that record depositional units separated by nondepositional intervals marked by unconformities, soils, organic layers, or abrupt changes in lithology; and, in addition, contain organic materials and artifacts datable by C-14, dendrochronologic, or archaeologic means.

The Time-Stratigraphic Record

The alluvial sections presently dated in the region are concentrated in Dinnebito Wash (Dead Juniper Wash and Dinnebito Bridge

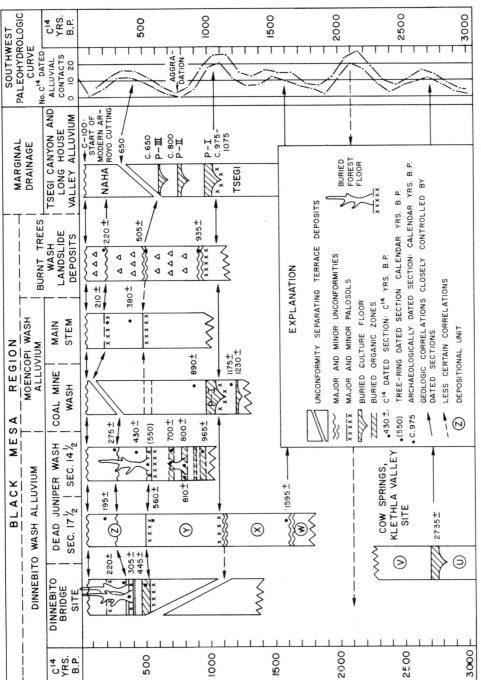

53. *Graphic summary of developing Black Mesa time-stratigraphy, relative to Tsegi Canyon deposits of Naha and Tsegi age, and to principal Southwest time-stratigraphic boundaries derived from time-frequency curve showing distinct groupings of C-14 dated alluvial contacts in the Southwest (unpublished compilation from radiocarbon volumes nos. 1–15). Left-hand curve: sum of C-14 dated events centered in overlapping 200-year intervals; right-hand curve: sum of events centered in 300-year intervals*

sites) and in the Moenkopi Wash system (Coal Mine Wash and Moenkopi Bridge sites) (Fig. 1). Landslide deposits have been dated from exposures of buried trees at the head of Burnt Trees Wash, south of Kayenta.

The developing time-stratigraphy is summarized in Figure 53. The dated nondepositional intervals in these three widely separate drainage areas strongly suggest essentially synchronous periods of aggradation (and accompanying landslide impulses) immediately following regional nondepositional or erosional intervals centered ca. 240 ± B.P. (ca. A.D. 1710); ca. 478 ± B.P. (ca. A.D. 1472); ca. 1,060 ± B.P. (ca. A.D. 890); and ca. 1,595 ± B.P. (ca. A.D. 350).

Three main depositional intervals (units X, Y, and Z), best defined in the Dead Juniper Wash area (Fig. 53), are suggested for the interval 1,600 B.P. to the present. The older units, U, V, and W, are at present only partly time-stratigraphically defined by our Black Mesa data. Based on regional data the unconformity between units W and V is provisionally placed ca. 2,200 B.P.

An important but subordinate nondepositional and erosional interval occurs ca. 240 ± year B.P. near the middle of unit Z. At least four minor interruptions in deposition are indicated by the forest litter zones in unit Y at section 14½, the first and third of which date 965 ± 80 years B.P. (I-7511) and 810 ± 80 years B.P. (I-7613). The uppermost forest litter zone in the same depositional unit from a nearby exposure dates 705 ± 80 years B.P. (I-6951), and overlies a stump exposed in the arroyo floor. A wood sample with 10–12 tree rings, estimated 50–60 years from the center of the decomposed core of this stump, dates 740 ± 80 years B.P. (I-6950). This result is consistent with stratigraphic position and suggests a germination date of ca. 800 years B.P. (740 ± 55 years) for the tree, and contemporaneity with the third forest layer directly dated ca. 810 ± years B.P. By stratigraphic interpolations in section 14½, the second from the bottom forest litter zone is placed ca. 890 B.P.

Assessment of Dating Accuracy

The question of the accuracy of C-14 results obtained from different materials collected in the region remains a notable and continuing concern in the project because of the importance of refined correlations between the archaeological and geological chronologies. Twenty-one of the twenty-four samples analyzed from the region by C-14 are consistent with stratigraphic placements and correlations as shown in Figure 53. The remaining three provide results that are seemingly anomalous. Two of these (I-6920: 3,685 ± 115 B.P. and I-6921: 34,300 ± 1,800 B.P.) seemingly date too old for their stratigraphic position. Since these results were the only ones obtained from fine-grained organic silt samples in sections generally rich in clastic coal, it is possible that they date spuriously old because of fine detrital coal contamination. The third sample (I-7520) collected from what appeared to be a deeply buried juniper tree near Kayenta dates modern. The reason for the anomalously young age, whether analytical or geological, remains obscure.

Two samples (I-6919: 1,175 ± and I-7543: 890 ± 80) were collected from separate sections in Coal Mine Wash and from horizons considered to closely bracket the buried Pueblo I site archaeologically dated between 1,075 and 975 years B.P. The C-14 results of these two samples conform to the assumed stratigraphic placements and the archaeologic age of the buried culture.

Results of tree-ring dating of nine buried trees in the Dead Juniper Wash (Fig. 54) also seemingly confirm the local C-14 dating of the contact between depositional units Y and Z at ca. 430 ± 80 years B.P. (I-7521). This date was obtained from outer wood collected from a tree trunk lying parallel to the contact. *In situ* trees buried in unit Z that are dated by tree rings record germination dates restricted to an interval between 500 and 600 B.P. (Jeffery S. Dean, oral communication, 1973) or just before burial of the forest floor by initial deposition of unit Z as C-14 dated

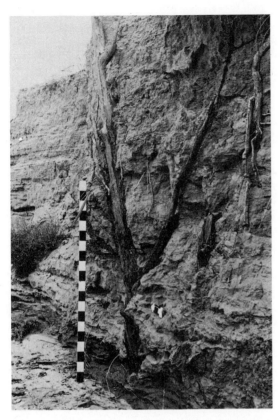

54. *Exposed buried juniper tree killed by alluviation*

by sample I-7521. Tree-ring analysis of the more deeply buried trees located along the arroyo axis suggests sudden death, presumably as a result of a major depositional episode ca. 300 years B.P. Less deeply buried trees along valley margins died more gradually; some survived progressive burial up to eighty years ago, a few have survived to the present (Jeffrey S. Dean, oral communication, 1973).

Samples of C-14 dated wood from forests buried by landslide deposits at the head of Burnt Trees Wash are pending tree-ring dating as a further check on the validity of the C-14 results.

The agreement of nearly all C-14 results with stratigraphic position, and with stratigraphically associated archaeologically and dendrochronologically dated materials, supports confidence in their general accuracy.

The agreement in age of the major Black Mesa alluvial contacts with the principal time-stratigraphic boundaries delineated by the regional time-frequency curve (Fig. *53*), indicates that the Black Mesa record may be generally representative of hydrologic and climatic history throughout the Southwest (Hevly and Karlstrom 1974).

RECONSTRUCTED PALEOHYDROLOGIC CURVE AND COLLATED DATA

Hydrologic and Pollen Curves

A qualitative hydrologic curve (Fig. *55*) may be derived from the Black Mesa time-stratigraphic data by considering the temporal positions of the major and minor nondepositional horizons, and by equating the intervening depositional (aggradational) intervals with increased hydrologic competence, higher water-table levels, and thus presumably more mesic climates. Numerous samples collected from dated sections in Dead Juniper Wash and in Coal Mine Wash are awaiting both mechanical and pollen analyses. Results of the mechanical analyses should provide for a more quantitatively detailed hydrologic reconstruction. A preliminary pollen profile from Dead Juniper Wash, section 14½ (Ward and Hevly, written communication, 1973) provides a sensitive record of vegetation changes as illustrated by the double-fixed sum piñon pine curve in Figure *55*. Both in broad trends and in some of the lesser fluctuations, the pollen curve parallels the hydrologic reconstruction, suggesting that piñon pine pollen production, relative to that of juniper, was favored during the inferred intervals of higher water table and more mesic climate.

Alluvial Data in Northern Arizona

The Black Mesa alluvial record of four main depositional epicycles during the past two thousand or so years is consistent with

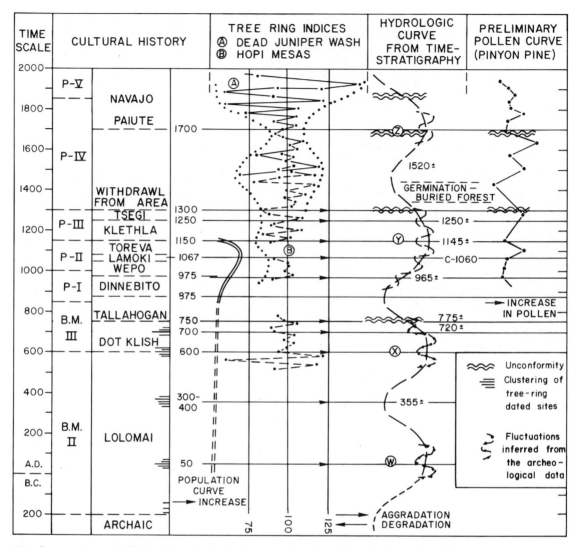

55. *Comparison of Black Mesa hydrologic record with cultural chronology (Gumerman, Westfall, and Weed 1972), tree-ring indicies (Dean, Robinson, and Lamarche, personal communication), and pollen curve (Ward and Hevly, personal communication)*

other detailed regional geoclimatic and bioclimatic records for this same time interval (Hevly and Karlstrom 1974). Other locally dated alluvial sequences in northern Arizona record contemporaneous aggradational impulses. The archaeologically dated terrace deposits of Naha age (<650 years B.P., Hack 1942) in Tsegi Canyon are in whole or in large part the time-stratigraphic equivalent of Black Mesa depositional unit Z. Deposits considered upper Tsegi in age in Tsegi Canyon

and in Long House Valley locally bury Pueblo I and include Pueblo II sites (Alexander J. Lindsay, Jr., and Jeffrey S. Dean, written communication, 1972–73), and are therefore the time-stratigraphic equivalent of Black Mesa unit Y (Fig. 53). The buried hearth horizons in alluvial fan sediments of designated Naha age in the Hopi Buttes are C-14 dates 1,040 ± year B.P. (Sutton 1974) and is thus contemporaneous with the buried P I horizon that separates Black Mesa units

X and Y. The erosional interval, archaeo-logically dated between ca. A.D. 200 and 400 in Cooley's (1962 alluvial sequence of part of the Colorado River system, is contempo-raneous with the Black Mesa W/X time-stratigraphic boundary. The last three of the major time-stratigraphic boundaries on Black Mesa are thus recorded locally in other parts of northern Arizona.

Data in Navajo Reservoir

The sophisticated cultural-alluvial-pollen reconstruction of the environmental history of the Navajo Reservoir District in nearby New Mexico (Schoenwetter and Eddy 1964; Eddy 1966; and Schoenwetter 1966) resembles our Black Mesa reconstruction in some re-spects and differs from it in others. Two al-luvial units are delineated, unit II from A.D. 1 to 800, and unit I from A.D. 1550 to 1700. The Laguna Seca soil at the top of unit II is dated A.D. 800–900 or contemporaneous with our X/Y time-stratigraphic boundary. How-ever, a significant gap in the Navajo Reservoir alluvial record of A.D. 1050–1550, and increas-ing uncertainties in the dating and subdivi-sions of the older deposits, complicate com-parisons with other parts of the Black Mesa record. The same discontinuities and dating uncertainties affect correlation with Schoen-wetter's pollen record. Nonetheless, the fol-lowing broad similarities between the Navajo District pollen-derived effective moisture rec-ord and the more continuous and closely dated Black Mesa alluvial sequence are sug-gested.

The Los Pinos (ca. A.D. 1–400) section of Schoenwetter's (1966) revised New Mexico record is the only part seemingly out-of-phase with our Black Mesa data in that it suggests high effective moisture between A.D. 300 and 400, or during the culmination of the W/X drought interval. However, it is not entirely clear whether this discrepancy represents real regional climatic differences or interval dat-ing by ceramics and C-14 and correlation problems. Other pollen data, dated to this

late Los Pinos time interval at sites La. 4289, 5843, and 4169 (Eddy 1966), suggest semi-arid or arid conditions contemporaneous with the X/Y drought culmination. The following interval of inferred generally high effective moisture (interrupted by separate returns to moisture conditions much like the present ca. A.D. 600, 700, and 750) and a final trend toward arid conditions traced out between early Sambrito and late Rosa phase (ca. A.D. 400–800) falls in the same time interval as Black Mesa depositional unit X. We have already noted the striking coincidence in time of the Laguna Seca soil as dated A.D. 800–900 with the Black Mesa X/Y time-stratigraphic boundary. Along with the pollen evidence for the ensuing Piedra and Arboles phases (ca A.D. 900–1050) interpreted as marking deep-ening and then lessening arid conditions, we note that this part of the record is from allu-vium postdating the Laguna soil. These re-lations suggest initial phases of aggradation following an interval of slope stability and soil formation. The interval of aggradation as dated is contemporaneous with the begin-ning of Black Mesa Y deposition.

In assessing regional history for the time interval represented by their information gap from A.D. 1050–1100 to 1550, Schoenwetter and Eddy mention pollen evidence from else-where in New Mexico (Leopold, Leopold, and Wendorf 1963) indicating an increased arboreal pollen peak between A.D. 1200 and 1400, or contemporaneous with the last half of Black Mesa depositional unit Y. The pre-ceding, pronounced short-term shift in ar-boreal pollen composition in Tesugue Valley, New Mexico, dated by Leopold and others between A.D. 1100 and 1200, coincides with the ca. A.D. 1150 secondary drought inferred from the Black Mesa hydrologic record.

Following the information gap, the higher, fluctuating effective moisture regime between A.D. 1550 and 1880, as tentatively inferred from the Navajo Reservoir pollen data, falls in the same time interval as deposition of Black Mesa unit Z.

Thus, the Navajo Reservoir pollen record,

as interpreted in terms of total effective moisture, seemingly traces out despite some gaps and dating uncertainties, many of the same general climatic trends as inferred from the Black Mesa data. On the other hand, the periods of summer-dominant precipitation versus winter-dominant precipitation proposed by Schoenwetter are more difficult to relate to the new Black Mesa alluvial and erosional evidence.

The basic assumption of Schoenwetter's seasonal variation hypothesis is that erosion accompanying high effective moisture conditions is a function of summer-dominant precipitation, whereas alluviation accompanying high effective moisture conditions is a function of winter-dominant precipitation. If this assumption is correct, and not an oversimplification of complex biologic-geologic-meteorologic interrelations, the new Black Mesa data indicate that summer-dominant precipitation regimes may have generally occurred between A.D. 50 and 350, A.D. 600 and 875, A.D. 1150 and 1450, and A.D. 1700 and present, and that winter-dominant precipitation may have generally occurred between 250 B.C. and A.D. 50, A.D. 350 and 600, A.D. 875 and 1150, and A.D. 450 and 1700. This tentative conclusion is based on a small but internally consistent sample of dated unconformities which suggests that arroyo-cutting episodes were favored during intervals of increasing drought and generally subsiding regional water-table levels.

Tree-Ring Data

In Figure 55 are plotted the dendroclimatic records, previously unpublished, obtained from the Dead Juniper Wash area (No. 113000 tree-ring, indices, Jeffrey S. Dean and Valmore C. Lamarache, Jr., written communication, 1973) and from the nearby Hopi Mesa area (No. 100199 tree-ring indices, Jeffrey S. Dean and William J. Robinson, written communication, 1973). For comparative purposes the tree-ring curves are smoothed by plotting means centered in nonoverlapping twenty-year intervals. The comparative data suggest some critical interrelations between local tree growth and changing ground moisture, or edaphic conditions.

There is a strong tendency for complacent, near-average growth rates during the aggradational intervals of inferred higher water-table levels, and for violent fluctuations between extremely low and extremely high growth rates during the degradational intervals of inferred lower water table levels. The resulting tree-ring curves show hourglass profiles with minimum cross-sections or necks coinciding with aggradational peaks (Fig. 55). These temporal coincidences indicate that the relatively complacent growth periods may have resulted from higher groundwater supplies tappable by root systems, whereas the violent fluctuations in growth rates may reflect cyclical variations in total and seasonal precipitation during periods when more constant groundwater supplies were generally below the root zones. The general profile traced out by the recurrent periods of minimal growth rates reproduces with some fidelity the broad general trends of the hydrological curve. Secondary drought and erosion intervals in the hydrologic curve generally coincide with periods of lower growth rates, or gaps, in the tree-ring indices; larger growth trends as well as accompanying larger climatic trends are removed from the record. (Fritts 1965) may provide an explanation of why some paleoclimatic reconstructions based on tree-ring analysis have missed the major geologically recorded drought intervals in the region.

CULTURAL-ENVIRONMENTAL RELATIONS

The primary and secondary hydrologic pulsations, as presently dated, correspond closely to cultural change on Black Mesa (Fig. 55). The major periods of aggradation are generally indicative of more mesic climate, and, where our data are most complete, record a series of secondary climatic fluctuations superimposed on the major trends. The archaeologically and tree-ring dated phase boundaries closely coincide with the C-14 dated secondary climatic oscillations toward more xeric, or drought, conditions. The major Toreva/ Klethla cultural boundary coincides with an important drought interval ca. A.D. 1150 at the apex of the major mesic epicycle, and marks the beginning of progressively worsening but fluctuating climatic conditions that culminated ca. 1450. The Klethla and Tsegi phases coincide with secondary mesic pulsations during this progressively worsening climatic trend. By A.D. 1300 climatic conditions had apparently deteriorated to the point that displaced Kayenta populations did not again return to the region.

Our archaeological data from early phases on Black Mesa are insufficient to indicate precise correlation between environmental change and cultural adaptation. The clustering of Basketmaker sites ca. A.D. 300–400 in adjacent Kayenta and Durango regions (Jeffrey S. Dean, oral communication, 1973) coincides with the nondepositional interval centered ca. A.D. 350 in the hydrologic curve, possibly indicating general abandonment of sites at this time because of major drought conditions or burial. Similar clusterings at A.D. 50 and A.D. 600 coincide with mesic epicycle peaks, comparable to that of the later important A.D. 1150 drought, and therefore may also reflect similar drought intervals, as provisionally plotted in Figure 55.

Black Mesa ruins of Tallahogan and Dinnebito phases are commonly located along the terraces and benches above the floodplains of primary drainage. The hydrologic curve suggests drought conditions during the eighth and ninth centuries A.D. Thus, closer locations of these sites to more assured sources of water appears logical.

By the beginning of the Wepo phase, when climatic conditions became more favorable for dry farming, the northern Black Mesa population began to increase, and moved into the uplands away from the major drainage systems. The population peaked during the Toreva phase at the crest of a mesic cycle about A.D. 1100. Then, as conditions became drier, the population dropped markedly and a general exodus from the mesa began.

In the Tsegi Canyon system, where the Kayenta lived until about A.D. 1300, or the end of the Tsegi phase, that date also marked the end of a mesic climatic period, with a subsequent unconformity that probably accounts for the headward cutting erosion that brought about the final Anasazi abandonment. Thus, the hydrologic curve seems to bear out our thesis that cultural adaptations, as delineated by our phases, were largely produced by environmental alterations.

Another more regionally based hypothesis may now be adopted. If the paleoclimatic reconstruction that we suggest for Black Mesa, and as supported by other regional data, is applicable to other parts of the Colorado Plateau, comparable climatic changes may have been in large part responsible for cultural dynamics throughout the region. The movement of people, in regions west and east of Black Mesa, especially about A.D. 1150, appears to have been a result of degradational sharp drought interval noted in our hydrologic curve at that time.

NOTE

This article has been authorized by the Director, U.S. Geological Survey.

7 Black Mesa: Retrospect and Prospect

GEORGE J. GUMERMAN and
ROBERT C. EULER

Rather than writing the usual conclusions summarizing the results of our surveys and excavations to date, we have chosen not only to synthesize our operations, but also to put into perspective eight years of archaeology and to prognosticate future work.

Introspection seems to be enjoying a vogue in archaeology (Binford 1972; Willey 1974) and for good reason. It is necessary, at certain intervals, to reexamine the underlying principles and goals of any major research project, and to modify those principles and goals according to the results of the ongoing research. This reexamination should not only be approached in a formal systematic way as we have done on Black Mesa, but should also include a more subjective, self-searching type of reanalysis. Thus competencies and weaknesses of various specialists can be assessed, real reasons for particular research strategies can be understood, and easier rectification of mistakes and honest appraisal of performance permitted. Willey (1974:ix) succinctly made the point when he stated that "While the measurements of a pyramid are immutable and the contents of a tomb remain the same, our perspective on these data and the interpretations that we derive from them are constantly being seen anew from the never-static present."

The first Black Mesa volume (Gumerman 1970:2–3) set forth a list of the questions we hoped to address as research objectives in the following years. These goals varied in scope from extremely limited (Are pithouses a common Pueblo II type of dwelling on Black Mesa?) to wide-ranging concerns (How do regional traditions evolve?). Most of the research questions were generated by asking scholars of the Anasazi tradition what questions they thought were important, and answerable, by work on Black Mesa.

Other research problems were gleaned from the published literature. While a considerable amount of survey and excavation had been done in surrounding regions, only one site had been previously excavated on northeastern Black Mesa, and that in 1936 (Beals, Brainard, and Smith 1945). Hence, many archaeologists (Brew 1946:302; Lindsay and Ambler 1963:91) felt the answer to their questions lay in the large, archaeologically unknown area of Black Mesa. Therefore, we did go to Black Mesa armed with questions and some largely poorly developed hypotheses.

Another major reason for our archaeological attack on Black Mesa was to train undergraduate students in field techniques and anthropological problem solving. Black Mesa, per se, was not the necessary locality for our archaeological field school, but offered the best possibility because money was available for excavations. That has been, in reality, the ultimate reason for the Black Mesa Project.

162

Funds were made available because of the strip-mining of coal that Peabody Coal Company was to be doing on the Mesa.

Thus, the Black Mesa Project was to be a salvage archaeological project, or in the idiom of the day "contract archaeology." But unlike most salvage projects, we did have some long-range goals, albeit poorly formulated and without well articulated hypotheses and test implications. Nevertheless, these were developed in time.

The first season of large-scale excavation (Gumerman 1970) was largely devoted to comprehending the kinds of archaeology with which we would be dealing, with the training of students, and above all with the logistical problems of setting up a long-range research project. The 1968 season would undoubtedly have been classified by new archaeologists as inductively oriented. In following years, however, this emphasis would change so that publications emanating from the Project are represented by the mix in this volume: straight descriptive site and survey reports, and highly imaginative and undoubtedly somewhat idealized theoretical articles.

The fact that the Black Mesa Project is a salvage program has, of course, profoundly influenced the direction of the progam. Most obviously we could not have mounted such a well-funded, long-range program without the financial assistance of a corporation required to abide by federal and tribal antiquities acts. Even the National Science Foundation does not generate the funding capability in archaeology that is now necessary to have long range interdisciplinary research goals. The funding aspect is, of course, a plus for the project. Absolute freedom of action obviously cannot be guaranteed, however. It is necessary to excavate where the coal will be mined and before it is mined. As a result, our survey and excavation sample is biased and we cannot always excavate the sites in the order that is most desirable.

The bias due to the salvage nature of the project is, however, not as restricting as it may seem. Since the coal company is mining

a large area rather than a single narrow right-of-way, it is possible to survey and excavate in large natural areas. The coal slurry line, power lines, and conveyor belt route, however, give a great lateral extent to the project so that we have had the advantage of understanding distributional characteristics of the archaeological record, as well as restricted areal knowledge. In addition, the mining areas cover all major environmental subzones on northeastern Black Mesa, except the Ponderosa Pine region at the extreme northeast edge of the Mesa. As a result, we feel that the surveyed areas reflect the actual situation and have not greatly biased the sample.

In addition, our philosophy is that not only can salvage archaeology be oriented to the solving of broad problems that are the archaeologists concern—that is, the understanding of extinct cultural systems—but that it must be if archaeologists and funds are to be utilized to their fullest advantage (Gumerman 1973).

In spite of what we feel are some significant contributions made by the project, there are some disappointing results, some goals of the research design that have not been accomplished, and some glaring errors. While some of these will be discussed in the culture-history section of this chapter, some may be commented upon here.

A major weakness is the inadequacy of the first two years of survey in 1967 and 1968. We feel confident that most visible sites were recorded, but the data recorded, the collections made, and their locations on maps were all in great need of improvement. The survey mistakes were largely due to inadequately prepared survey crews. Not enough time was spent instructing the students in survey techniques. Further, our concerns with types of relevant data to be collected were not as sophisticated as they should have been.

A great disappointment has been our inability, in spite of great effort, to achieve a base-line study of the present environment on Black Mesa. We have excellent studies of the faunal materials from excavation (Douglas

1972), but it is necessary to have a detailed biological study of the current condition of northeastern Black Mesa and vicinity if we are to understand the past environmental situation. We are presently still attempting to accomplish these studies.

One advantage of the Black Mesa archaeological record is that the sites are small, usually consisting of a single phase, and were not occupied for long periods. As a result, it is relatively safe to assume that observable differences in artifacts at a site are due to factors other than temporal. Unfortunately, except for ceramics, artifacts are exceedingly scarce; even the ubiquitous mano and metate are rare. Therefore it is difficult to devise tests for hypotheses that involve the concept of tool kits or functionally specific areas of sites. Sherds and architecture have to provide the major resources for hypothesis testing.

Well-preserved burials are also rare and, therefore, many questions we have concerning mortality rate or paleopathologies cannot be answered. It is doubtful if we will ever recover a large enough population to make significant statements about human biological characteristics on Black Mesa.

Finally, it would be advantageous to be able to compare the Black Mesa archaeological manifestations with those in the immediate vicinity. Although, there has been considerable work immediately north on Black Mesa, which would be valuable to compare with the Black Mesa data, none of this has yet been published. This necessitates that we view the Black Mesa Anasazi operating as a relatively closed system, especially since we have little evidence of Black Mesa interaction with other areas.

BLACK MESA CULTURE HISTORY

A major task of the project has, of course, been devoted to understanding the regional Black Mesa sequence. Before detailing a phase-by-phase summary a few prefatory comments are in order. Originally, in 1968, we used the Pecos Classification as a means of

assigning cultural-temporal labels to the various constellations of traits. After the first year, however, because of what we perceived as variations from the Pecos Classification, we defined a provisional regional phase sequence (Gumerman, Westfall, and Weed 1972:28). This was largely based on the ceramic sequence which is essentially that of the Kayenta tradition of the Anasazi. Rather than use the already established Kayenta phase sequence (Colton 1939), however, we devised a new system, because of what we perceived in the archaeological record as significant differences from established Kayenta traits and because we recognized a need for a greater number of phases.

In retrospect, the establishment of the new phase system has been justified because as excavations continue we see greater and greater discrepancies between the originally defined Kayenta Anasazi and what we have informally called the *Black Mesa Anasazi*. The differences between the more traditional Kayenta and the Black Mesa Anasazi appear to be due to a more impoverished environment on Black Mesa and also to a greater degree of isolationism.

Since the Black Mesa phase sequence was first devised, a number of modifications seem in order. A new phase, the Lolomai, roughly equivalent with the Basketmaker II stage in the Pecos Classification, has tentatively been identified (Karlstrom, Gumerman, and Euler, this volume).

For a fuller description of each phase than that which follows see Gumerman, Westfall, and Weed (1972:189–98).

The Lolomai Phase

In the summer of 1973 we recognized the existence of a Basketmaker II occupation on Black Mesa proper. This we have tentatively called the Lolomai Phase. Excavations at the one site of this phase (Ariz. D:7:152) over two field seasons suggest the following diagnostics: large open pit structures, probably for storage, dug into decomposing bedrock and partially slab-lined; large slab-based circular cists, smaller circular and ovoid cooking pits with fire-cracked rock-filled alcoves; extramural slab- and clay-lined hearths; corn; primarily small animal bones such as rabbit; coiled basketry fragments; fragmentary ground stone mano and metates; and chipped dart "points" and knives of silicious materials similar to those recovered from White Dog Cave in Marsh Pass about 15 miles north (Guernsey and Kidder 1921:87 and Plate 35); and shell and stone beads. Preliminary radiocarbon results obtained from burned logs in one structure, range from 630 B.C. to 65 B.C. The site is at an elevation of about 6,700 feet on a piñon- and juniper-covered rocky hillside overlooking Coal Mine Wash.

It must be emphasized that as this is being written the site is still being excavated, analysis of the artifactual and nonartifactual remains is incomplete, no tree-ring dates have been attainable, and more radiocarbon samples are in the process of being submitted.

Yet, while similarities with the previously described White Dog Cave Basketmaker II period, especially in the chipped stone artifacts and basketry fragments are apparent, the characteristics of the open structures suggest to us the provisional description of a new phase for Black Mesa.

Dot Klish Phase

The first Dot Klish phase villages to be reported were excavated along the coal slurry line (Ward, this volume). No Dot Klish phase sites have been excavated in the coal strip-mine areas, which demonstrates the environments which Dot Klish people exploited. Although only a few Dot Klish phase villages have been recorded and only three excavated, a number of generalizations can be made from this small sample. Dot Klish phase sites, equivalent in the Pecos Classification to Basketmaker III, are usually situated on low knolls, or the lowest terraces along the major drainages. In addition, they have been noted in heavy sand dune areas

and along major washes immediately north of the Mesa. All these environments are the most favored areas for agriculture. The number of recorded Dot Klish phase sites may not reflect the true situation, since alluviation has buried many of them (Ward, this volume; Karlstrom, Gumerman, and Euler, this volume). Most sites of this phase were discovered by construction activity which exposed burial cultural materials, or by eroding alluvial terraces. Consequently there might be a greater population for the Dot Klish phase than survey data suggests.

A summary of the Dot Klish phase follows.

"The sites of this time period are not large, but few villages on the northern part of the Mesa are. Although the number of sites in this phase is very low, the size of individual sites does not vary much from phase to phase suggesting that the primary social unit did not change much during the length of occupation of Black Mesa. The primary social unit was most likely the extended family or several extended families which occupied a single site.

"On the basis of such a small sample, it is dangerous to generalize about the village orientation and architectural patterns, especially since no pattern is apparent. There seems to be no particular orientation of the dwellings which are usually shallow oval pithouses or small jacal structures. Storage rooms are mostly slab or even masonry lined and semi-subterranean. In no instance was there a linear village orientation of contiguous storage cists, pithouses, and trash deposit as has been suggested as the classic 'type site' for Basketmaker III.

"Dot Klish phase artifacts are not greatly different or represented in impressively different percentages than other phases with the exception of mano types. One-hand manos represent over 50 percent of the hand grinding implements. Pottery types representative of the Dot Klish phase are Lino Black-on-gray, Lino Fugitive Red, and Lino Gray. Two Lino Black-on-gray sherds with a yellow cast were recovered, indicative of the probable use of coal for firing vessels. Coal found in a hearth of Ariz. D:9:2 also establishes the use of coal for household fuel at this early date. No burials have been found in this phase so nothing can as yet be discussed about interment patterns.

"Evidence of the subsistence base is both direct and indirect. A handful of charred corn was recovered from the excavations as well as the bones of animals which are also represented in the later phases. From the settlement pattern we can assume that two types of agriculture were practiced. The selection of sites on the lowest terraces and knolls in the major drainages suggests that floodwater farming was practiced in these situations. The location of sites in sand dune areas indicates dry-farming techniques in moisture-holding dunes similar to that described by Hack (1942b) for the Hopis. Dry-farming in upland, unduned areas apparently was not practiced.

"From a study of human fecal material on the floor of a pithouse at Ariz. D:9:2 (Ward, in press), it is apparent that at least one Dot Klish phase individual suffered from a massive infestation of spiny-headed worms (*Acanthocephalans*) (John Ubelaker, personal communication). The infestation was sufficiently severe that the individual may have suffered from internal bleeding eventually causing death. Since spiny-headed worms are extremely infectious, their presence may have been a severe problem to the Dot Klish phase people" (Gumerman, Westfall, and Weed 1972:190–91).

Tallahogan Phase

The sample of Tallahogan phase sites, equivalent to the Basketmaker III-Pueblo I "transition" period is small, consisting of one excavated and five surveyed sites. The number may, however, like the Dot Klish phase sites, be deceptively small because of alluviation. The single excavated site, Ariz. D:11:113, was deeply buried on the first terrace of

MoenKopi Wash and was exposed by a water pipe trench.

There appears to be a slight locational shift of sites in the Tallahogan phase. Sites are now located above the floodplain on the first terrace. This may indicate an increased population which had to utilize the lower, former habitation areas for agriculture. Perhaps because of the smallness of the sample no village orientation is apparent except at a single site, Ariz. D:11:10. This site, which was previously thought to be a Dinnebito phase site, is located on a high terrace above MoenKopi Wash and has contiguous, slab storage cists projecting above the surface. In front of these cists are several depressions suggesting pithouses. Trash appears deeply scattered over most of the site.

The single excavated pithouse at Ariz. D:11:113 bears a close resemblance to several pithouses excavated off the southern edge of Black Mesa at Jeddito 264 (Daifuko 1961). The most obvious similarity is the double opening ventilator shaft at floor level.

Little more can be said about the Tallahogan phase than was reported earlier (Gumerman, Westfall, and Weed 1972:191–92), since no additional sites have been recorded.

Dinnebito Phase

There are fourteen recorded Dinnebito phase sites, one of which has been excavated. At this writing one more is being excavated. The Dinnebito phase is equivalent to Pueblo I in the Pecos Classification. There is again a shift in settlement patterns from the previous phases. Most living locations are still along the primary streams, but there is a tendency for more sites to be situated in the uplands, possibly because of population pressure.

The one excavated Dinnebito phase site, Ariz. D:11:57, appeared unusually small compared to other surveyed Dinnebito phase sites. Three recently recorded sites of this phase seem to show a pattern of a single large depression with rubble from masonry on one side, or on two sides forming an L-shaped unit. Some tendency toward a formal community layout seems to exist at this period and probably tends toward later Wepo phase forms. The Dinnebito phase dates approximately from A.D. 875 to A.D. 975.

Wepo Phase

The Wepo phase sites number twelve surveyed and two excavated sites, dating from about A.D. 1000 to 1050. The phase was formerly called the Pueblo I-Pueblo II transition period.

The tendency to settle in the uplands increases during this time. The following quotation (Gumerman, Westfall, and Weed 1972: 193–94) summarizes the settlement pattern, community layout, and architecture.

"The Wepo phase, formerly called the Pueblo I-Pueblo II transition period, is represented by nine surveyed and two excavated sites.

"The Wepo phase settlement pattern evidences a shift away from the confines of the Moenkopi and its major tributaries and there is a trend towards the settlement of the upland region. In addition, there is a tendency during this phase toward the clustering of sites in certain locations which increases during the later periods. . . . Settlements are much better represented in the various sub-environments of the northern part of the Black Mesa than they were in earlier phases, but at the same time they tend to cluster within these sub-environments.

"The village plan begins to stabilize during the Wepo phase, taking on some of the characteristics of later phases, and yet some of the sites show an incredible amount of casualness in their orientation. For example, Ariz. D:7:11, located on the north bench of Black Mesa, shows a certain degree of orientation. The surface dwellings are to the north, a kiva is situated in front to the south and to the southeast and down slope is the trash deposit. A pithouse and storage room are also to the

southwest. Ariz. D:11:18, on the other hand, is located in the uplands on the Mesa proper and appears to have no orientation. The three kivas, numerous storage rooms and dwellings, both pithouses and jacal units, appear scattered throughout the site with the only orientation being that the three kivas' recesses are to the northeast.

"In the Wepo phase, there is a slight suggestion of seasonality of site occupation. At Ariz. D:7:11, Pithouse 1 was re-utilized as a cooking area but apparently not until after the site had been abandoned for perhaps a season or two as evidenced by the culturally sterile layers on the floor and below the hearths built in the fill of the structure. Of course, the site may have been abandoned for a short time for other reasons than because of the seasonality of economic pursuits.

"The architectural form of the individual structures is amazingly varied. The Wepo phase appears to be the period when there was considerable shifting from subsurface to surface dwellings and consequently, experimentation with architectural form. Dwellings at both Ariz. D:7:11 and Ariz. D:11:18 have combinations of jacal and masonry construction. Both have pithouses and surface dwellings but the pithouse at Ariz. D:7:11 is more or less Anasazi in form while the structures at Ariz. D:11:18 immediately strike one as much more Mogollon or Hohokam-like (Bullard 1962) than they do Anasazi. They are usually shallow, rectangular with rounded corners and often have a ramp entry. One unit at Ariz. D:11:18 is a deep pit structure with masonry walls built above the old occupation surface, thereby combining subsurface with surface construction. It is in the Wepo phase that large contiguous jacal structures become common. The jacal unit at Ariz. D:11:18 is unusual in that it is circular, shows evidence of much remodeling and seems to have both storage and dwelling facilities.

"The first kivas excavated on the Mesa appear in the Wepo phase complete with all the features that characterize them in later phases. They are circular, sometimes masonry lined, have a wide variety of form in bench or recess style, and many have a foot drum behind the hearth. Also in this phase as in later ones, there is a high ratio of kivas to dwellings."

The great variation in community layout, the tremendous range in architectural form, and these deviations from many Kayenta Anasazi sites especially obvious in the Wepo phase encourages us to think of the archaeological manifestations as Black Mesa Anasazi. We do not propose a separate branch, but instead prefer to think of the Black Mesa record as a regional variation, hence the phase sequence was developed.

There are no artifacts which are distinctive of the Wepo phase, with the exception of two coal "buttons" but their occurrence in this phase is probably fortuitous. Certain classes of artifacts, however, are highly represented in the Wepo phase. Bone awls and worked sherds from two Wepo phase sites are greater in number than from excavated sites of all other phases combined. No explanation for this "over-representation" exists. The ceramic types indicative of the Wepo phase are Wepo Black-on-white and various types of neck molded plain jars.

The Wepo phase appears to be a major turning point in the culture history of Black Mesa. The trend is to increased population, a shift from usually subsurface to surface dwellings, the formalization of kiva features, and an increasing utilization for habitation of the upland areas.

Lamoki Phase

Although twenty-one Lamoki phase sites have been recorded, none have been excavated. As a result, there is little that can be said about this phase, except that which can be deduced from surface evidence.

The tendency for sites to be situated away from the major washes increases during this period. More sites are located along secondary washes and in the uplands. Surface indications suggest that the most common village layout is similar to the following Toreva phase. The common pattern is a masonry room block with a kiva depression in front and a refuse deposit beyond the kiva. If the pattern is similar to the Toreva sites, there are presumably jacal structures extending at right angles from the ends of the masonry room block.

Since the Lamoki phase is short, possibly fifty years, and no Lamoki phase sites have been excavated, a major question concerns the cultural validity of the Lamoki phase. The phase was largely defined as the result of research in other Kayenta areas, and on Black Mesa is identified from the ceramic type Black Mesa Black-on-white. Perhaps future excavations will demonstrate that the Lamoki phase is not valid in a cultural sense and that the phase should be deleted or perhaps incorporated into the early portion of the Toreva phase. Because the Lamoki phase is at a critical period when population is starting to greatly expand, it is profitable to continue to delineate the phase rather than eliminate it, since the narrow temporal span of the phase might provide the basis for a close examination of change over a short period.

Two large Lamoki phase cliff dwellings near the northeastern rim of Black Mesa have been recorded. One hypothesis that may be presented here is that short term climatic conditions at this time may have caused the Black Mesa people to move into these higher areas near springs, thus beginning a socially oriented pattern that flourished in the later Tsegi phase to the north. This, however, remains to be tested.

Toreva Phase

The Toreva phase has by far the largest number of sites, one hundred and four surveyed and twelve excavated. It includes the period of greatest population and also the termination of the phase, at about A.D. 1150, which signals the abandonment of northeastern Black Mesa. Unfortunately the chronological controls are not sufficiently fine to isolate the phase into the period when adoption to the environment appeared to be excellent, from that period when stress is apparent, to the time of final abandonment. Perhaps as the chronological control becomes refined the Lamoki phase can be extended into the early part of what is seen as the period of increasing population in the Toreva phase.

There is an increased utilization of the uplands during this period from A.D. 1050 to 1150 paralleling the situation for much of the Anasazi area. That there was an increased emphasis on dry farming is indicated by the clustering of sites around the edge of sage covered flats and basins in the uplands.

During the Toreva phase the distinction between primary and secondary sites can be made, although the dichotomy may have existed earlier. Phillips (1972) has suggested that the primary site, or mother village, was relatively autonomous, consisting of habitation, storage, corn mealing rooms and a kiva. The secondary, or daughter site, Phillips contends, is smaller and does not have a kiva. The secondary site may be a response to increasing utilization of the uplands and an increasing population necessitating the budding off of population to secondary sites which returned to the primary site for religious activity at certain times of the year. Clemmen (this volume) suggests that the primary site was occupied by two social units who occupied the separate jacal habitation units and who shared the mealing room, kiva and perhaps the storage rooms.

The distinct clusters of primary sites with secondary sites that Phillips perceived probably do not exist but are more likely an artifact of the necessity to survey coal strip areas. This, however, does not invalidate the concept of primary and secondary sites and their implication. The secondary site still appears to be a result of increasing population and a greater reliance on dry farming in the uplands.

An alternate hypothesis for the primary-secondary site dichotomy is that the secondary sites are not contemporaneous with the primary sites, but represent a breakdown in social organization in a stress period toward the end of the Toreva phase. In order to test this hypothesis finer chronological control would be necessary. With the data at hand Phillips's hypothesis seems the most likely.

Not only is there a change in the settlement pattern and an increasing reliance on dry farming, but there are also other indications of a shift in the subsistence base from pre-Toreva phase to the Toreva phase. Douglas (1972:230–31) has demonstrated that while the ratio of carnivores, lagomorphs, and rodents remains relatively constant throughout the phase sequence, the number of artiodactyl bones drops significantly in the Toreva phase. The virtual lack of deer and antelope long bones in the Toreva phase is so marked that it can almost be used as a dating technique during excavation. Ariz. D:7:98, excavated in 1972, is a double component site in which it was possible in some instances to separate the Toreva phase component from the Wepo phase by the varying numbers of artiodactyl bones. In addition, deep slab-lined roasting pits exist only in pre-Toreva phase sites suggesting different cooking techniques, or perhaps the cooking of different types of food.

That the decrease of deer and antelope bones coincides with certain changes in hearth configuration and also with a decrease in chipped stone artifacts and debitage suggests that in the Toreva phase there was an increasing reliance on agriculture. The decrease in artiodactyls may be due to some depopulation of the species from the human population increase in earlier phases, a destruction of their habitat by upland farming, and to the greater human reliance on domesticated plant foods.

Abandonment

The abandonment of northeastern Black Mesa at the end of the Toreva phase ca. A.D.

1150 has been "explained" in two different ways in this volume. Swedlund and Sessions suggest that the cause of abandonment might be overpopulation and Karlstrom, Gumerman, and Euler offer an environmental explanation. Both explanations accounting for abandonment have an internal, logical consistency, and yet superficially, they are incompatible in that they posit different causes for abandonment.

The two hypotheses are not, however, incompatible. It is likely that a shift in the climatic regions along with an increased population made the habitation of northeastern Black Mesa unfeasible. In the last several years, a number of post-Toreva phase sites (Klethla and Tsegi phases in the Kayenta Anasazi phase system) have been recorded in the interior of the Mesa. These sites, both cliff dwellings such as Hawk House, and open sites like Fat House, are usually situated where more water is available. At least two seeps are located near Hawk House and a flowing spring is near Fat House. In addition, it is apparent that there is today a greater abundance of grasses and trees toward the southern end of the Mesa. This situation is apparently due to the basinlike character of the Mesa and the surfacing of local aquifers toward the central and southern portions of the Mesa (Thor Karlstrom, personal communication).

It appears then that the abandonment of northeastern Black Mesa was due to a worsening climate and overpopulation, and that at least some of the Black Mesa Anasazi re-treated to the interior of Black Mesa where more water was available.

We have often used the term "abandonment" in the preceding paragraphs without amplification. Southwestern archaeologists often use the term "abandonment" in a general sense, but there are a number of types of abandonment which can be distinguished in the archaeological record, and these types may reflect the reason for the movement of the people.

In the Kayenta Anasazi country to the north of Black Mesa often when sites were abandoned, artifacts that were difficult to transport, such as metates, were purposely destroyed, the people realizing that they were not returning (Jeffry Dean; Alexander Lindsay, personal communication). In other places, such as the large pueblo of Grasshopper in the White Mountains, large numbers of artifacts were left when the site was abandoned. Often food remains in jars and tools are left on floors (William Longacre, personal communication). On Black Mesa at the end of the Toreva phase almost all artifacts were taken by the people. Even manos and metates were taken. Of over one hundred mealing bins that have been excavated, not one had a metate still in place. The artifact yield of a Toreva phase site is far less than earlier phase sites. It might be hypothesized that the people of Black Mesa, unlike the other two examples, left in an orderly fashion, knowing where they were going and moving only a short distance away, to the interior of the Mesa or off the north edge.

Bibliography

Index

Bibliography

Allen, William L. and James B. Richardson III
1971 The reconstruction of kinship from archaeological data: the concepts, the methods, and the feasibility. *American Antiquity* 36, no. 1, January.

Amsden, Charles Avery
1949 *Prehistoric Southwesterners from Basketmaker to Pueblo*. Los Angeles: Southwest Museum.

Bartlett, Kathrine
1935 "Prehistoric mining in the Southwest." *Museum of Northern Arizona*, Notes, vol. 7, no. 1, pp. 41–44. Flagstaff.

Beals, R. L., G. W. Brainard, and W. Smith
1945 *Archaeological studies in northeastern Arizona*. University of California Publications in American Archaeology and Ethnology, vol. 44, no. 1.

Bennett, Kenneth
1972 *The Indians of Point of Pines, Arizona*. Anthropological Papers of the University of Arizona, no. 18. Tucson.

Binford, Lewis R.
1962 Archaeology as anthropology. *American Antiquity* 28, no. 2, pp. 217–25.
1965 Archaeological systematics and the study of culture process. *American Antiquity* 31:203–10.
1968 Archaeological perspectives. In *New perspectives in Archaeology*, edited by Lewis R. and Sally R. Binford, pp. 5–32. Chicago: Aldine Press.
1972 *An archaeological perspective*. Chicago: Seminar Press.

Binford, Lewis R., and Sally R. Binford, eds.
1968 *New perspectives in archaeology*. Chicago: Aldine Press.

Bliss, Wesley L.
1960 Impact of pipeline archaeology on Indian prehistory. *Plateau* 33, no. 1, pp. 10–13.

Bogue, Donald
1969 *Principles of demography*. New York: John Wiley & Sons.

Breternitz, David A.
1962 Excavations at the New Leba 17 site, near Cameron, Arizona. *Plateau* 35, no. 2, pp. 60–68.
1966 *An appraisal of tree-ring dated pottery in the Southwest*. Anthropological Papers of the University of Arizona, no. 10. Tucson.
1967 The eruption (s) of Sunset Crater: dating and effects. *Plateau* 40, no. 2, pp. 72–76.

Brew, J. O.
1946 *Archaeology of Alkali Ridge, southeastern Utah*. Papers of the Peabody Museum of American Archaeology and Ethnology, vol. 21. Cambridge: Harvard University.

Brew, J. O., and J. T. Hack
1939 The prehistoric use of coal by Indians of northern Arizona. *Plateau* 12, no. 1.

Bullard, W. R. Jr.
1962 *The cerro Colorado site and pithouse architecture in the southwestern United States prior to* A.D. *900*. Papers of the Peabody Museum of American Archaeology and Ethnology, vol. 64, no. 2. Cambridge: Harvard University.

Carlson, R. L.
1963 *Basketmaker III sites near Durango, Colorado*. University of Colorado Studies, Series in Anthropology, no. 8. Boulder.

Christaller, W.
1933 *Die Zentralen Orte in Suddeutschland: Eine ökonomisch-geographische. Untersuchung über die Gestzmässigkeit der Verbeitung und Entwicklund der Siedlungen mit städtischen Functionen*. Jena.

Cockrum, E. L.
1960 *The recent mammals of Arizona: their taxonomy and distribution*. Tucson: University of Arizona Press.

Colton, Harold S.

1936a "Hopi coal mines." *Museum of Northern Arizona*, Notes. vol. 8, no. 12, pp. 59–61. Flagstaff.

1936b The rise and fall of the prehistoric population of northern Arizona. *Science* 84: 337–43.

1938 Names of four culture roots in the Southwest. *Science* 87, no. 2268, pp. 551–52.

1939 *Prehistoric culture units and their relationships in northern Arizona.* Museum of Northern Arizona, Bulletin no. 17. Flagstaff.

1945a The Patayan problem in the Colorado River valley. *Southwestern Journal of Anthropology* 1, no. 1.

1945b Sunset Crater. *Plateau* 18, no. 1, pp. 7–14.

1946 *The Sinagua: a summary of the archaeology of the region of Flagstaff, Arizona.* Museum of Northern Arizona, Bulletin no. 22. Flagstaff.

1949 The prehistoric population of the Flagstaff area. *Plateau* 22:21–25.

1955 Wares 8A, 8B, 9A, 9B. In *Pottery types of the Southwest,* edited by Harold S. Colton. Museum of Northern Arizona, Ceramic Series, no. 3A. Flagstaff.

1956 Wares 5A, 5B, 6A, 6B, 7A, 7B, 7C. In *Pottery Types of the Southwest,* edited by Harold S. Colton. Museum of Northern Arizona, Ceramic Series, no. 3C. Flagstaff.

1958 San Francisco Mt. Gray Ware. In *Pottery Types of the Southwest,* edited by Harold S. Colton. Museum of Northern Arizona, Ceramic Series, no. 3D. Flagstaff.

1960 *Black sand: prehistory in northern Arizona.* Albuquerque: University of New Mexico Press.

Colton, H. S., and L. L. Hargrave

1937 *Handbook of northern Arizona pottery wares.* Museum of Northern Arizona, Bulletin no. 11. Flagstaff.

Cook, Sherburne

1972 Prehistoric demography. *Addison-Wesley Modular Publications* 16. Reading, Mass.

Cook, Sherburne, and W. Borah

1971 *Essays in population history: Mexico and the Caribbean.* Vol. 1. Berkeley: University of California Press.

Cooley, M. E.

1958 Physiography of the Black Mesa Basin Area, Arizona. In *Guidebook of the Black Mesa Basin, northeastern Arizona.* New Mexico Geological Society Ninth Field Conference, 1958, pp. 146–49.

1962 Late Pleistocene and recent erosion and alluviation in parts of the Colorado River system, Arizona and Utah. In *Short Papers in the Geologic and Hydrologic Sciences.* U.S. Geological Survey Professional Paper 450-B, pp. 48–50.

Cutler, H. C.

1966 *Corn, cucurbits, and cotton from Glen Canyon.* University of Utah Anthropological Papers, vol. 80, pp. 1–62. Salt Lake City.

1969 *Plant remains from sites near Navajo Mountain.* Museum of Northern Arizona, Bulletin no. 45, pp. 371–78. Flagstaff.

Cutler, H. C., and Winton Meyer

1965 Corn and cucurbits from Wetherill Mesa. *American Antiquity* 31:136–52.

Daifuku, Hiroshi

1961 *Jeddito 264: Reports of the Awotovi expedition, Report no. 7.* Papers of the Peabody Museum of American Archaeology and Ethnology, vol. 33, no. 1. Cambridge: Harvard University.

Dean, Jeffrey S.

1969 *Chronological analysis of Tsegi phase sites in northeastern Arizona.* Laboratory of tree-ring Research. Tucson: University of Arizona Press.

1970 Aspects of Tsegi phase social organization. In *Reconstructing prehistoric Pueblo societies,* edited by Wm. A. Longacre, pp. 140–74. Albuquerque: University of New Mexico Press.

Deetz, James D. F.

1960 An archaeological approach to kinship in eighteenth century Arikara culture. Ph.D. dissertation, Harvard University.

1965 *The dynamics of stylistic change in Arikara ceramics.* Illinois Studies in Anthropology, no. 4. Urbana.

Dellenbaugh, F. S.

1932 The painted desert. *Science* 76, no. 437.

Dittert, A. E., Jr.

1968 Some factors affecting southwestern populations during the period A.D. 900–1540.

In *Contributions to southwestern prehistory* 4, edited by Cynthia Irwin-Williams. *Proceedings VII Congress International Association for Quaternary Research, Eastern New Mexico University.* Contributions in Anthropology, vol. 1, no. 1.

Dobyns, H. F.
1956 Prehistoric Indian occupation within the eastern area of the Yuma complex. Master's thesis, University of Arizona.

Douglas, Charles
1972 Analysis of faunal remains from Black Mesa: 1968–1970 excavations. In *archaeological investigations on Black Mesa: the 1969–1970 seasons,* George J. Gumerman, Deborah Westfall, and Carol Weed. Prescott, Ariz.: Prescott College Press.

Dozier, Edward P.
1970 *The Pueblo Indians of North America.* New York: Holt, Rinehart, and Winston.

Eddy, Frank W.
1961 *Excavations at Los Pinos phase sites in the Navajo Reservoir District.* Museum of New Mexico Papers in Anthropology, no. 4. Santa Fe.

1966 *Prehistory in the Navajo Reservoir District, northwestern New Mexico.* Museum of New Mexico Papers in Anthropology, no. 15. Santa Fe.

Eggan, Fred
1950 *Social organization of the western pueblos.* Chicago: University of Chicago Press.

Elmore, Francis H.
1944 *Ethnobotany of the Navajo.* University of New Mexico Bulletin with the School of American Research. Monograph Series, vol. 1, no. 7. Albuquerque.

Ember, Melvin
1973 An archaeological indicator of matrilocal versus patrilocal residence. *American Antiquity* 38, no. 2, pp. 177–82.

Euler, Robert C.
1958 Walapai culture-history. Ph.D. dissertation, University of New Mexico.

1963 Archaeological problems in western and northwestern Arizona, 1962. *Plateau* 35, no. 3, pp. 78–85.

1973a Attributes of prehistoric Pueblo settlement patterns on Black Mesa, Arizona. *Pro-ceedings of the 40th International Congress of Americanists,* Rome, Italy, pp. 77–81.

1973b Exploring the past on Black Mesa. *American West* 10, no. 5, September.

Euler, Robert C., and Henry Dobyns
1958 Tizon Brown Ware. In *Pottery types of the Southwest,* edited by Harold S. Colton. Museum of Northern Arizona, Ceramic Series, no. 3D. Flagstaff.

1971 *The Hopi people.* Indian Tribal Series. Phoenix.

Euler, Robert C., and Albert Ward
1971 Excavations on Black Mesa, 1971: preliminary report. Mimeographed. Prescott, Ariz.: Prescott College.

Euler, Robert C., and George J. Gumerman
1974 A résumé of the archaeology of northern Arizona. In *The geology of northern Arizona with notes on archaeology and paleoclimate,* edited by Thor N. V. Karlstrom. Twenty-seventh Annual Meeting, Rocky Mountain Section, Geological Society of America. Flagstaff.

Fenenga, Franklin, and Fred Wendorf
1956 Excavations at the Ignacio, Colorado, field camp: site LA 2605. In *Pipeline archaeology,* edited by Fred Wendorf, Nancy Fox, and Orian L. Lewis, pp. 207–14. Sante Fe and Flagstaff: Laboratory of Anthropology and Museum of Northern Arizona.

Fewkes, J. W.
1895 *Cliff villages of the Red Rock Country.* Smithsonian Institution Report for 1895. Washington, D.C.

Fox, Robin
1967 *Kinship and marriage.* Baltimore: Penguin.

Freeman, Leslie G., Jr., and James A. Brown
1964 Statistical Analysis of Carter Ranch Pottery. In *Chapters in the Prehistory of Eastern Arizona, II,* P. S. Martin et al. *Fieldiana: Anthropology* 55. Chicago: Chicago Natural History Museum.

Fritts, H. C.
1965 Dendrochronology. In *The quarternary of the United States,* edited by H. Wright and D. Frey, pp. 871–80. Princeton, N.J.: Princeton University Press.

Fritts, H. C., D. G. Smith, and M. A. Stokes
1965 The biological model for paleoclimatic interpretation of Mesa Verde tree-ring series. In *Contributions of the Wetherill Mesa Archaeological Project,* assembled by Douglas Osborne. Society for American Archaeology, Memoirs, no. 19, pp. 101–21.

Gladwin, Harold S.
1945 "The Chaco Branch: excavations at White Mound and in the Red Mesa Valley." *Medallion Papers,* no. 33. Gila Pueblo. Globe, Ariz.

Goodenough, Ward H.
1956 Residence rules. *Southwestern Journal of Anthropology* 12:22–37.

Green, Christine R., and William D. Sellers
1964 *Arizona climate.* Tucson: University of Arizona Press.

Guernsey, Samuel J.
1931 *Explorations in northeastern Arizona.* Papers of the Peabody Museum of American Archaeology and Ethnology, vol. 12, no. 1. Cambridge: Harvard University.

Guernsey, Samuel J., and A. V. Kidder
1921 *Basketmaker caves in northeastern Arizona.* Papers of the Peabody Museum of American Archaeology and Ethnology, vol. 8, no. 2. Cambridge: Harvard University.

Gumerman, George J.
1966 Two Basketmaker II pithouse villages in eastern Arizona: a preliminary report. *Plateau* 39, no. 2, pp. 80–87.
1970 *Black Mesa: survey and excavation in northeastern Arizona, 1968.* Prescott, Ariz.: Prescott College Press.
1973a A rural-urban continuum for the prehistoric pueblo Southwest: Black Mesa and Chaco Canyon. *Proceedings of the 40th International Congress of Americanists, Rome, Italy.*
1973b The reconciliation of theory and method in Archaeology. In *Research and Theory in Current Archaeology,* edited by Charles Redman. New York: John Wiley & Sons.

Gumerman, George J., Deborah Westfall, and Carol Weed
1972 *Archaeological investigation on Black Mesa. the 1969–1970 seasons.* Prescott, Ariz.: Prescott College Press.

Hack, John T.
1942a *The changing physical environment of the Hopi Indians of Arizona.* Papers of the Peabody Museum of American Archaeology and Ethnology, vol. 35, no. 1. Cambridge: Harvard University.
1942b *Prehistoric coal mining in the Jeddito Valley, Arizona.* Papers of the Peabody Museum of American Archaeology and Ethnology, vol. 35, no. 2. Cambridge: Harvard University.

Haggett, Peter
1965 *Locational analysis in human geography.* London: Edward Arnold.

Hargrave, Lyndon L.
1937 A new sub-culture in Arizona. *Southwestern Lore* 3, no. 2.
1938 "Results of a study on the Cohonina Branch of the Patayan culture in 1938." *Museum of Northern Arizona,* Notes, vol. 11, no. 6. Flagstaff.

Harrill, Bruce G.
1968 A small prehistoric rockshelter in northwestern Arizona. *Plateau* 40, no. 4, pp. 157–65.

Hassan, Ferri A.
1973 On mechanisms of population growth during the Neolithic. *Current Anthropology* 14:535–40.

Haury, E. W.
1940 Excavations in the Forestdale Valley, east-central Arizona. *University of Arizona Bulletin* 21, no. 4., *Social Science Bulletin* 12. Tucson.
1956 Speculation on prehistoric settlement patterns in the Southwest. In *Settlement patterns in the New World.* Viking Fund Publications in Anthropology, no. 23, pp. 3–10.

Helms, Mary W.
1970 Matrilocality, social solidarity, and culture contact: three case histories. *Southwestern Journal of Anthropology* 26, no. 2, pp. 197–212.

Hester, James J.
1962 *Early Navajo migrations and acculturation in the Southwest.* Museum of New Mexico, Papers in Anthropology, no. 6. Santa Fe.

Hevly, R. H., and T. N. V. Karlstrom
1974 "Southwest paleoclimate and continental correlations. In *The geology of northern Arizona with notes on archaeology and paleo-*

climate, edited by Thor N. V. Karlstrom. Twenty-seventh Annual Meeting, Rocky Mountain Section, Geological Society of America. Flagstaff.

Hill, James N.
1968 Broken K Pueblo: patterns of form and function. In *New perspectives in archaeology,* edited by Lewis R. and Sally R. Binford, pp. 103–42. Chicago: Aldine Press.
1970*a* Prehistoric social organization in the American Southwest: theory and method. In *Reconstructing prehistoric pueblo societies,* edited by Wm. A. Longacre, pp. 11–58. Albuquerque: University of New Mexico Press.
1970*b* *Broken K Pueblo: prehistoric social organization in the American Southwest.* Tucson: University of Arizona Press.

Hodge, F. W.
1904 Hopi pottery fired with coal. *American Anthropologist,* n.s. 6, no. 4, pp. 581–82.

Jennings, Jesse D.
1966 *Glen Canyon: a summary.* University of Utah Anthropological Papers, vol. 81. Salt Lake City.

Jett, S. C.
1964 Pueblo Indian migrations: an evaluation of the possible physical and cultural determinants. *American Antiquity* 29:281–300.

Johnson, Stephen C.
1968 *How to use HICLUS—a Hierarchical Cluster Analysis Program.* Stanford Computation Center. Stanford, Calif.

Karlstrom, Thor N. V., George J. Gumerman, and Robert C. Euler
1974 Paleoenvironmental and cultural changes in the Black Mesa Region, northeastern Arizona. In *The geology of northern Arizona with notes on archaeology and paleoclimate,* edited by Thor N. V. Karlstrom. Twenty-seventh Annual Meeting, Rocky Mountain Section, Geological Society of America. Flagstaff.

Karlstrom, Thor N. V., ed.
1974 *The geology of northern Arizona with notes on archaeology and paleoclimate.* Twenty-seventh Annual Meeting, Rocky Mountain Section, Geological Society of America. Flagstaff.

Kearney, Thomas H., Robert H. Peebles, and collaborators
1951 *Arizona flora.* Berkeley and Los Angeles: University of California Press.

Kluckhohn, Clyde, and Paul Reiter, eds.
1939 *Preliminary report on the 1937 excavations, Bc 50–51, Chaco Canyon, New Mexico.* University of New Mexico Bulletin, Anthropological Series, vol. 3, no. 2.

Kunitz, Stephen, and Robert C. Euler
1972 *Aspects of southwestern paleoepidemiology.* Prescott College Anthropological Reports, no. 2. Prescott, Ariz.

Leopold, L. B., E. B. Leopold, and F. Wendorf
1963 Some climatic indicators in the period A.D. 1200–1400 in Mexico. In *Changes of climate, Proceedings of the Rome Symposium,* organized by UNESCO and the World Meteorological Organization. Liege, Belgium.

Lévi-Strauss, Claude
1967 *Structural anthropology.* Garden City, N.Y.: Anchor Books.

Lindsay, Alexander J., Jr., and J. Richard Ambler
1963 Recent contributions and research problems in Kayenta Anasazi prehistory. *Plateau* 35, no. 3, pp. 86–92.

Lindsay, Alexander J., Jr., J. Richard Ambler, Mary Anne Stein, and Philip M. Hobler
1968 *Survey and excavations north and east of Navajo Mountain, Utah, 1959–1962.* Museum of Northern Arizona, Bulletin no. 45, *Glen Canyon Series,* no. 8. Flagstaff.

Lister, R. H.
1966 *Contributions to Mesa Verde archaeology, III, site 866, and the cultural sequence at four villages in the Far View Group, Mesa Verde National Park, Colorado.* University of Colorado Studies, Series in Anthropology, no. 12. Boulder.

Lockett, H. Claiborne, and Lyndon L. Hargrave
1953 *Woodchuck Cave, a Basketmaker II Site in Tsegi Canyon Arizona.* Museum of Northern Arizona, Bulletin no. 26. Flagstaff.

Long, Paul V., Jr.
1966 *Archaeological excavations in Lower Glen Canyon, Utah, 1959–1960.* Museum of Northern Arizona, Bulletin no. 42, *Glen Canyon Series,* no. 7. Flagstaff.

Longacre, William A.
1964 Sociological implications of the ceramic

analysis. In *Chapters in the Prehistory of Eastern Arizona, II*, P. S. Martin et al. *Fieldiana: Anthropology* 55. Chicago: Chicago Natural History Museum.

1968 Some aspects of prehistoric society in east-central Arizona. In *New perspectives in archaeology*, edited by Lewis R. and Sally R. Binford, pp. 89–102. Chicago: Aldine Press.

1970a *Archaeology as anthropology: a case study.* Tucson: University of Arizona Press.

1970b *Reconstructing prehistoric Pueblo societies*, Albuquerque: University of New Mexico Press.

Lösch, A.
1938 The nature of economic regions. *Southern Economic Journal* 5:71–78.

1954 *The economics of location.* New Haven: Yale University Press.

Lowe, Charles H.
1964 *The vertebrates of Arizona.* Tucson: University of Arizona Press.

McGregor, John C.
1951 *The Cohonina culture of northwestern Arizona.* Urbana: University of Illionis Press.

1965 *Southwestern archaeology.* Urbana: University of Illinois Press.

1967 *The Cohonina culture of Mount Floyd, Arizona.* University of Kentucky Studies in Anthropology vol. 5. Lexington.

McKee, B. H.
1933 The naming of the Grand Canyon. *Grand Canyon National Park Notes* 9:310–21.

Martin, P. S., J. B. Rinaldo, W. A. Longacre, L. G. Freeman, J. A. Brown, R. H. Hevly, and M. E. Cooley.
1964 *Chapters in the Prehistory of Eastern Arizona, II. Fieldiana: Anthropology* 55. Chicago: Chicago Natural History Museum.

Martin, P. S., and Fred Plog
1973 *The archaeology of Arizona.* New York: Natural History Press.

Michaels, J. W.
1972 Dating methods. In *Annual Review of Anthropology* 1, edited by B. J. Siegel, A. R. Beales, and S. A. Tyler, pp. 113–26. Stanford, Calif.: Stanford University Press.

Mindeleff, Cosmos
1898 Navaho houses. *Seventeenth Annual Report of the Bureau of American Ethnology*, pp. 475–517. Washington, D.C.

Morris, Earl H.
1939 *Archaeological studies in the La Plata District, southwestern Colorado and northeastern New Mexico.* Carnegie Institution Publication 519. Washington, D.C.

Morris, Earl H., and Robert Burgh
1941 *Anasazi basketry: Basketmaker II through Pueblo III.* Carnegie Institution Publication 555. Washington, D.C.

1954 *Basketmaker II sites near Durango, Colorado.* Carnegie Institution Publication 604. Washington, D.C.

Nequatewa, Edmund
1946 The place of corn and feathers in Hopi Ceremonies. *Plateau* 19, no. 1, pp. 15–16.

Nichol, A. A.
1937 The Natural Vegetation of Arizona. *University of Arizona Agricultural Experiment Station Technical Bulletin* 68:181–222. 2d ed. (1952), *Technical Bulletin* 127:189–230.

Odum, Eugene
1971 *Fundamentals of ecology.* 3d ed. Philadelphia: W. B. Saunders.

Olsen, Stanley J.
1972 The small Indian dogs of Black Mesa, Arizona. *Plateau* 45, no. 2, fall.

Olson, Alan P.
1962 A history of the phase concept in the Southwest. *American Antiquity* 27, no. 4, pp. 457–72.

Ortiz, Alphonso
1969 *The Tewa world.* Chicago: University of Chicago Press.

Phillips, David A.
1972 Social implications of settlement distribution on Black Mesa. In *Archaeological investigations on Black Mesa: the 1969–1970 seasons*, George J. Gumerman, Barbara Westfall, and Carol Weed. Prescott, Ariz.: Prescott College Press.

Reed, Eric K.
1954 Transition to history in the Pueblo Southwest. *American Anthropologist* 56:592–97.

1956 Types of village-plan layouts in the

Southwest. In *Settlement patterns in the New World*. Viking Fund Publications in Anthropology, no. 23, pp. 11–17.

Robert, Frank H. H., Jr.
1929 *Shabik'eshchee Village, a Late Basketmaker site in the Chaco Canyon, New Mexico*. Bureau of American Ethnology, Bulletin no. 92. Washington, D.C.

1931 *The ruins at Kiatuthlanna, eastern Arizona*. Bureau of American Ethnology, Bulletin no. 100. Washington, D.C.

1940 *Archaeological remains in the Whitewater District, Eastern Arizona, part II, artifacts and burials*. Bureau of American Ethnology, Bulletin no. 126. Washington, D.C.

Robinson, W. J., and J. S. Dean
1969 *Tree-ring evidence for climatic changes in the prehistoric Southwest from A.D. 1000 to 1200*. Laboratory of Tree-Ring Research. Tucson: University of Arizona Press.

Rohn, A. H.
1963 Prehistoric soil and water conservation on Chapin Mesa. *American Antiquity* 29:441–45.

Sanders, W. T.
1972 Population, agricultural history, and societal evolution in Mesoamerica. In *Population growth: anthropological implications,* edited by B. Spooner. Cambridge: M.I.T. Press.

Schneider, David M., and Kathleen Gough
1962 *Matrilineal kinship*. Berkeley: University of California Press.

Schoenwetter, James
1966 A Re-evaluation of the Navajo Reservoir pollen chronology. *El Palacio* 73, no. 1. Santa Fe.

1970 Archaeological pollen studies of the Colorado Plateau. *American Antiquity* 35, no. 1, pp. 35–48.

Schoenwetter, James, and F. W. Eddy
1964 *Alluvial and palynological reconstruction of environments, Navajo Reservoir District*. Museum of New Mexico Papers in Anthropology, no. 13. Santa Fe.

Schoenwetter, James, and A. E. Dittert, Jr.
1968 An ecological interpretation of Anasazi settlement patterns. In *Anthropological archaeology in the Americas*, pp. 41–66. Washington, D.C.: Anthropological Society of Washington.

Schroeder, Albert H.
1957 The Hakataya cultural Tradition. *American Antiquity* 23, no. 2.

1960 *The Hohokam, Sinagua, and Hakataya*. Society for American Archaeology Archives of Archaeology, no. 5. Madison: University of Wisconsin Press.

Schwartz, Douglas W.
1956a Demographic changes in the early periods of Cohonina prehistory. In *Prehistoric settlement patterns*. Viking Fund Publications in Anthropology, no. 23.

1956b The Havasupai, 600–1500 A.D.: a short cultural history. *Plateau* 28, no. 4, pp. 77–85.

Simpson, Ruth DeEtte
1953 The Hopi Indians. *Southwest Museum Leaflets*, no. 25.

Skinner, S. Alan
1967 Four historic sites near Flagstaff, Arizona. *Plateau* 39, no. 3, pp. 105–23.

Smiley, Terah L.
1958 The geology and dating of Sunset Crater, Flagstaff, Arizona. In *Guidebook of the Black Mesa basin, northeastern Arizona,* edited by R. Y. Anderson and J. W. Harshbarger, pp. 186–90. New Mexico Geological Society, Ninth Field Conference, Socorro.

Stanislawski, Michael B.
1973 Review of *Archaeology as anthropology: a case study,* by Wm. A. Longacre. *American Antiquity* 38, no. 1, pp. 117–22.

Steward, Julian H.
1955 *Theory of culture change*. Urbana: University of Illinois Press.

Sutton, R. L.
1974 The geology of Hoppi Buttes, Arizona. In *The geology of northern Arizona with notes on archaeology and paleoclimate,* edited by Thor N. V. Karlstrom. Annual Meeting, Rocky Mountain Section, Geological Society of America. Flagstaff.

Swedlund, A. C., and D. B. Hanson
1972 Human skeletal remains from Black Mesa: 1969–1970. In *Archaeological investigations on Black Mesa: the 1969–1970 seasons,* George J. Gumerman, Deborah Westfall, and Carol Weed. Prescott, Ariz.: Prescott College Press.

Taylor, W. W.
1948 *A study of archaeology*. American Anthropological Association Memoirs, no. 69.

Titiev, Mischa
1944 *Old Oraibi: a study of the Hopi Indians
of Third Mesa*. Papers of the Peabody Museum
of American Archaeology and Ethnology, vol.
22, no. 1. Cambridge: Harvard University.

Trewartha, Glenn
1970 *The geography of populations: world
patterns*. New York: John Wiley & Sons.

Turner, Christy, and Laurel Lofgren
1966 Household size of prehistoric western
Pueblo Indians. *Southwestern Journal of Anthropology* 22:117–32.

Vivian, R. Gwinn
1970 An inquiry into prehistoric social organization in Chaco Canyon, New Mexico. In *Reconstructing prehistoric Pueblo societies*, edited
by Wm. A. Longacre, pp. 59–83. Albuquerque:
University of New Mexico Press.

Wade, William D.
1970 Skeletal remains of a prehistoric population from the Puerco Valley, eastern Arizona.
Ph.D. dissertation, University of Colorado,
Boulder.

Ward, Albert E.
1968 Investigation of two hogans at Toonerville, Arizona. *Plateau* 40, no. 4, pp. 136–42.

Weiss, Kenneth
1973*a* A Method for approximating age-spe-
cific fertility in the construction of life tables
for anthropological populations. *Human Biology*
45:195–210.

1973*b* Demographic models for anthropology.
Society for American Archaeology Memoir 27.
American Antiquity 37, no. 2, pt. 2.

Wendorf, Fred
1953 *Archaeological studies in the Petrified
Forest National Monument*. Museum of Northern Arizona, Bulletin no. 27. Flagstaff.

Wendorf, Fred, Nancy Fox, and Orian L. Lewis,
eds.
1956 *Pipeline archaeology*. Santa Fe and Flagstaff: Laboratory of Anthropology and Museum
of Northern Arizona.

Whiting, Alfred F.
1939 *Ethnobotany of the Hopi*. Museum of
Northern Arizona, Bulletin no. 15. Flagstaff.

Willey, Gordon R.
1966 *An introduction to American archaeology*.
Vol. 1. Englewood Cliffs, N.J.: Prentice-Hall.

Willey, Gordon R., ed.
1974 *Archaeological researches in retrospect*.
Cambridge, Mass.: Winthrop Publishers.

Woodbury, Richard
1954 *Prehistoric stone implements of northern
Arizona*. Papers of the Peabody Museum of
American Archaeology and Ethnology, vol. 34.
Cambridge: Harvard University.

1961 Climatic changes and prehistoric agriculture in the southwestern United States. *Annals
of the New York Academy of Sciences* 95:705–
9.

Wormington, H. Marie
1947 *Prehistoric Indians of the Southwest*.
Denver Museum of Natural History, Popular
Series, no. 7. Denver.

Wyman, Leland C., and Stuart K. Harris
1951 *The ethnobotany of the Kayenta Navajo*.
University of New Mexico Publications in Biology, no. 5. Albuquerque.

Zubrow, Ezra
1970 Carrying capacity and dynamic equilibrium in the prehistoric Southwest. *American
Antiquity* 36:127–38.

Index

Abandonment: causes, 28, 102–3, 137, 146–47, 151, 161, 169–70; during Toreva phase, 114, 154, 169; purposeful destruction of artifacts, 170; removal of artifacts from site, 170; definition of, 170

Actinea, 43, 85

Agave, 9

Agriculture: dry farming, 4, 6, 35, 70, 84, 153–54, 161, 165, 166, 169; during Dot Klish phase, 43, 52, 104, 153, 166; during Toreva phase, 85, 153, 154; in matrilineal clan system, 123; technological innovations, 145–46; as resource base, 146; as affected by rise in population, 147; spur to population growth, 148; water and soil conservation systems, 151; abandonment of farmland, 151, 154; adaptive action of agriculturalists, 152; floodwater farming, 166. *See also* Abandonment

Alluvial data: regions presently dated, 154, 156; developing Black Mesa time-stratigraphy showing alluvial contacts in the Southwest, 155

Alluvial sequences, 157–58, 159

Anglo-American Period, 11–13, 18

Anglo homesteader's jacal house, 7, 12, 13

Anglo line-camp, 7

Architecture: of excavations, 31–95

—Ariz. D:13:4: jacal dwelling, 31, 32, 34

—Ariz. D:13:1: circular pithouse, 35, 39; plan and profile of, 36; oval subsurface storage room, 37, 39; circular subsurface storage room, 37, 39; summer shade or ramada, 38, 39; circular jacal dwelling, 38, 39; extramural storage pits, 39, 40

—Ariz. D:9:2: plan and profile, 44; oval pithouses, 45, 46, 47, 48

—Ariz. D:10:1: view of, 53; circular storage cists, 53, 55, 56, 60–61, 62; plan and profile, 54; oval storage cist, 55, 56, 61, 62; oval surface dwellings, 56, 57, 58, 59, 62; subrectangular surface dwelling, 57, 59–60, 61–62; jacal dwelling, 60, 62; plaster-mixing cists, 61, 62

—Ariz. I:3:1: rectangular pithouse, 70, 78; three-room pueblos, 70, 74, 75, 78; plan and profile, 71; profiles of fill, 72; stratigraphy of structure, 73; oval pithouse, 75, 78; jacal multiroomed dwelling, 77, 78; front-orientation plan, 78

—Ariz. D:9:1: kiva, 87, 95; plan and profile, 88; pithouse, 89, 90; subrectangular pithouse, 91, 92, 93, 95; rectangular masonry storage room, 92, 95; jacal dwelling, 93, 95; front-orientation plan, 94–95

Arizona bull snake, 10

Arizona cottontail, 10

Arizona pack rat, 10

Arrow shafts, 28

Artiodactyla, 108–10

Aster, 43

Awls: at Ariz. D:13:1, 37, 42, 110; at Ariz. D:10:1, 56, 61, 66, 67, 110; at Ariz. D:9:1, 94, 101, 110; summary of bone implements from six sites, 110; from Wepo phase sites, 168

Banana yucca, 9, 10

Basketmaker II: site, 6, 30, 103; importance of jacal architecture, 34; architecture of, 34, 164–65; demographic change, 149, 164; Lolomai phase, 164; artifacts, 165

Basketmaker III: sites, 6, 29, 34, 35, 52; ceramics, 41–43, 64, 103; architecture, 62, 68, 102; settlement of, 103. *See also* Dot Klish phase

Basketry, 48, 51

Bear grass, 9

Big sage, 85

Bilocal residence pattern, 115

Biotic communities, 8–10, 30, 68

Birds, 10

Black bear, 10

Black Mesa Pipeline Company, 3

Black Mesa project: reasons for, 162–63; description of, 163; an overview of, 164

Black-tailed jackrabbit, 10

Bobcat, 10

Bones, 108, 110, 167

Bracken fern, 10

Broken K Pueblo: matrilocal residence pattern at, 114

Buckhorn, 4, 9

Burials, 64, 94, 102, 138

Calcite, 41

Canadian elder, 10

Cane cholla, 30, 34, 43, 52, 85

Carrying capacity: factor in abandonment, 147

Carter Ranch: matrilocal residence pattern at, 114; distribution of traditional ceramic types, 121

Catclaw, 9

Cattlemen's line-shack, 11–12

Ceramic analysis: as archaeological test for matrilineal and matrilocal societies, 127

Ceramics: Kayenta Branch, 17, 21, 22, 23, 24; Cohonina Branch, 17, 22, 26, 27; Parker Red-on-buff, 18; Tizon Brown, 18, 26; Cerbat Branch, 18, 26, 27–28; Lino Gray, 21, 22, 35, 39, 40, 41, 42, 46, 50, 51, 64, 103, 165; Lino Black-on-gray, 21, 22, 37, 41, 42, 47, 48, 50, 56, 58, 60, 64, 66, 104, 165; Abajo Red-on-orange, 22; Deadmans Black-on-gray, 22; San Juan Red Ware, 22, 23, 26, 69, 83, 100; Deadmans Gray, 22, 26; Tallahogan Red, 22, 41, 42, 46, 50, 64, 66, 104; Kana-a

181